FROM BOW STREET TO BAKER STREET

Also by Martin A. Kayman

*THE MODERNISM OF EZRA POUND
REVOLUTION AND COUNTER-REVOLUTION IN PORTUGAL

*Also published by Macmillan

From Bow Street to Baker Street

Mystery, Detection and Narrative

MARTIN A. KAYMAN

*Associate Professor and Director of the English
Institute, University of Coimbra, Portugal*

MACMILLAN

First published 1992

Published by
MACMILLAN ACADEMIC AND PROFESSIONAL LTD
Houndmills, Basingstoke, Hampshire RG21 2XS
and London

Companies and representatives
throughout the world

Edited and typeset by Grahame & Grahame Editorial, Brighton

Printed in Great Britain by
Billing & Sons Ltd, Worcester

British Library Cataloguing in Publication Data
Kayman, Martin A.
From Bow Street to Baker Street
I.   Title
823
ISBN   0–333–46766–3

This book is dedicated to the memory of John Kassman,
Dickens scholar, teacher, conversationalist, and friend

Contents

Part I
Rite and Writing

1
Mystery

'Popular fictions . . . need to be read and analysed not as some sugar-coated sociology, but as narratives which negotiate, *no less than* the classic texts, the connection between "writing, history and ideology".'[1]

MYSTERY AND DETECTION

Discussions of what is commonly called 'detective fiction' seem obsessed with discovering 'who done it', who founded the genre. In pursuing this inquiry the literary scholar may be tempted by an analogy with the detective gathering the material evidence and proposing a retrospective theory which situates every event in its appropriate place in an orderly and totalizing narrative leading from origin to explanatory conclusion. A similar analogy may be (and often is) invoked for the scientist, and especially the psychoanalyst – indeed, for anyone who reads the present for or through an explanation that is perceived as 'buried' in the sequences of the past. But before we don the deerstalker we should be advised that there can be a dangerous tautology in the detective's 'double logic' which uses 'the plot of the inquest to find, or construct, a story of the crime which will offer just those features necessary to the thematic coherence we call a solution, while claiming, of course, that the solution has been made necessary by the crime.'[2] Many accounts of 'detective fiction' have been bedevilled by this sort of teleological fallacy, especially the orthodox theory which presents Conan Doyle as the model of the genre and in consequence treats earlier writing as a simple anticipation of his 'classic'. This approach comes close to realizing the analogy in terms of the characteristic which Julian Symons identifies as central to detective writing: the 'manner of working back from effect to cause, from solution to problem.'[3]

3

Ian Ousby and R. F. Stewart alert us to the historical anomaly
of treating as 'detective fiction' texts written before the existence
of detectives or of a perceived genre of writing sufficiently dif-
ferentiable and specific to warrant the name.[4] In this sense it is
obviously absurd to call *Oedipus Rex* a 'detective story'. But whilst
a rigorous historicism may save us from anachronisms it must
still account for the formal and functional continuities which even
historically-minded readers have observed. In a formal sense, there
is a relation between what the 'classic' detective does and what,
for example, Oedipus or Pip or Freud do. Notwithstanding all the
necessary qualifications, much of the fascination and power of modern detective stories does indeed rely on the way they foreground
structural or functional tropes which inform a wide range of narrative discourses – literary, scientific, forensic, diagnostic, theoretical
and critical. Studying such texts may therefore first be justified in
terms of the acute problems they pose to models of reading and
analysis. Precisely because of both its paradigmatic properties and
the fact that it is a specific product of the nineteenth century, this
sort of writing resists equally purely formalist and purely historicist
approaches; rather, 'detection' obliges us to the sort of articulation
of history and form proposed by Franco Moretti: 'Literary texts
are *historical* products organized according to *rhetorical* criteria. The
main problem of a literary criticism that aims to be in all respects
a *historical discipline* is to do justice to both aspects of its objects: to
work out a system of concepts which are both historiographic and
rhetorical.'[5]

In this context, the links between modern detection and its corol-
laries are, to my mind, best established through the prior object that
each presupposes, a *mystery*. What we call 'detection' is most use-
fully construed as a historically specific strategy for mastering what
are designated as the mysteries which, at various moments, a range
of discourses, structures and institutions claim the privilege and
power of being able to read/write. For this reason, I have chosen to
study here not a formally pre-defined category of 'detective fiction',
but a wider territory of narratives, mainly of the nineteenth century,
concerned with the reading of mysteries of various sorts (including
monsters) – what I have called 'mystery/detective fiction'. What
interests me in this book is the *range* of strategies and positions, and
how, largely in the hands of Conan Doyle, one particular reading
of mystery, a historically specific 'detective fiction', emerged as the
master. A more precise and developed discussion of the problems

of definition will be found in Chapter 5; in this chapter I wish not to define, but to circumscribe that territory in terms of its formal framework and pre-history.

The formal relation between modern mystery fiction and earlier 'mysteries' is decidedly double-edged. Whilst permitting the former to be taken seriously, at the same time it inevitably makes us aware that when we witness features in modern popular works formally or functionally comparable to those of more ancient and classic mysteries, we also observe that their transformation into modern forms seems to offer no more than a decayed residue of earlier, more dignified experiences – less a genre than a deposit for the decayed paradigms of a pre-history of modes – tragic, epic, romantic – all of them lacking some essential ingredient which makes them what they are.[6] The fact that ritual becomes commercial formula, sin becomes crime, awe sensation, tragedy melodrama and the saviour becomes, eventually, a smart-assed tough-guy, serves at first to denigrate the literary value of mystery/detective fiction, making it little more than a theoretical curio, a pedagogic instrument or cultural source. But I see no need to explain the success of these stories through the spiritual infirmity of the reader (like, presumably, oneself) for whom they provide genuine narrative satisfactions; nor do I feel the need to start from a judgement of modern popular mystery stories as a lesser genre because they, unlike much Modernist (and even more, 'Post-Modernist') literature, do not manifest a parodic nostalgia for the religious or tragic grandeur of the past. The difference between them is not a matter of spiritual judgement but of historical analysis. What in fact informs such qualitative judgments is clearly that our very sense and experience of the mysterious has changed. It is this dislocation that has to be historically specified if we are to account for the particular forms of reading/writing mystery which concern us: the process of the *secularization of mystery* which determines the transformations in the discourses and institutions which claim it as their territory.

Thus this sense of banality, still the most salient feature of the genre, is a useful starting-point; it is its absence of aesthetic value which, for professional literary criticism, most defines mystery/detective fiction as a form of 'popular literature'. In this sense, one of the phenomena which registers the apparent decadence of the modern sense of mystery at the same time as it characterizes the genre is the role attributed to plot in the discrimination between 'high' and 'low' culture. Whereas, in one context, Aristotle could argue the

primacy of plot in the 'highest' of cultural forms, nowadays 'Plot
has been disdained as the element of narrative that least sets off and
defines high art – indeed, plot is that which especially characterizes
popular mass-consumption literature.'[7] The classic novel of 'character' and the Modernist 'anti-novel' are taken as perpetuating the
spiritual mysteries and mission of Literature, whilst popular fiction,
no more than a 'superficial' exploitation of the mere 'mechanics' of
narrative, maintains an empty husk of ritual degraded to formula,
itself as it were a parody of art. Yet this reversal of course has a
history, as much a product of the period as is the emergence of the
detective story: the lengthy struggle of that innovative, low-born,
heterogeneous and problematic modern form, the realist Novel,
to emancipate itself from the reputation of its origins in popular
narrative fiction as a 'low-mimetic', frivolous, unimproving and
eventually pernicious entertainment, and to claim its right to be
treated as art. The defenders of what Terry Lovell calls 'the novel
as literature' differentiated it from 'the novel as commodity' by
redirecting the accusations of 'lowness' aimed at narrative fiction
as a whole against the commercially successful sub-genres – those
species of narrative, like the gothic novel and horror and sensation
fiction, which 'serious novelists' disparaged for their reliance on
'unnatural' plots.[8] In other words, the Novel concealed its own
hybrid origins by accusing its popular competitors of being a
monster. This will play a large role in selecting the texts under
study here: like its objects, the criminal and the monster, mystery
fiction is located historically by a process of exclusion, the way that
the other discursive institutions which claim a particular privilege to
narrate modern mystery deny them respectability. In this sense, they
can be circumscribed in the first place by a boundary imposed by the
efforts of what was to become the classic realist Novel to legitimate
itself aesthetically by differentiating itself from their lesser fictions.

Yet what makes mystery/detective fiction particularly interesting
is that, being constitutionally barred from these more respectable
discourses whilst being obliged to refer constantly to them, it is
uniquely placed to put in question the former's ability to narrate
modern mystery. It is by no means incidental that it is precisely
in the 'low' genre that we find major narrative experimentation
with point-of-view, character and plot. Such experimentation is
a constant from the early days of the Novel to the most recent
'Post-Modernist' metafictions: crime, detective, horror and mystery
stories may on the one hand exploit the mechanics of narrative

fiction, but they may also be used to put those mechanics in question. I shall therefore be arguing that, whilst the classic Novel goes about establishing its respectability by denigrating popular commercial fiction, the foregrounding of certain tropes of fictional narrative in mystery/detective stories explores and challenges the formal limits of realism's claims to represent modern mysteries.

In this context, another accusation directed against mystery/ detective fiction as evidence of its 'lowness' and spiritual poverty is its modish fascination with that discourse which most reflects the intellectual secularization of mystery, scientific rationality. But this criticism tends, curiously, to involve two contradictory charges. These stories are accused on the one hand of articulating a repressive scientism which reduces all the complexities of experience to rationalistic and mechanical categories, and on the other hand of indulging in pseudo-science, a sensationalism of technology and theory or an abusive methodology which falsifies nature through a hyperbolic, inaccurate, fanciful, artificial or 'unscientific' science. The discourses and theoretical positions of Science certainly play an important part in mystery/detective fiction, but rarely (at least until Holmes) at the price of forgetting their status as fiction. As a consequence, the stories which are informed by a scientific 'spirit' as often as not draw critical attention to the limitations of contemporary orthodoxy (on occasion in relation to an alternative phantasy of science or theory). This is particularly true of the presence of those sciences most directly concerned in the secularization of the human, and which play such a large part in nineteenth-century mystery fiction: medicine and psychology. Thus, to the extent that mystery/detective fiction is a form of science fiction (or more accurately, a 'fiction of science'), it is in the second place bordered by the orthodox science and theory which it questions or transforms in its fictions. In this way it is able to inquire into the boundaries between the narratives of fiction and those of science and theory, questioning here too the capacity of determinate discourses to narrate modern mysteries.

The third, and perhaps most characteristic, horizon which encloses mystery/detective fiction and to which it directs its attention and experimentation is, clearly enough, the Law. Whilst the police and criminal lawyers are often the first to criticize detective fiction for its unfaithfulness and ignorance, many critics attack it for being the slave of a legalistic, policial mentality. In contrast to the realist Novel's profound moral sensibility, the detective story is accused of being 'moralistic' and hence 'realistic' in only a superficial and topical sense, a modern echo of Mrs. Oliphant's complaint in 1863 against 'the police-court aspect of modern fiction'.[9] This attitude borders on snobbishness. Mystery/detective fiction *is* rather unashamedly interested in the 'truth' – or more often, we should note, the lack of it – of the 'police-court', its concepts of justice explicitly and deliberately engaged with contemporary legal frameworks, both institutional and discursive. But these stories are not primarily exercises in practical ethics any more than they are exercises in practical science. Alongside the intellectual secularization of Science, the rise of Law is perhaps the most important single aspect of the secularization of mystery. If the sciences of medicine and psychology come first to complement and gradually to substitute religious codes in determining the constitution of the physical and spiritual human subject, the social and ethical subject becomes rewritten by modern law as the privileged paradigm for the achievement of secular justice and truth. Here again, in articulating the paradigms of Law on those of its fictional narrative, mystery/ detective fiction offers a critical stance, continuing its investigation into discourse, narrative and mystery by examining the capacity of the Law to fulfill the preeminent claim it shares with Science and, indeed, the Novel, to encompass modern mysteries.

If our texts are bordered by these three major discursive institutions, the latter in their turn are themselves interrelated by sharing something fundamental to the secularization of mystery: they all rely on a *modern paradigm of realism.* The realism of English nineteenth-century culture is certainly not that of a materialist philosophy (however materialistic its fascination with objects). Rather, the rejection of the 'marvellous' and the adoption of Aristotelian criteria of probability in plot development committed the Novel already in the eighteenth century to criteria of verisimilitude which may be characterized as fundamentally empiricist. The Novel obtains legitimation as a 'natural' or 'reliable' discourse by maintaining a methodological horizon based on the sensations, perspectives and experiences of the 'ordinary' event and the 'normally-constituted' individualized but universal subject – the same criteria, in effect, which found scientific positivism and democratic legality.

On the other hand, the sort of texts we will be considering deal generally with degrees of the extra-ordinary – with natural, social and psychological pathologies. The extra-ordinary is, like the genres which narrate it, a field constructed by exclusion. The Law, the classic Novel and orthodox Science are, in their different registers, both the appropriate reflections and the *sources* of the positive self-image of nineteenth-century bourgeois society. This is a process central to the construction of the modern state and of modern mystery. Through the eighteenth and nineteenth centuries, the traditional institutions of religion were supplemented by an elaborate range of scientific, legal and medical discourses and authorities to serve ostensibly as mechanisms for mastering and controlling what is dangerous to orderly society. However, as Foucault and others have shown, the categories, constitution and imagery of danger, deviance and pathology are in fact produced by the modern strategies of expulsion, dehumanization, repression, ghettoization, confinement and silencing invented to define and control the poor, the unemployed, the migrant, the factory worker, the criminal, the insane, the sick, the female, the juvenile, and the savage, along with the personal impulses and behaviours which are held to define and be defined by these categories – that is to say, those aspects of society and the psyche which do not conform to the paradigms of the 'human nature' described by the dominant discourses. In sum, the ordinary, as ideological and institutional category, is itself called into being by the demarcation and delegitimatization of what is constructed as the extra-ordinary. So if Victorian society presents an image of respectable and natural rationality, it is obviously at the price of social and personal repression, the production of a social and psychological 'underworld', and it is in very large part the mysteries of this 'underworld' which are explored by the fiction of detection and horror. Monstrosity, insanity and crime, dream and sexuality, all return, particularly in reference to women, with a vengeful violence which these texts refer to the modern narrative, scientific and juridical structures of control. The very sensationalism of the genre registers the limits of the empiricist models which lie behind the three discursive institutions which serve as the horizons of the genre.

In this book, I shall therefore be viewing mystery/detective stories as narratives concerned with a modern territory of the repressed, perceiving its mysteries in terms of monstrosity, insanity, and crime, and which offer experimental and critical images, narrative frames and authorities for their mastery, bounded by the discourses of the realist Novel, Science and Law. My 'case' will be that these narratives are best read not as mere puzzle or sensation – and even less as, *a priori*, contributions to a repressive system of control – but as symbolic and formal explorations in the representation of the mysterious territories of society and of the psyche which cannot be captured within the narrative strategies of literary realism, scientific positivism and contemporary legal structures. As we shall see, it is not in the victory of control (as in Conan Doyle), but in the violence that is contained by the attempt to control that the literary and social energies of these texts lie. Their experimental importance derives in the end from the way that, by questioning the dominant paradigms of authority and the relations between them, they open a breach in their model of mastery and foreshadow and contribute to the production of new narrative forms and narrative subjects designed to deal with modern mysteries. By imposing itself retrospectively as the dominant tendency in this sort of writing, the nostalgia for mastery of Conan Doyle has foreclosed on these earlier strains; the effort here therefore is to reinstate their contribution to the literary and epistemological revolutions of the Modernist period, in which Freud appears not as a corollary but as an alternative to Sherlock Holmes.

MYSTERY AND NARRATIVE

What articulates my interest in the historical specificity of mystery/detective fiction with its formal properties and what guides my attempts to historicize mystery and the strategies for its reading/writing are questions to do with narrative and power. This is because the first aspect of mystery which we encounter in our literary experience is that which is most conspicuously exploited in mystery/detective fiction: the mystery of narrative itself. At its worst, this is reduced to little more than the suspense of wanting to know what happened or what happens next, achieved by imposing a spurious ignorance on the reader and moving to a fabricated and reassuring knowledge – as in David Grossvogel's characterization of the detective story as a low form, where 'the mode . . . is to create a mystery for the sole purpose of effecting its effortless dissipation'.[10] But even if we take this as an absolute and unquestionable index of the decadence of mystery, reduced to a mere sensationalism of reading, what could be a more important area of modern mystery for the literary scholar than the reading experience as such?

Narrative can be related broadly to two concepts: to the mimetic, an accounting (or 'telling') of the things in the world, and, as Jean-Pierre Faye points out, to the *epistemological* (from the root *gnarus*), an imitation of the things of the world ordered in such a manner as to embody a knowledge about them.[11] The point is that if narrative is fundamentally epistemological, so too is mystery – not an absolute unknown but precisely something that is known by someone who is not telling it to others (in its etymological derivation from the Greek root verb 'to close one's eyes or lips'). As a knowledge concealed by the knower from those who are defined by their exclusion, mystery is obviously the source and result of an asymmetry of power. This power has a specific structure for its exercise, in the sense of the word enacted in the pagan Mysteries or the Christian Mystery of the Mass. Here mystery is not a concealment but the special condition of the revelation of a secret knowledge, a ritual of initiation (cf. *mystes* [initiate]) in which a *master* (or priest), whose power is guaranteed by his secrecy and his status as officiate of the ritual, presides over the unfolding of what is hidden for a specific community which is defined and transformed by its collaboration in the ritual.

Such an asymmetry obviously has a literary corollary in the relation between narrator and reader. The narrator exercises power on the reader at the beginning of his tale by letting the latter know that there is a mystery, a knowledge (a story) to be told. The nature of the mystery is not of course necessarily religious or metaphysical, but syntactic – in the sense in which Todorov identifies the 'poetics of prose' as a mystery of predication.[12] Every narrative gesture generates syntagmatic gaps by revealing that it is concealing what it knows, opening up, in place of an immediate totalizing predicate, a space which the act of reading is driven to fill with hypothetical continuations. These gaps are 'mysterious' because they are not absolute absences; they represent knowledges known to the (ideal) author but as yet concealed from the reader until they are filled by the rest of the text. We keep on turning the pages as we follow the sequences which eventually foreclose the promiscuous alternatives of predication towards a coherent meaning. This movement corresponds to Lacan's sense of the syntagmatic axis as 'the metonymy of desire', the simultaneous opening up and attempted foreclosure of the gaps provoked by the non-coincidence of signifier and signified. Whereas Lacan identifies the driving lack of what is for him an interminable speech in an original splitting of the subject, Peter Brooks, citing Walter Benjamin's observation that 'Death . . . is the sanction of everything that the storyteller can tell', sees the motivating absence as determined and resolved by ending: we read in what he calls an *'anticipation of retrospection . . . in a spirit of confidence, and also a state of dependence, that what remains to be read will restructure the provisional meanings of the already read.'*[13] The power of the ideal author resides in the fact that what he or she knows most of all (and what he or she systematically denies to the reader) is how it will end and only thus what it will have meant.

Since the end is then, necessarily, already contained (and concealed) in the beginning, the act of narrating depends on a process of postponement:

> We have a curious situation in which two principles of forward movement operate upon one another so as to create retard, a dilatory space in which pleasure can come from postponement in the knowledge that this – in the manner of foreplay? – is a necessary approach to the true end . . . . As Sartre and Benjamin compellingly argued, the narrative must tend towards its end, seek illumination in its own death. Yet this must be the right death, the correct end. The complication of the detour is related to the danger of short-circuit: the danger of reaching the end too quickly, of achieving an im-proper death.[14]

The price of meaning is the sacrifice of the text, the abolition of the epistemological asymmetry through which the author exercises his power over us and, in a powerful text, its replacement by our adherence to the author's 'vision'. In this way the text, like us, must make a 'good end' – which neither should be in too great a hurry to achieve. Thus, the deviations by which that end is both postponed and achieved – in Lacanian terms, the defiles of the metonymic chain which register the movement of desire – constitute the dynamic and inevitable pleasure of reading, corresponding for Brooks to the double movement of Freud's two basic instincts: 'the two antagonistic instincts serve one another in a dynamic interaction that is a complete and self-regulatory economy which makes both end and detour perfectly necessary and interdependent. The organism must live in order to die in the proper manner, to die the right death. One must have the arabesque of plot in order to reach the end. One must have metonymy in order to reach metaphor.'[15] Brooks' use of metaphor here returns us to the articulation of narrative as account and as knowledge, and to a central source of its mystery: what, or rather, how the story *means*, how an imitation of events comes to embody a significance. If this is the end to which the syntagmatic gaps of temporality and syntax move, then this, the paradigmatic closing of the semiotic gap between signifier and signified, is the 'ultimate' mystery of narrative.

Simply enough, we know that in narrative something else – something other than a mere accounting – is at issue. This is because narratives do not in fact ac-count but re-count. Narrative is both mimesis and meaning, referent and significance, a sequence of events and their meaning – what modern narratology distinguishes as *sjuzet* (discourse) and *fabula* (story). According to Brooks, 'Plot [is] . . . the active process of *sjuzet* working on *fabula*, the dynamic of its interpretive ordering.'[16] The *sjuzet* is thus necessarily a repeated image, or metaphor, of the *fabula*, in the sense of Todorov's '"narrative transformation", where start and finish stand in the relation – itself metaphorical – of the "same-but-different."'[17] Here of course the classic detective story foregrounds the process in the transformation of the *fabula* of the 'meaningless', gap-ridden story of the crime into the 'same-but-different' *sjuzet* of those events rewritten into plenitude, coherence and significance by the detective's closing explanation. But well before this, we find a clear example in the Romance – for Todorov, a model of narrative in that it is a text which 'contains its own gloss'. Here,

> We are confronted, then, from the outset and in a systematic fashion, with a double narrative, with two types of episodes, of a distinct nature but referring to the same event and alternating regularly . . . . the interpretation is included within the texture of the narrative. One half of the text deals with adventures, the other with the text which describes them. Text and meta-text are brought into continuity.[18]

Because, as Todorov also notes, both types of episodes are equally narratives ('The narrative of an adventure signifies another narrative'), narrative can be seen as fundamentally *allegorical* (*allos* = other; *agoreuein* = to speak); the possibility of meaning in the recounting of events resides in the fact that one reads on two narrative levels. What enables us to mediate instantly between them, translating the one into the other, is 'the existence of a code'.[19]

Allegory as a complete and transparent system is of course restricted to a particular stage of Christianity, in which the 'code' in question is necessarily communal and sacred – a single, unified and exhaustive 'master code'. And it is clearly the loss – or rather fragmentation – of such a 'master code' that identifies the modern condition of secular mystery. None the less, as Frederic Jameson argues, the tendency to read allegorically survives – even (or especially) in criticism, formalism and historicism itself. Jameson cites Deleuze and Guattari's attack on 'a system of allegorical interpretation in which the data of one narrative line are radically impoverished by their rewriting according to the paradigm of another narrative, which is taken as the former's master code or Ur-narrative and proposed as the ultimate hidden or unconscious *meaning* of the first one'.[20] However, Jameson maintains that the alternative to such a reductive form of reading the significance of events is not the spurious 'pluralism' of contemporary deconstruction. Meaning, and hence code, still exist. What is at issue is a question of power: the installation of a particular code as 'masterful' or authoritative.

Instead of the convenient dissolution of meaning, Jameson proposes an articulation of the notion of genre with a historicization of code.[21] Effectively endorsing (in a qualified way) Northrop Frye's identification of Romance as 'the ultimate source and paradigm of all storytelling',[22] he suggests that the development of narrative be perceived in terms of historical – and hence generic – transformations in the Romance mode, imposed upon it by the fragmentation caused by the disappearance or collapse of the sacred master code:

> From this point of view, then, the problem raised by the persistence of romance as a mode is that of substitutions, adaptations, and appropriations, and raises the question of what, under wholly altered historical circumstances, can have been found to replace the raw materials of magic and Otherness which medieval romance found ready to hand in its socioeconomic environment. A history of romance as a mode becomes possible, in other words, when we explore the substitute codes and raw materials, which, in the increasingly secularized and rationalized world that emerges from the collapse of feudalism, are pressed into service to replace the older magical categories of Otherness which have now become so many dead languages.[23]

These transformations or substitutions consist in the creation of other levels (what Jameson calls 'new positivities') which *struggle* to offer themselves as, or to integrate themselves within, a privileged master code which might permit the translation of event into meaning by unifying the disparate paradigms of which the text is composed into a single, transparent and totalizing significance. As in the original Romance model, we encounter a layering of narratives; only, in the fragmented post-Romance world, lacking the sacred master code, these layers cease to be homogeneous. What a history of narrative hence reveals is 'the coexistence or tension between several generic modes or strands',[24] of which the most vigorous and complex form is precisely that peculiarly hybrid but ostensibly most 'natural' discourse which lay claims to the inheritance of the Romance, the Novel. By tracing the substitutions of Romance elements and the tensions between the generic modes which compose the discourse,

> the 'novel' as an apparently unified form is subjected to a kind of x-ray technique designed to reveal the layered or marbled structure of the text according to what we will call *generic discontinuities*. The novel is then not so much an organic unity as a symbolic act that must reunite or harmonize heterogeneous narrative paradigms which have their own specific and contradictory ideological meaning.[25]

Here then we have a means of understanding not only the mystery of narrative as such but also a formal register, in specific narrative practices, of the secular transformation of the historical experience of mystery. The ancient experience and structures of mystery – the celebration of a universal and unchanging knowledge in ritual – is possible only in a homogeneous universe of meaning, a world whose significance is indivisible and immediately intelligible to an entire community through its sharing of a necessarily centralized, sacred master code. In modern times, the allegorical nature of narrative meaning is not a unified given, in which the existence of the master code permits each level transparently to imitate or reflect the other. Yet event still has to be translated into significance through code; the problem now is that in place of one 'master code', we find a disparate range of codes vying for the power of mastery, the ability to hold the various narrative levels in the semblance of unity and truth and thus to determine the meaning of events as self-evident. The experience of mystery changes as it comes to inhabit *the gaps between conflicting codes* which a new mastery aims to fill.

The modern experience of mystery – doubt, perplexity, isolation, suspense – can therefore be seen as the consequence of this fragmentation. If we no longer *feel* the mystery of the inevitability of repeated plots and already-known meanings but are awed more by the suspense of 'what will happen next?' and 'what does this mean?', this is because, despite retaining our nostalgia for a stable and transparent universe of meaning, we no longer have a master code of plots through which to identify our knowledge of the truth. As Peter Brooks puts it:

> The enormous narrative production of the nineteenth century may suggest an anxiety at the loss of providential plots: the plotting of the individual or social or institutional life story takes on a new urgency when one no longer can look to a sacred master-plot that organizes and explains the world. The emergence of narrative plot as a dominant mode of ordering and explanation may belong to the large process of secularization, dating from the Renaissance and gathering force during the Enlightenment, which marks a falling-away from those revealed plots . . . that appeared to subsume transitory human time to the timeless.[26]

If the ancient experience, plots and rituals of mystery belong to the realm of the timeless, the modern experience indeed has to do with 'what comes next' (or, reversing the question, 'how did we get here?'): it is the mystery of History. It is also, as I have suggested, the mystery of Language ('what does this mean?'), located in the paradigmatic gaps of narrative, the relation between signifier and signified. Thus, Grossvogel is right to observe but, I think, wrong to complain that 'The characters of *Oedipus the King* and the rest of us read the same signs: the mystery that lies beyond them concerns us equally. But the modern reader tends to seek his truth elsewhere, transferring the mystery to the signs themselves, questioning them rather than himself',[27] for these signs *are* our mysteries. As he himself observes earlier in his book, 'mystery must be decipherable – has indeed been deciphered: there remains only to decipher the decipherer.'[28] This is the project of Theology, the study of the Godhead. For us, the mystery is different but no less mysterious and no less powerful. As subjects not of a Godhead but of 'mysterious' personal and social forces which escape our control, we are driven to decipher the decipherer by seeking the non-metaphysical masters and authorities who, in the material dimensions of history and language, are writing our plot and speaking in us.

MYSTERY AND SECULARIZATION

This book seeks to relate the development of police and detection as social forms of mastery to the development of modern forms of narrative mastery in fiction. Its scheme is fairly simple, as the chapter titles indicate. It deals with a period from roughly the Constitutional Settlement of 1688 to the end of the nineteenth century, but obviously with a greater emphasis on the period of some forty years which, in orthodox histories of detective fiction, represents a perverse and puzzling hiatus, from the social invention of the detective – or, effectively, what is not at all the same thing, the literary invention of the Chevalier Dupin – to the creation of Sherlock Holmes. Throughout the discussion, I shall be concentrating on the fragmentation, conflict and coherence of codes in the constitution of social and literary mystery and mastery, in particular in reference to the development of Law and Medicine, the conflicts between them and within them, and to their relations with narrative fiction. In the context of the dialectic of the ordinary and extraordinary discussed above, I shall be endeavouring to relate these developments to empiricism and to questions of ideology, sexuality, language and subjectivity, and to the rivalry between the novel and the so-called 'sub-genres' of popular literature. Thus the part that follows this introduction, 'Wronging Rights and Righting Wrongs' (chapters 2–4), traces the substitution of an imminent providential narrative order by the development of a model of mastery by 'police', in which we shall see how the detective emerges as the highly ambivalent inheritor of the Reform model of management in the wake of its failure. In the next part, 'Writing Wrongs and Wrong Writing' (chapters 5–7), I begin with a discussion of the history of 'detective literature' and a study of the popular literature which directly celebrated the police detective before moving on to look at the mysteries which are created by and wreak their revenge upon the dominant 'police' of social and literary mastery, the monstrous beings, women and secrets of horror and sensation fiction. The book ends with the attempted foreclosure of the latter tradition by what I shall argue is Conan Doyle's 'masterly' *invention* of 'detective fiction'. Rather than finding in Holmes a modern hero who serves as a culmination of the earlier traditions and a model for Freud, I shall be arguing that the former represents the final victory of a conservative and repressive model of mastery, whereas the latter looks towards a new, albeit persistently problematic, articulation of the subject in history and language.

I would like to end this introductory chapter by specifying in a little more detail the fragmentation of code which pre-conditions both the development of the novel as a new mode of narrative (Chapter 2) and that decay from ancient and classical 'mystery' which, as I observed in the first part of this chapter, is such a striking and problematic feature of modern mystery/detective fiction. We are drawn back then to a mythical 'origin' in classical tragedy, the first literary expression of the mysterious rite of natural and social renewal as realized in the sacrificial moment when the hero discovers the secret of the past through a cathartic matching of signifier and signified – the catastrophic climax when Oedipus finally learns to read the meaning of his own acts and, in so doing, acts out the words of the prophecy. This ritual possibility of a semiotic plenitude is made utopically rather than tragically possible by the coming of Christ and his sacrifice. Christ immediately fulfills all prophecies (providing, in his person and life, the typological signified of the earlier signifiers) and at the same time resolves the mystery of our acts, giving all of them meaning in terms of an unalterable and already finished master plot. Not a human hero but the incarnation of God in Man, the synthesis of spirit and matter, Christ is himself a matched and fixed sign ('I am what I am'). As such, the central figure of the Christian mystery produces the unique trope of transubstantiation, that sign in which both object and symbol are indissociably one, enacted regularly in the liturgical rite of the Mass and expressed in the allegorical translation which this figure makes possible. Although the liturgy of the Christian story is still tragic in origin in the sense that it too bears the residues of pagan fertility rites, the new tropic possibilities of the Christian semiotic become the occasion for major dislocations in the sense of mystery in the later Middle Ages, as it is 'enromancié', or translated into vernacular literary forms: the 'Mystery or Miracle Plays' and the English 'Romance'.[29]

In the first case, the dislocation of mystery from its tragic and liturgical origins to those of the bases for a new, popular and, in due course, realist secular drama is initiated by the low-mimetic elements introduced when 'ordinary' men, rather than priests, represent to their colleagues the holy figures and events of the Bible. 'Mystery Play' is, of course, a later misnomer (OED, 1744), inasmuch as what is enacted is not the sort of ceremony or rite hitherto associated with the concept of mystery, reserved still for the Mass and the liturgical drama.[30] But the source of the misunderstanding points precisely in the direction of a major moment of secularization. The 'Mystery' refers less to the content than to the performers – the guilds or 'mysteries' whose rise during the second half of the fourteenth century provided them with the respectability and the means to take on the responsibility of edifying the populace at the time of the Corpus Christi procession more efficiently than the priests.[31] 'Arts and mysteries' read the indentures of apprentices in the Middle Ages. In the guilds, production itself is structured as a mystery, by secret knowledges, symbols, languages and rites of passage, masters and initiates, an institutional process through which signifiers (instructions and raw materials) are translated into signifieds (commodities), and those signifieds translated into signifiers (money). Whilst not surrendering its association with the religious rite, as the dramatic ritual begins its process of secularization, so too does the concept and source of mystery, in the most material sense: 'mystery' becomes conflatable with the *means of production* of the ritual itself and, at the same time, with the productive structure of the society which supports it.

Important as the new popular drama is to the modernization of mystery that will concern us in the following chapters, both in terms of its shift of mystery into the realm of economic power and in its introduction of a mode of popular realism, of equal importance for us is the transformation, in quite another class context, of the pagan rites in the Romance – a model, as we have seen, for fictional narrative itself. The original European Romances and *chansons de geste* of the twelfth century recounted adventures as idealized and exemplary trials of aristocratic social codes. However, since England never achieved the sort of hegemonic feudal structure seen for example in the France of Chrétien de Troye, the English Romance appears already as a decadent form, a late derivation from the epic stories of Arthur, the 'master-plot' of the destiny of Britain, incorporating popular magical folk traditions within the ethnic struggles which determined the nation's history. According to W. Lewis Jones, what in effect transforms the English epic into the Romance is the introduction of two motifs conveying the chivalric values of courtoisie and courtly love – the Lancelot tales –, and the religious values of asceticism – the Quest for the Grail.[32]

The fact that these elements are introduced when the Romance form itself was already past its heyday and the social class to which it theoretically corresponded was already on the way out does much to explain the role of the Grail, especially in the most important English prose Romance, Thomas Malory's *Morte d'Arthur*.[33] If the motive which sets the narrative of epic in motion and sends the hero forth upon the world is that of conquest, the introduction of this very special element in the English Romance, which portrays a society whose domestic expansion has been consolidated, gains a particular significance. Generally speaking, 'the quest for the Grail is the quest for a code. To find the Grail is to learn how to decipher the divine language'.[34] But if the Grail represents the possibility of decodification, then its most pertinent quality is that it has been lost. Whereas in the ritual the elements of meaning are present in the objects and events of the rite, here the master-symbol is reified, an object defined by absence. What then is the Grail and, above all, why should it be missing? According to Marc Shell, it is, in all senses, the 'means of life': first a religious symbol of transubstantiation, the Eucharist itself (brought to Britain by Joseph of Arimathea); second, a cornucopia, the possession of which will restore the Waste Land to fertility and prosperity; and third, in a rhetorical sense, it is the 'trope of tropes' which unites the two realms of the spiritual and the material in a unique manner: 'The tales represent the grail as being a thing both of this world and not of this world, or as being a thing both homogeneous and heterogeneous with all things. The grail, which is the source of all things, is the source of itself; to put it another way, one of the contents of the container that is the grail is the container itself.'[35] The importance of this unique spiritual, material and tropic phenomenon, entering and transforming the British epic at the time it does, derives from its relation to a new semiotic mystery which above all links the mystery of production, referred to above, to that of language. This is the mystery of *money*:

how can anything be both the symbol of all things and the source of them? The etynomic Word in the Gospel of Saint

John suggests an answer, for in some Christian theology the problem of symbolization and production is expressed in terms of the relationship between God the Father and God the Son, who is sent to earth or made flesh . . . . Theories of metallic money tend to share with discussions of the Eucharist the problem of homogeneity and heterogeneity, or confusion of representation with production. It is unclear whether metallic money is a member of the group of commodities (a group that includes coins *qua* metal) or another kind of thing (a symbol). Nominalist theorists noted that coined money, like the Verbal Eucharist, seems to constitute a common or architectonic denominator for all things. This simultaneous homogeneity and heterogeneity in the relationship between money and commodity, or between inscription and thing, raises the same metonymic problem of genus that makes mysterious the grail, the Eucharist, and the Word.[36]

The fact that the Grail only appears when the class which is represented in the Romance is already in decline, and that it appears as an absence, is explained then by the relation between this new semiotics and changes in the social structure.

Shell follows Wagner in arguing that feudal power derived from the distribution of the cornucopic capacity for wealth contained in the figure of the magical but real 'Hoard'. After its pre-historic, mythical past, this economic topos and its 'union of real and ideal' is found only once: in the archetype of Romance and feudal authority, Charlemagne, 'during whose reign as the first Holy Roman Emperor (A.D. 800–814) the secular ruler and the religious ruler were reunited "as body and spirit of mankind"'.[37] The substitution of the Hoard by the Grail as the cornucopic topos, both religious and economic, represents a new mystery, a novel relation between signifier and signified which, in Shell's account, corresponds to the increased importance of money during this period and particularly to the associated emergence of 'money of account', the instrument which, in the thirteenth century, accompanied the rise of a new class that, generating its wealth through trade, would challenge the feudal aristocracy for power.

At this stage, coin itself is still an ingot with a real, albeit (as the history of the debasement of coin testifies) highly vulnerable value content. But, in the 'money of account' which progressively supplemented and gradually replaced the actual exchange of specie, increasingly the signifier of value becomes the incarnation of its real value in only an ideal or theoretical sense. The relationship between the signifier and signified is underwritten not by a real hoard but by an authorial guarantee, the inscription on the ingot, commonly represented by an image of the temporal authority, in a similar way to that in which the image and honour of the King symbolically underwrites that of his knights and, in terms of the feudal contract between lord and vassal, vice versa. In other words, the authority of the King derives from his possession of an *ideal* hoard and is signified by the coin that this *symbolic* possession enables him to issue and stamp with his presence, whilst the value of the coin in its turn derives from his authority. The value of the King's coin may be enforced by purely temporal or military power: that is, as in Herodotus' story of Gyges, by simple tyranny.[38] But in symbolic terms, the gap between signifier and signified can only be closed by the invocation of the unique trope which unites both temporal and spiritual authority: the King has to show that his authority is 'backed' not only by temporal power but by the authority of God and Nature. In this way the obverse of the image of the monarch on the coin is commonly a text or an image referring either to God's or Nature's bounty, most often, in the latter case, a cornucopia. The Grail – the container which contains itself – serves as the symbol that might, in place of the Hoard, secure the semiotics of the peculiar magic of money by itself being an image of that very semiotics.

But, without the Hoard, the monarch has repeatedly to prove his right to possess the Grail. Just as the Romance becomes a pretext for the regular trial of the King and his nation through the testing of the code of values of one of his knights, the second guarantee of money's value in the absence of a mythical real Hoard is the regular testing of an example of the specie, conducted, we should note, by the guilds, and known as the 'trial of the pyx'. What is on trial here, again as in the Romance, is not so much the coin itself, but the issuing authority whose virtue, and the virtue of the society over which he rules, is judged in terms of the honesty of the circulating symbols of his power. It is precisely here that we find the register of another crucial moment in the process of secularization: the 'pyx' is the box in which the specie is kept for testing; it is also the name given to the cabinet in which the Eucharist is kept.[39] In sum, coin, as it substitutes barter as the mechanism of exchange and physical wealth as a mechanism of account, is 'mysterious' because the idealization of its referent increases the gap between signifier and signified. The quest for the Grail can thus be understood as the search for the symbolic object which guarantees the social order, the fertility of the land and the possibility of decodification (the mysterious attachment of signifier to signified), underwriting the new means of exchange and the temporal authority which issues and controls it.

The new mystery and the new mode of social relations under development in a mercantile economy dislocates the hegemony of code and generates a new narrative dynamic of conflict and dilemma which profoundly affects the 'questor', as can be seen in the 'further adventures' of a leading example of the class, Sir Gawaine. The occasion for trial in *Gawain and the Green Knight* is not the pursuit of the Grail but a game, a feat of arms which involves the hero also in a contest of 'love-talking'. The ritual games which structure the tale significantly take the form of a series of *exchanges*. The first exchange – blow for blow – is the result of the Green Knight's challenge, to be realized, like a contractual debt, in a year and a day. Having chopped the Knight's head off, Gawain lives his year and undergoes his adventure on credit. The adventure involves him in two further and only apparently subsidiary exchange-games. At the castle his host offers to exchange what he wins at hunting with what Gawain obtains at home; at the same time he is involved in a sexual language-game with the host's lady, in which he has to use all his skill to return her courtesy and affection without betraying his code of honour in relation to himself and his host. Gawain twice discharges the contract with Birtilak; but on the third occasion, he pays him in debased coin – giving him another kiss in place of the girdle he had received from the lady. He keeps the girdle because it promises to save him from the blow he is bound to receive for his original contract with the Green Knight: it offers him the possibility of saving both honour and life.

The nature of Gawain's trial depends on his ability to articulate the various levels of code which constitute the society he represents, codes of martial, sexual, comradely and religious behaviour, in a series of exchanges involving the means of life – the exchange of codes itself being the means of life of the knight as such. The first contract with the Green Knight implies values of courage in an exchange of honour and life (in order to honour the contract Gawain will have to die); the second contract, with Birtilak's lady, implies the successful articulation of honour and love; and the third – where Gawain defaults – involves the exchange of food (what Birtilak brings back from the hunt) and love (the kisses Gawain receives from the lady and gives to his host). The point is that, in terms of the ideal chivalric code of the feudal world, where exchanges are ideally between equivalent use-values (such as protection/service, food/labour, charity/power), these are all exchanges of absolute equivalents. Gawain's problem – and the narrative fascination of the tale – results from the fact that here the codes, which should be homogeneic (i.e. equally exchangeable), *enter into conflict*: they put him in a situation of a double-bind. Rather than maintaining the stable state of the Romance by accepting the exchange-sacrifice of his life for the honour of the court, Gawain survives by *making a profit*, by receiving more than he gives, when the whole economy of chivalry relies on not doing so. This profit (made, we should recall, on a debt) comes at the price of his code of honour and is signified by his return to court wearing the magic girdle, traditional and explicit symbol of invulnerability, which he now wears as a token of his shame and hence of the shame of the society of which he is such an exemplary representative – although, fatally, the decadent court fails to recognize it as such. As a Romance knight confronted now with a world not of homogeneous codes but of dilemmas, Gawain can only apply his codes with as much skill as he possesses; what he – and the court – cannot do, is reflect on the dilemma, change and seek to redeem the flaw in his society. That is to say, Gawain cannot yet become Hamlet; there is no possibility of generic renewal.

But if Gawain needs to become Hamlet, the *Morte d'Arthur* needs to become Shakespeare's Second Tetralogy. In compiling the epic/romance of the Civil Wars, the absolute end of England's quasi-feudal period, Malory locates his story in a Romance past without being able to synthesise the sources he claims to be editing into a modern historical narrative. There are many signs of decadence in Malory's text, particularly in the part which most concerns us, the Sangreal episode. Its structure is strictly episodic rather than ritualistic, its series of adventures and trials much more dispersed, lacking in connective coherence, than the antecedents it claims to compile. The multiplication of heroes, involving the whole court, reflects a fragmentation and distribution of virtue, rather than its centralization in one perfect representative knight. Rather than the site of universality, the court itself becomes the originating point for a simple circulation, existing as a court only so long as its population is absent on the quest. The Grail does not repair the land; the flower of knighthood is disillusioned or decimated.

The trial of the knights is increasingly less a test of valour than of their ability to solve riddles and make choices in situations of conflict. Much of the action depends, as in the traditional Romance, on the interpretation of dreams, visions, phenomena and experiences. Only here not only are the experiences perversely ambiguous, such as Lancelot's misreading of the black and white knights (Book XV, chapter 5), but the interpreters themselves are potentially deceitful – as, for example, with Percival: 'but late here I spake with a good man that fed me with his good words and holy, and refreshed me greatly. Ah, sir knight, said she, that same man is an enchanter and a multiplier of words. For an ye believe him ye shall plainly be shamed' (XIV, 8). Linguistic authority is constantly shifting. The knights not only lack a code-book to their visions, but also one which would help them identify authoritative or trustworthy interpreters. In such an unstable and conflictual universe of meanings, the knights are constantly being required to choose between absolute equivalents in deals in which they can only lose. The very first crossroads they come to offers a choice between the path of goodness and the path of prowess (XIII, 12); in Romance these should amount to the same thing. Similarly, Bors, for example, is put in the cruel position of having to choose between saving a lady and saving a comrade (XVI, 9–10), and Ector is accused by Nacien the hermit of being 'an untrue knight, and a great murderer' (XVI, 5) – a harsh accusation for a knight who is obliged to fight in honour. The breakdown in the homogeneity of codes represented by the dilemmas and discriminations to which the knights are subjected is, I think, best explained by this last charge. Under a regime of imperial conquest, the nature of the trials and particularly the relationship between self, comrade, and enemy may have been clear; but in a civil war the man you kill may prove to be a member of your own class and nation, as happens here with Gawaine (XVI, 3–4). All that can provide stability in this universe is its most anachronistic element: Malory's re-invention of the spiritually and martially ideal Romance hero, the Christ-like and newly-minted Galahad, and the Grail – itself defined as unattainable to all but the most perfect knight, the one who wishes to die when he obtains it. When it is found and placed in its proper location (outside the world), the occasions for chivalry fulfill their destiny and die and Arthur's court collapses into civil war.

Written in jail by a supporter of the losing side in the Civil War, Malory's archaic narrative represents a crisis in authority brought on by the loss of the Romance master-plot of feudalism. Mystery develops in the gaps of language and plot created by the conflict of codes and reflects the social conflict of power-centres which characterizes the moment of its composition. In its symbolic instability and lack of overall narrative cohesion, the *Morte d'Arthur* seems a somewhat inconsequential epitaph to a period which has ceased to make sense, without the new period providing a new sort of sense. If, as Shell maintains, the authority of the Hoard derives from the power to dispense or distribute its wealth, and the authority of the Grail derives from its possession, for the Tudors it derives, as Moretti argues and as both Hamlet and Hal have to learn, from the power to *decide*.[40] Where codes enter into conflict, what is needed is a new discourse with the power to impose its homogeneity on conflicting sources, like, in a first moment, the sort of myth of nation provided by the Tudors and, in the later moment where our study begins, the hegemonizing myth of parliamentary democracy, the state of law, developed from the late seventeenth century. In other words, the redistribution of the asymmetries of power caused by new modes of production and exchange, and the social conflict they generate, determine that mystery unfolds towards the increasingly temporal, political power which determines the attachment of signifieds to signifiers and the articulation of personal and social histories – the power of what, as we shall see below, may be called 'police'.

What then does Malory's text display as missing that prevents it from developing into coherence, into a form which might recodify the various levels it inherits and marshals? The anachronism of Romance provides a first explanation: the lack of a form of narrative organization which, in the absence of the feudal master-plot, permits the episodic to transcend its incidental nature. This lack can be specified in terms of what we might call a *syntax of causality*, a means of articulating events into meaning according to principles, like those enunciated by Francis Bacon for a secular science, which are no longer the self-repeating patterns of the residues of fertility ritual, magic and Divine intervention. This problem is in its turn related to the limitation of the reality of the Romance to a specific – and increasingly less hegemonic – class. Malory's text is condemned to speak of another land and another time; the knights ride through a landscape which is effectively devoid of labourers and peasants, are sustained without a glimpse of any process of production, and conduct exchange without trade. The collapse of the feudal order is the consequence of the rise of other classes which had hitherto been excluded from the social narrative. In this way, the absence of a syntax of causality is linked to the simultaneous lack of a coding which would allow the text to speak of what presses most urgently upon it: a *mimesis of the contemporary*. This then is the modern condition of mystery: no longer the knowledge of the plots of the metaphysical and the timeless, but the struggle for the authority to narrate a knowledge of the contemporary and its causal sequences.

But if the *Morte d'Arthur* is the end of Romance, it is also the beginning of something else. Malory's purported compilation of lost or imaginary sources based on a mythical French original was published after the death of its author, in 1485, the same year that Henry VII put an end to the Civil War and inaugurated a new dynasty. To discuss that dynasty, and the drama which, as I have already indicated, provides a major literary form for modern mystery, would take us in quite another direction. My concern here being more strictly with particular strategies of modern power in narrative, I shall stay generically closer to Malory's work of prose fiction. In this context particularly, the *Morte d'Arthur* is a text which, however anachronistic its world, looks forward to a new era. After Chaucer's attempt to portray the languages and characters of contemporary reality in a new form, *The Canterbury Tales* (1476), it is the first book written originally in English to be *printed* on Caxton's Westminster Press. It is worth noting that the other major work issued by the Press in 1485 was a *Life of Charles the Great*, and the text whose sales exceeded both Chaucer and Malory was *The Book of Good Manners* (1487). Malory's compilation of codes which is lacking a code-book is thus bracketed by two non-fictional code-books, the one still looking back to the exemplary life of the incarnation of Romance and feudalism and the other a handbook to teach the rising classes how to behave. Just as the mint provides political power in a mercantile economy, Malory's heterogeneous and fragmented text is related to the development of a market in writing and its new sources and forms of authority. It is this novelty – the commercial printing press – which will in large part concern us in Chapter 2.

Part II
Wronging Rights and Righting Wrongs

2
Crime

We observed in the previous chapter that 'detection' can best be construed through the historicization of the mysteries which are its object. In this context the eighteenth century presents itself as a central moment of coincidence for our theoretical and historical concerns in that it sees, on the one hand, the emergence of the novel as a new and peculiarly modern narrative form for the developing industry of print and, on the other hand, an intense development in the figure of crime – precisely that figure specific to detection as a form for mastering mystery – as a central means of representing social conflict. More to the point, we find that the novel at its inception is haunted by this eminently secular topic. Why was it then, as Lennard Davis puts it, that 'There seems to have been something inherently novelistic about the criminal, or rather the form of the novel seems to demand a criminal content'?[1] One answer, Davis suggests, lies in its own discursive antecedents, particularly in relation to the new press. The orthodox view of the novel underwrites its modern literary status by viewing it as the realist descendent of the high-cultural prose romance. But the term 'novels' is to be found as early as c. 1566 as a synonym for 'newes', the 'low' literature of popular ballads which constituted the main product of the new press, a growing industry of entertainment and information embracing traditional songs and stories of monsters, scandals and murder.[2] As the industry developed in response to the urbanization of its audience, the traditional folk tale declined in relation to what Davis calls 'the journalistic ballad' and, from the 1620s, the prose 'newsbook', texts which functioned 'as newspapers to inform primarily the literate and illiterate lower classes of public events such as earthquakes, wars, murders, freaks of nature, and supernatural happenings, as well as to preach religious homilies to

31

those considered most likely to commit violent acts'.[3] The 'novelty' of the new popular form resided precisely in its being printed, in its capacity, in other words, not only to reach a wider readership but also to transcribe event into text with much greater rapidity.

The 'novel' emerged as a form of literary fiction in the eight-eenth century through the splitting of this undifferentiated 'news/novel' discourse into separate discourses of fact and of fiction. The growing commercial and ideological importance of newssheets and pamphlets and their threat to the ruling class' monopoly on the circulation of information led the government to attempt to control them through the Stamp Acts of 1712 and 1724. The printers' reaction to the latter law in particular, with its tax on 'news' itself, makes it, for Davis, 'a turning point in the history of the press and consequently of the novel': they divided up 'a previously intact discourse – narrative – into the taxable (news) and the untaxable (fiction, history)', publishing the former on one sheet and shifting the latter to a separate 'literary' section.[4] In short, 'novel' begins to distinguish itself as fiction from 'news' as fact as a result of competing imperatives of state control and commercial and ideological interests.

The tradition of balladry, early printed sheets, pamphlets and 'novels' dealt with various popular areas of interest – traditional songs, collections of jests, current events, tales of witches, mon-sters and 'strange happenings' in general, plus romance and love-intrigues (indeed Dr. Johnson defined 'novel' in his *Dictionary* as 'A small tale, generally of love'). But their most frequent subject by far was criminal (auto)biography, confessions and tales. These were particularly suited to the 'news/novel' discourse inasmuch as not only did they reflect a felt contemporary reality but they themselves played on the ambiguously factive status of the discourse, being simultaneously sensationalist but none the less attested as authentic, recent journalistic accounts frequently claiming to be written by or based on the testimony of the criminals themselves.[5] If then the Novel, as it emerges in the eighteenth century, is in large part descended from the popular ballad and newsbook, and if the latter are preeminently concerned with narratives of crime, this brings us to the obvious question: why the popular and literary obsession with crime? In what sense does the topic of crime articulate the new mysteries of the modern period?

The common assertion that the early eighteenth century was characterized by a 'crime wave' does not really bear scrutiny: rather than more crime, what we are probably witnessing is either more offences, more efficiency in apprehension, or better records. Indeed, the intensity and the very image of criminality gleaned from the popular literature does not bear comparison with the available court records.[6] But this surely is the point: whether or not the 'crime wave' existed, what the statistics and narratives prove beyond doubt is an intense contemporary concern with crime, a marked coding of behaviour in terms of the criminal and the lawful. What is being registered in the focus on crime is thus the growing centrality of Law.

To the extent that prose fiction exists as a form of moral fable, its overall structure is determined by a literary code which guarantees the victory of the good and the punishment of the bad as the ending to which the narrative proceeds and which determines its retrospective meaning. This is sustainable as the moral realism of Romance so long as reader and writer share a unifying social code. The literary element which assures moral structure is the convention that the very principle of the mystery of narrative – its imminent authority – is inherently providential. The cohesive narrative code is in its turn sustained by and produces the complementary ideas of the active intervention of God and the myth of community. Both these are synthesised in the figure of the divinely appointed monarch ruling over a united nation. However, it is clear that there is a complex historical process through which the generalized belief in the active intervention of God, in the community of interests of a society, the workings of a Hookerian Providence and the divinity that hedges the King, begin to break down. It is in this way that the Civil War and the execution of Charles I was accompanied by searching examinations of the relation between History and Providence, and the urgent need for new safeguards against the collapse into an anti-providential world in which personal and social narratives had no pattern but strife and were in consequence 'nasty, brutish, and short'. Whereas Hobbes still clings to his nostalgia for absolutism, arguing that 'Where there is no common Power, there is no Law',[7] for 'liberals' like Locke, where there was no Law there was no legitimate power. Sovereignty was a 'compact', 'contract' or, in Locke's legalistic term, a 'trust', an authority not merely to be instituted, but constituted by rules.

The shift is particularly clear in the constitutional debates of the 'Glorious Revolution' of 1688–9. To legitimize its own action, Parliament needed to claim that James II had acted illegally, particularly in using the key and exclusive power of the monarch to grant individual dispensation from the effects of the Law to suspend the Test Acts wholesale. This was achieved through the concept of 'contract'; on 28 January 1689 the Commons ruled 'That King James II, having endeavoured to subvert the constitution of the kingdom, by breaking the original contract between king and people; and by the advice of Jesuits and other wicked persons having violated the fundamental laws; and having withdrawn himself out of this kingdom; has abdicated the government; and that the throne is thereby vacant.' Whilst the traditional royalists maintained, through inheritance and custom, that it was the monarch who had brought Parliament into being as an instrument of his authority and was hence the source of Law, the latter could only justify itself by claiming the superior sovereignty of the legislature – or, in other words, the ultimate sovereignty of legislation, the Law as the *source* of authority rather than its instrument. But when the Lords turned to the lawyers to explain the terms of the 'original contract', they were unable to do so, as Sir Robert Atkyns confessed: 'I believe none of us have it in our books or cases; nor anything that touches on it.'[8] In the absence of an explicit 'original compact', as both Locke's *Two Treatises of Government* (1690) and the Bill of Rights (1689) testify, it was necessary to 'invent' a contract that would bind the monarchy within legal and rational terms. The significance of this moment is its affirmation that the organic tradition which underwrote authority in England was not that of the ancient mystery of the monarchy, but that of the Law as the discourse of social contract.

There is of course precedent, and no part of the historical process I am sketching can be identified as original or decisive. Rather, what exist are moments in the secularization of the mysteries of authority and fate, in the fragmentation of codes and cultures and their reassembly in a modern consensus. But what we find in these moments is not only that they tend to mark what are retrospectively seen as the keystones of the English legal system, but that they each in their turn represent the growing importance and extension of that system as the foundation of authority, identity, and the regulation of social destiny. This is, in an important sense, an English epic – its peculiar and much-vaunted common law constitution, perceived as an organic and traditional expression of English nationhood and democracy. It is in that sense the narrative of the emergence and construction of the Law as the master code, the central mystery, of the modern secular state.

Once again, there is a simple metonymic explanation inasmuch as the development of the English legal system is in practice a secondary consequence of the development of a system of administration of power. The very notion of the 'common law' ('common' not in being equal for all but in being geographically uniform) derives from the first two Henries' attempts to centralize local administration through their itinerant justices. However at the ideological level the practical structures of power have always been raised to the level of mysteries, their instruments legitimized by attributing transcendental, metaphorical qualities to the Law – its translation, for example, into the singularly providential notion of Justice. Magna Carta and the Bill of Rights become popularly perceived less as pragmatic divisions of power between competing factions than as sets of transcendental social values of universal application, transhistorical guarantees of individual freedoms. The English Law, as it evolved from the peculiarly quasi-feudal system of the Middle Ages, is particularly suited to this role in that it is based on contract and not on command.[9] The Common Law codifies relations of identity and authority as relations of tenure, expresses them in contractual terms of rights and duties, and imbues them with the mysteries of community: universality, liberty, equality and justice. The Law is superior to the institution of sovereign precisely because the latter (the 'tenant-in-chief') is constituted as such by the Law. Authority is not the emanation of a person but a consequence of the code which constitutes his identity and that of all subjects as a contractual relation of rights and duties. By this token, the Law becomes the simultaneous guarantee of authority and of both individual and national identity – the birthright of the free-born Englishman.

In this way then the Constitutional Settlement founds the modern state by establishing the Law as its master code (resolver of conflicting codes): 'the notion of "the rule of law" was central to seventeenth- and eighteenth-century Englishmen's understanding of what was both special and laudable about their political system . . . an idealization, a potent "fiction" . . . which commanded widespread assent from both patricians and plebeians.'[10] Thus it was that the eighteenth century saw a general expansion and systematization of the role of Law in social life. The first government attempts to regulate the profession in 1729 and the founding of the first 'Society of Gentleman Practitioners in the Courts of Law and Equity' in 1739 (later to become the Law Society in 1826) demonstrate the new power lawyers themselves began to wield. The 'torrent of new law books' which flowed from the printing press included not only technical books for the growing profession but the major classic texts which are as close as English Law gets to a systematic 'legal code', the most important of which was undoubtedly Sir William Blackstone's pioneering lectures at Oxford (1753), the *Commentaries on the Laws of England* (1765) – 'the first comprehensive survey of English law since Bracton'.[11] More important still is the fact that the attempted textual systematization of existing law was accompanied by extensive legislation: the new criminal law statutes, which, as if in testimony to their comprehensive and exhaustive nature, were known popularly as the 'Bloody Code'. More than 187 capital statutes were enacted between 1660 and 1819, in an increasingly wholesale incorporation of social life under the criminal law which goes a long way to explain the contemporary obsession with crime as an expression of the mystery of the modern state.

Although comprehensive, the 'Bloody Code' was not deliberately systematic; superficially it was a series of *ad hoc* and often originally temporary laws, a simple succession of specific protective measures aimed at isolated disruptions of the social order. But it possessed an implicit systematic rationality founded not so much on juridical as on larger socio-economic terms: put simply, on the protection of property through the uniform and totalizing enforcement of law and order by the terror of execution. The rise of 'absolute private property' is commonly seen as the key element in the transformation from feudalism to capitalism, particularly in relation to the new social 'trust' as expressed by Locke and the distinctive English legal system articulated by Blackstone.[12] If then the obsession with crime, the Constitutional Revolution, the rise of the legal profession, the systematization of the Law and the 'Bloody Code' reflect the centrality of the eighteenth century in the establishment of the rule of Law as the social master code, then what this in turn preeminently reflects are the new mysteries engendered by the socio-economic transformations associated with the early development of modern capitalism.

The use of legislation against specific offences as the occasion for a general and comprehensive control of populations, aimed at mastering a global transformation of English society, is patent in its most significant and notorious example, the Waltham Black Act of 1722, an emergency measure which was extended and prolonged as a matter of course, becoming permanent in 1758 and only abrogated in general in 1823: 'There is hardly a criminal act which did not come within the provision of the Black Act . . . [It] constituted in itself a complete and extremely severe criminal code which indiscriminately punished with death a great many different offences,' amounting to 'a kind of "ideological index" to the large body of laws based on the death penalty' of the period.[13] Studies of punishable offences in the seventeenth and eighteenth centuries demonstrate that what was being punished to a large extent was not, strictly speaking, new. Rather, activities which were previously either legitimated or at least tolerated by custom became criminalized under the pressure of developments directly associated with the emergence of modern capitalism in England in the period: the increasing commercialization of agriculture, the intensification of land-use, enclosure, the transformation of the peasantry into mobile or seasonal labourers, the development of the cities and new relations of production, and the extension of the state. This can be seen, for example, in the multiplication of statutes dealing with poaching (from the 1671 Act instituting a property qualification for hunting to the Game Duty Act of 1784), gleaning and common-land grazing. By the same token, the prosecution of smugglers – another customarily tolerated activity – can be seen as reflecting the increasing importance of international trade and of state control, particularly the development of state financing by taxation. Finally, the increase in internal trade and of the expansion of the state through its channels is reflected in the building of the turnpikes and the laws relating to them, as well as in the phenomenon, so much an image of eighteenth-century crime, of the highwayman.

In the second place these transformations produced reactions in the population which another body of legislation was directed specifically at de-legitimizing and controlling: in particular, the comprehensive laws against arson and the issuing of threats, and above all the 1715 Riot Act aimed at assembly and protest. This Act not only involved the harsh repression of popular unrest; its importance also lies in the fact that, inasmuch as popular riots can be viewed as the customary political expression of the disenfranchised, it also reflected the development of a modern attitude to political action: contemporaneous with the development of political parties, it implied the incorporation of all legitimate political activity exclusively within the parliamentary party system.[14] Yet another body of legislation relates more directly to the disciplining of the workforce. The again comprehensive Vagrancy Act of 1740 linked rural 'criminality' to more specifically urban activities by providing control over the increasing number of dispossessed and unemployed rural workers, travelling people (including ballad singers), and the urban 'Mob'. The severe punishment of petty theft by employees and servants – a customarily tolerated activity as an unofficial supplement to wages – sought to discipline the workforce to new relations of production and payment, and the laws against combination (1720, 1744) limited the workers' means of organization. By the same token, the laws against prostitution and infanticide reflected changing structures in the family and the fate of women, particularly in the cities, at the same time bringing the state's control to bear on sexuality. Here too we should include the beginnings of state involvement in marriage, the 1754 Marriage Act.[15] Finally then, legislation began to extend state control into not only the economic but also the personal and ideological lives of the population through the increasing use of licensing mechanisms, such as the Gin Act of 1736 and similar acts for the licensing of places of entertainment and gambling, the Stamp Acts and the censorship of the theatre (1728 – in response to John Gay's satire based on Jonathan Wild, *The Beggar's Opera*), and developments in the laws of defamation.

In other words, eighteenth-century criminal legislation represents a new form of control using the concept of crime as the all-encompassing and uniform category for behaviour which failed to conform to the emerging modern code, and to use the comprehensive terror of punishment to destroy, exclude, or alter that behaviour. One of its major consequences, from our point of view, was then the creation of a new and mysterious class. Just as certain previously common practices were uniformly recoded as criminal, so too the groups of people for whom they constituted a customary way of life were comprehensively re-categorized as criminals – that is to say, as outside of and threatening to the hegemonic codes. J. A. Sharpe refers to this process as 'the "criminalisation" of the poor', since the population at which it was directed was precisely that created by the emerging regime of property, trade and state, its transformation of the way of life of the peasantry and its partial and progressive conversion into a body of seasonal labourers, peripatetic poor, 'masterless men', and an urban working class. As soon as serious contemporary attention was paid to crime, we find that it was viewed as an alternative, contrary and evil cultural code, a counter-plot, governing the activity of almost an entire social class. Between the sixteenth- and seventeenth-century stereotype of the 'vagrant' and the nineteenth-century notion of the pervasive urban 'dangerous classes', the eighteenth century suffered from a chronic fear of an amorphous mass of unruly elements, 'the Mob', supporting organized and professional criminals operating in specific impenetrable and interconnecting geographical locations, a society closed upon itself, but constantly reaching out literally to touch and threaten ordered society.

The literature of the developing 'news/novel' discourse of the seventeenth and eighteenth centuries seeks to penetrate this 'underworld' and to represent it to ordered society. What identified the class and indicated it as a mystery was precisely its secret code of language ('cant') and behaviour. Daniel Defoe, ever the spy, pursued information by entering the underworld journalistically and fictitiously. The sort of pragmatic advice on how criminals talk, think, behave and organize themselves that Moll Flanders and Colonel Jack pretend to give us as a justification for their stories is in fact the staple fare of a large number and variety of texts, narrative, didactic or both, be they criminals' tales and confessions or legal and religious tracts. Thus, not the spy but the magistrate, Henry Fielding wrote a number of campaigning tracts on crime, such as the influential *Inquiry into the Cause of the late Increase in Robberies* (1750), the most cogent contemporary portrait and analysis of the circuits and localities of crime. He too, in his seriously 'factual' discourse, concentrates on providing the public with revelations not only of the tricks of the 'trade' but also particularly of the language and means of communication and identification of a community which was clearly perceived as knowable only through its secret code.

This code of language and behaviour was seen not only as the means of identification but the very cause of the criminal way of life. The extremely high incidence of criminal behaviour in the metropolis, according to Fielding, derived simply from the abominable manners and life-style of the poor (drinking, swearing, gambling and prostitution) – the 'torrent of luxury', 'habit of idleness' and 'Multitude of Place of Entertainment for the lower Sort of People'.[16] As Jonas Hanway the philanthropist, writing in the midst of the Age of Reason, put it: 'The Present time is distinguished as the *age of Pleasure*: her altars are erected in every street and corner: the common people are initiated into her *mysteries* . . . '[17] Criminality functioned in these pamphlets as a concept governing not only an entire class but also the entirety of its form of life, 'the manners of the people, their social intercourse and the way in which they spent their leisure'.[18] It was this that the Law had to master if it was to establish itself as the homogeneous code.

The notion of a mysterious 'underworld' registered a genuine conflict. The culture of the poor increasingly ceased to be the tolerable disorder of a distant and controllable class. The growth of the cities brought the 'lower orders' into closer and ill-defined contact with the middle and ruling classes – as we see in the obsession with pocket-picking, that image of the dirty urchin brushing up against a gentleman or lady in public places and invading the privacy of the pocket. The notion and imagery of the uncivilized 'Mob' transformed the lives of the poor from a low culture into something which was no more than the locus of unregulated and vicious behaviour threatening the social order.

To this mysterious life the Law responded with its own quasi-religious rituals of mastery, consisting basically in two key moments, the first of which was the twice-yearly local assizes. These – and to a lesser extent the quarter sessions – were special social events, attracting both 'the county' and a popular crowd. The court arrived in town in a majestic parade, the judges dressed in elaborate, archaic and symbolic garb and accompanied by representatives of the church. There would be a special church sermon; the court displayed its learning in an arcane language and strange ritual practices which marked the impenetrable mystery of the Law itself. The climax of the assize was the ceremonial of sentencing, itself designed to achieve maximum effect as a drama of mystery, and again accompanied by sermonizing on the part of the judge. Indeed, according to Douglas Hay, 'In its ritual, its judgements and its channelling of emotion the criminal law echoed many of the most powerful psychic components of religion . . . .The secular mysteries of the courts had burned deep into the popular consciousness, and perhaps the labouring poor knew more of the terrors of the law than those of religion. When they did hear of hell, it was often from a judge.'[19]

This rite served as a preface to the second key moment of the mystery of the criminal law, the public ceremony of execution. With its 'doctrine of maximum severity', the 'Bloody Code' took the narrative form of a closed, simple and univocal moral drama. By committing a felony, the subject lost all right to continue within the universe of the community and surrendered his or her body

and destiny to the will of authority. The individual was transformed from a free citizen to an object on which the state could
inscribe a 'sentence', whose life it could foreclose. The culminating
spectacle was thus the narrative conclusion of the discourse of the
criminal law, in which the disruptive sequence of events which
were signified by crime and its culture were finally ordered into
a spectacular proof and tragic enactment of the inexorable destiny
of evil, with the criminal law and its juridical institutions playing
the part of Providence.

Although the number of capital crimes and of convictions
increased enormously in this period, the number of actual executions
failed to keep pace. Radzinowicz has explained the mechanisms
by which felons evaded the penalty.[20] Of these, the use of Royal
Pardons on application by the magistracy had a particular value
in exploiting the mystery of 'Mercy' to reinforce the structure of
authority, so that, in sum, at this stage 'The Law made enough
examples to inculcate fear, but not so many as to harden or repel
a populace that had to assent, in some measure at least, to the
rule of property.'[21] Thus, although the statutory uniformity of
punishment encouraged a belief in the impartiality of the Law's
severity, the doctrine of maximum severity was not a literal system.
The execution was therefore preeminently a *symbolic* act which
relied above all on the pedagogic ritual of execution to extend its
reading of the life of the poor to the massed spectators. Following
on the rites of trial and sentence, its ceremonial, surrounded by a
mixture of custom, solemnity, license and superstition, transformed
the criminal into a symbolically tragic object of horror and pathos
around whom a moral community could be generated. The public
endorsed the terror of the Law at the moment that the disturbing
element of the peace was sacrificed to the values of the community
constructed or reinforced by the rite: 'In theory, the processional to
the gallows and the execution itself were supposed to be a carefully
stage-managed theater of guilt in which the offender and the parson
acted out a drama of exhortation, confession, and repentance before
an awed and approving crowd.'[22]

As a spectacle, 'A successful public execution justified justice, in
that it published the truth of the crime in the very body of the man
to be executed.'[23] But it was not only the body that was in question.
At the assizes, until 1836, felons were denied both speech and silence
– not having the right to council, they could not, in modern legal
slang, 'tell the tale', but they were compelled to answer guilty or

innocent, under the threat of the *peine forte et dure*. However, in the ceremonial of symbolic execution, the criminal's speech was a major element in the spectacle:

> the condemned was expected to make a 'good end', to show courage on the gallows . . . . One aspect of making a good end . . . was being launched into eternity in a contrite and penitent frame of mind. Proof of this was frequently offered in the 'last dying speech' or 'last dying confession' which the criminal was often recorded as delivering. Such speeches, far from being used as the occasion to hurl a final defiance at the unkind world, were usually marked by an acceptance of the justice and deservedness of the sentence which was about to be carried out, a warning to those present to avoid a similar fate, and a confession not only of the crime which had brought retribution, but also of a career of past sinfulness.[24]

At the moment of tragic catastrophe, the culmination of the terrible mystery of the criminal law occurs as the condemned, on the scaffold stage, publically confesses and repents of his life in endorsement of his end, his new identity, and the code of authority which determined them. And it is here that we find the first significance of the popular criminal tale or biography, based as it is on the drama enacted between the criminalized and the criminalizing codes, so central to the generation of a community around the culture of property and the rule of modern Law.

We have seen how Peter Brooks considers narrative as a retrospective account of events repeated and revised under the coherent and truthful meaning that only death can guarantee. In this way, as he argues, Rousseau's *Confessions* can be viewed 'at least symbolically [as] the *incipit* of modern narrative':

> the life histories of societies, institutions, and individuals assumed a new importance as the idea of a sacred masterplot lost its persuasive and cohesive force. From sometime in the eighteenth century onward, the interpretation of human plots took on a new urgency in response to a new centering of perspectives on the individual personality and a search for patterns in the individual existence and understanding of self that might recover some of the explanatory force lost with the decline of the collective myth. Rousseau's effort to get his life into a book that he might present to

the Sovereign Judge – if not God, then at least the reader – stands as the emblematic emergence of the biography of the individual personality, announcing the typical focus and concern of modern narrative.[25]

However, in our context, this privilege of retrospective repetition of a life is not that of the Catholic modeled on the privacy of the confessional, and it does not yet take the form of Rousseau's individual introspective personality. Rather is is part of the eminently social and symbolic spectacle of the secular Law. It is uttered by criminals, acting as representatives of their 'low' class, before their earthly as much as their divine judges, addressed as much to the state and the public as it is to God.

THE NOVEL

This ceremonial encounter of two orders of society, in which the criminal represented both the consequence and the symbol of the 'sub-culture' the ritual aimed to master, was not a mere formality but a real drama, fraught with potential tension and resistance by that 'sub-culture'. It would seem that, at least for a while, the ritual was in general successful; but speeches of defiance, drunkenness and rioting were not uncommon, and, as the century progressed, the consensus the ceremonial sought to encourage and embody became increasingly so fragile that it was in due course discontinued, in favour, as we shall see in Chapter 3, of new means for mastering the mysteries of the poor. But what should be noted here is that the criminal's confession and the popular printed genres which exploited it are defined by this tension between conflicting cultural codes – the narrative excitement of the ritual as its proper end is awaited – constituting a structure which is of major importance to the emerging novel.

The gallows confession is structured by a fundamental doubleness. First, to be effective, the criminal's autobiography had to be realistic – striking the audience as authentic by providing vivid details of a recognizable existence. But, in its raw form, this existence – normally of poverty, debauchery, daring and criminality – apparently only has the form of impulse and opportunity; it is a random and episodic picaresque, an autobiographical *discours sauvage*. Only the moment of confession and execution can reveal its shape, retrospectively re-ordering the accidental and opportunistic life in the light of a destiny, a masterplot which integrates the incidental adventures as moments in a fateful career of evil by means of a syntax of moral causality that endorses, in the criminal's own words, the narrative structure of the new order of property. Therein lies the repentance for the criminal and the generous moral lesson for the community from which he came: in his new identity within a moral frame as one who recognizes the evil of his ways and the inevitability and justice of his destiny by rewriting his life not as random excitement but as a tragic plot brought to order and meaning by the Providential intervention of the Criminal Law.

But to what extent did the moral frame which ordered the otherwise plotless *discours sauvage* resist the sensational realism of the adventure it sought to subdue to its moral syntax? The intrinsic doubleness of the cultural and narrative codes – adventure or morality, the culture of the 'mob' or its repudiator? – becomes markedly clearer when the ritual drama of the execution is displaced into the literary environment of the popular broadsheet or pamphlet. If, as Lincoln Faller maintains, there was a social consensus around the culprit of the *petit trahison* of the murder of father, husband or employer or the Cain-like fratricide in favour of the moral frame, this was no doubt due to the fact that these crimes usually went well beyond the cultural conflict expressed by the new property crimes. In any case, the same consensus by no means necessarily applied to the literature of thieves' and highwaymen's confessions and, particularly, the third-person tales which tended only superficially to encase the picaresque form of the adventures of the entertaining rogue in a moral frame. Whether Faller is right to separate the two generically or not, in both cases, inasmuch as they contain both the 'adventure' of a life and its retrospective moral framing, the public confession of the criminal can be described as constitutionally 'double': speaking as both complete criminal and sincere penitent (in Davis' words, 'both example to be avoided and example to be imitated'), equally convincing in both roles ('both the locus of fraud and the locus of truth'), he or she both appeals to and admonishes, thrills and reforms, the community.[26] This 'doubleness' is, for Davis, also constitutive of the emergent novel. The relation between the new narrative prose and crime is not only metonymic (through their contiguity in the popular printed 'news/novel' discourse and their content) but also metaphoric: what he calls the 'publication ritual' of confession and execution serves as a powerful analogy for the constitutive illicitness of 'fictionalizing, inventing, forging reality, and lying' which was the basis of the new writing.[27]

This has to do with the manner in which the discourse of crime relates to the emergence of the codes of the modern capitalist state in another, more strictly literary context. Since the Renaissance, the moral justification for imaginative prose against Platonic accusations of falseness and fraud were based on Sir Philip Sidney's argument that the Romance or Fable permitted an inspiring idealization of virtue precisely because it was archaic and 'marvellous' and did not attempt to imitate the real and the contemporary. But, as James Beattie wrote in 1783:

> *The History of Don Quixote* . . . brought about a great revolution in the manners and literature of Europe, by banishing the wild dreams of chivalry, and reviving the taste for the simplicity of nature. In this view, the publication of Don Quixote forms an important era in the history of mankind . . . . This work no sooner appeared, than chivalry vanished, as snow melts before the sun. Mankind awoke as from a dream . . . . It astonished them to find, that nature and good sense could yield a more exquisite entertainment, than they had ever derived from the most sublime phrenzies of chivalry.[28]

In the wake of the seventeenth-century revolutions, this sort of Romance – and especially its decayed French form – had come to be perceived as at least frivolous and at worst pernicious, as was the aristocratic life-style that bred it. Literature had other functions, and other classes, to serve in the modernizing state.

So alongside Cervantes we must again place Locke – on this occasion, his influential contribution to the emerging debate on child-rearing and on the imagination. In *Some Thoughts Concerning Education* (1693) Locke argued in defence of the pleasures of imaginative literature in terms of their ability to seduce the child into virtue. But such pleasures are a two-edged weapon; whilst Locke's argument defended imaginative literature against extreme Puritanism, it also implied the need for strict criteria of selection – he recommends only books in which 'the entertainment that [the child] finds might draw him on, and reward his Pains in Reading, and yet not such as should fill his Head with perfectly useless trumpery, or lay the principles of Vice and Folly'.[29] This discrimination of imaginations is again related to two cultures. As

Locke was at pains to point out, children were constantly exposed
to a form of extravagant, useless, and pernicious literature derived
from their contact with 'the most dangerous of all, the Examples of
the Servants', not the aristocratic but the popular culture of the marvellous – in Geoffrey Summerfield's ironic words, 'all the vulgar,
superstitious nonsense that servants indulge in below stairs'.[30] Thus
the influential Isaac Watts: 'Let not Nurses or Servants be suffered
to fill their Minds with *silly Tales and with senseless Rhimes*'; or the
anonymous author of *The History of Genesis* (1708): 'Let not our
Children read these vain Books, profane Ballads, and filthy songs.
Throw away all fond amorous Romances, and fabulous Histories
of Giants, the bombast Achievements of Knight Errantry, and the
like; for these fill the Heads of Children with vain, silly, and idle
imaginations.'[31]

Throw them away; but what to put in their place? The new form
of fictional writing for both children and young adults had to start
by disavowing the pernicious frivolities of the aristocratic and
popular marvellous and to stake its claim by contrast in the territory
of an imagination whose pleasures were sober and respectable:
'To the old romance, which exhibited exalted personages, and
displayed their sentiments in improbable and impossible situations, has succeeded the more reasonable, modern novel; which
delineates characters drawn from actual observation, and, when
ably executed, presents an accurate and captivating view of real
life.'[32] The restraint of imagination by reason, nature, observation,
experience and probability – the 'real life' of the new realism –
thus provided the emergent novel with an armoury of related
moral, didactic, and ontological claims for the techniques it carried over from the factual discourse of 'newes'. The equation of
this 'natural' realism with both mimesis and moral improvement
is made aggressively clear in Defoe's preface to his journalistic
account of Jonathan Wild: 'They that had rather have a falsehood
to laugh at, than a true account of things to inform them, had best
buy the fiction, and leave the history to those who know how to
distinguish good from evil.'[33] 'Truth to life' seeks to posit itself as a
sufficient guarantee of moral virtue. But, as the very aggressiveness
of Defoe's protestation suggests, such legitimization by disavowal
– that is to say the rejection of the codes of Romance and the
marvellous of the folk culture which informed the vast majority of
texts commercialized by the popular press as 'falsehood' or 'fiction'
– leads the new writers into a complicated double-bind.

First, as we have just seen in Defoe, although the terms 'novel' and 'romance' were developing distinct connotations, without yet any agreement as to the characteristics of the one or the other or a theoretical discourse to distinguish them, the new writers had little choice but to defend their new products from their proximity to romance by conflating their own fictions with fact, in a disingenuous pretence that, whilst they were clearly works of the imagination, they were none the less true – as in Defoe's *Roxana*: 'this Story differs from most of the Modern Performances of this Kind, tho' some of them have met with a very good Reception in the World: I say, It differs from them in this Great and Essential Article, Namely, That the Foundation of This is laid in Truth of Fact; and so the Work is not a Story, but a History'.[34] Even when the outrageousness of the claim does not extend to the explicit falsehood of claiming the historical truth of the fiction, it remained present in the very texture of the discourse, the technical apparatus of 'news' and realism which it deployed to convince the reader of the verisimilitude of the action, its implicit pretence that if the story did not in fact happen, it was as if it had.

The double bind derives from the fact that whilst the verisimilitude of the new writing provided a moral claim against the marvellous of Romance and popular literature, it did not in fact itself immediately raise 'factual fiction' from its 'low' status – rather the contrary. 'Fact' may be a virtue in relation to 'fiction', but, in relation to the proper moral purposes of literature, it was potentially dangerous, especially when it was most convincing. As Samuel Johnson was quick to point out in his classic essay on fiction in *The Rambler*, 4 (1750), it was the nature of empirical verisimilitude as a form of mimesis that the nearer one approached it, the greater the risk of deviation from moral truth. In this light, the fanciful irrealism of the old Romance becomes once more its (albeit ironic) defence: 'In the romances formerly written, every transaction and sentiment was so remote from all that passes among men, that the reader was in very little danger of making any applications to himself'. On the other hand:

It is justly considered as the greatest excellency of art, to imitate nature; but it is necessary to distinguish those parts of nature, which are most proper for imitation . . . . If the world be promiscuously described, I cannot see of what use it can be to read the account . . . . It is therefore not a sufficient vindication of a character, that it is drawn as it appears, for many characters ought never to be drawn; nor of a narrative, that the train of events is agreeable to observation and experience, for that observation which is called knowledge of the world, will be found much more frequently to make men cunning than good.

Observable life and the moral scheme of things do not follow the same plots, and the justification by 'fact' inclined the novel necessarily towards the former, exasperating the tension between the moral frame and the presence of the un(re)formed real.

The 'doubleness' of the emergent novel, like that of the criminal confession, lay in its difficult negotiation of the codes of empirical and moral verisimilitude. This negotiation becomes more tense when one bears in mind the first major distinction between the new writing and popular criminal biography on the one hand, and the actual confession on the other. In the latter case, the solemnity generated by the imminence of death was certainly a convincing guarantee of the framing of the code of events within the moral code. But the literature, like Locke's scheme of education, defended itself on its ability to instruct its audience through delight. As Terry Lovell reminds us, 'the novel is one of the earliest cultural commodities', a product of a commercial press that sought to found itself not only 'as literature, but also, necessarily, as entertainment'.[35] Thus the defining tension of the criminal confession between the adventurous picaresque life and its recuperation within a morally providential plot carries over into the new forms of narrative as the tension between entertainment and instruction, between the mimesis of the contemporary and its structuring by a moralizing syntax of causality. The anxiety is constantly present for example in *Moll Flanders*, where the editor's pious hope that 'the moral . . . will keep the reader serious, even where the story might incline him to be otherwise' is repeatedly echoed by Moll herself: 'many of those who may be pleased and diverted with the relation of the wild and wicked part of my story may not relish this, which is really the best part of my life, the most advantageous to myself, and the most instructive to others . . . . It would be a severe satire on such to say they do not relish the repentance as much as they do the crime.'[36] The 'doubleness' of the new narrative in denying its fictionality, like that of the criminal confession and tale, renouncing its false life, reflects the problematic status of fiction and the conflicting cultural roots of the discourses of adventure and moral and social instruction that the novel engages. This many-layered tension between mimesis and causality, realism and ideology, entertainment and instruction, popular sensationalism and didactic seriousness, transgression and conformity, vitality and death – the postponed but inevitable negotiation of a 'good end' to a potentially 'bad life' – is a crucially productive and problematic characteristic of the novel as a new literary form. As Davis again puts it: 'realism and moral probability, fictions and truths, plot and providence . . . wicked actions and feigned words' are the 'energetic principle . . . that powers the novel's form'.[37]

However, if the novel does emerge in large part from this popular literature and its occasions, then it obviously does so under the sign of difference. I have already mentioned the obvious distinction that arises, allowing the adventure to enjoy a more vital resistance to official morality, as the gallows confession passes into print. Within print the new novel distinguishes itself from the popular tale in that, whereas the confession and its printed form is directed primarily at the criminal's own class and hence has a premium on the use of his or her own words, the novelistic account of crime 'is put into new words', 'particularly . . . in modester words'.[38] The latter is directed at another class that certainly does not, *a priori*, share the former's social values: a new and highly sensitive audience – precisely that which required a Lockean 'education', such as Defoe and others provided in those other digests of social code, the conduct books.[39] This is indeed Dr. Johnson's anxiety: 'These books are written chiefly for the young, the ignorant, and the idle, to whom they serve as lectures of conduct, and introductions into life.' And those who were felt to be most at risk were precisely the most constitutionally idle, inexperienced and impressionable, middle-class adolescent females.

So, if Defoe's narratives penetrated the mysteries of the life of the 'Mob', they also to a large extent privileged the mysteries of the woman, particularly in her relations to marriage and money. It was strange enough that such lives should find their way into the drawing-room (or the boudoir) of the emergent middle-classes and their daughters. But there is of course a further and even greater difference between these narratives and those of the actual Tyburn criminal. Whereas the protagonists of the latter are allowed a voice only because they are about to die in justification of the morality they witness and in repudiation of the life they recount and disown, in the former they are not hanged. In the case of Moll in particular, the moral frame of repentance provides 'a new scene' in which she is reprieved, transported, reformed and, finally, makes her legitimate fortune. Here the 'double discourse' derives from the rewriting of the voice of the criminal precisely in that of the new bourgeoisie. The story and its subject are driven not only from crime to repentance but simultaneously from poverty to respectability. As Moll passes from the criminalized culture into the culture of property, she speaks not only of the mysteries of the mob and of women but also of another central – and, for the novel, crucial – mystery of the new society, the mystery of social mobility. This is no small matter for narrative in the transition from a quasi-feudalistic society where people live out the unchanging collective destinies of their birth. The model of the crime confession not only seeks to master the life of the Mob within the frame of dominant morality but, in the novelistic form where respectability is substituted for death, its very doubleness also provides a metaphorical vehicle for the contradictions and anxieties of a new social structure based on accumulation and exchange, in which individuals may actually make their own lives and change class – those new personal and social plots of which Brooks speaks.

Hence arises a metaphorical ambiguity between the criminal and the new property classes which is insistently exploited in these narratives – again particularly those of Defoe. Moll's very move into criminality arises because of her desire to change class: 'I had a thorough aversion to going to service, as they called it (that is, to be a servant)'. She wishes to be, precisely, 'a gentlewoman'; however, the meaning of the word is a mystery to her: 'they meant one sort of thing by the word gentlewoman, and I meant quite another; for, alas! all I understood by being a gentlewoman was to be able to work for myself'.[40] The conflicting codes which define 'gentlewoman' lay traps for the young Moll, whose mistaking a local prostitute as an example of a 'gentlewoman' sets the scene for much of her future career which (like that of Roxana) plays on the parallel metaphorical ambiguities and metonymic double-binds of the major vehicle of female class mobility – marriage – and the major signifier of female criminality – prostitution – in a society in which marriage has, like everything else, 'come to market'.

Indeed, marriage is constantly referred to in terms of 'trade', the very metaphor which, alongside (significantly) 'art', is so insistently used for crime here.[41] In this we may certainly mark the presence of the discourse of the popular culture. The strength of the metaphor of crime/trade as a reversible description of the underworld of the new economics derives from the authentic language of the 'Mob' and from the well-established conventions of highwayman narratives. These self-styled honourable 'gentlemen', often Royalists or Jacobites if not Robin Hood figures, have a particular penchant for robbing and humiliating the new ruling classes – Whigs, tradesmen and members of the new professions (particularly lawyers) – and ironizing on the relation between their respective 'trades'. This was not a simple matter of party; with these comparisons 'highwaymen attack not only the political tendencies of their time but the very nature of its economic relations'.[42] And this is nowhere clearer than in the case of a figure of obviously central importance to us: the hero who makes the transition from a narrative based on crime to one based on detection, the foremost criminal and, in historical terms, arguably the first 'detective' in literature, the 'Thief-Taker General', Jonathan Wild.

The different treatments of Wild by Fielding and Defoe (amongst the dozens of versions published in the eighteenth century)[43] reflect their different strategies for the new form of writing, as well as their different political positions and respective careers as magistrate and spy. In Fielding's *The Life of Mr. Jonathan Wild* (1743), Wild provides the occasion (in itself, of no great originality) for a metaphorical portrayal of the new form of government, not only a satire on a specific scandal in Walpole's corrupt administration, but on a system of government, taxation and party. Each detail of Wild's criminal activity is made satirically allegorical of contemporary social organization, with Wild/Walpole as the capitalist businessman turned governor. His formation of a gang begins as a justification of the wage-system: 'Why should you, who are the labourer only, the executor of my scheme, expect a share in the profit?' This division itself becomes the basis of the 'art of policy': 'Mankind are first properly to be considered under two grand divisions, those that use their own hands, and those who employ the hands of others.' In a world of class and competition, government becomes a matter of knowing 'how to play with the passions of men, to set them at variance with each other, and to work his own purposes out of the jealousies and apprehensions which he was wonderfully ready at creating by means of those great arts which the vulgar call treachery, dissembling, promising, lying, falsehood, etc., but which by great men are summed up in the collective name of policy, or politics, or rather *pollitrics'*.[44] The metaphor of crime organized as a trade offers an allegory of a state which conflates commerce and politics, a regime in which the codes of political government are structured by the new master-codes of contemporary economic organization: 'trade', the division of labour, cut-throat competition and obsessive accumulation, self-interest, profit and cartels.

In Wild's own version he claimed precisely the role which was to be that of the future police-force: the recovery of stolen property and the apprehension of criminals. Behind this façade, what he in fact commonly did was to buy back stolen goods from thieves and to sell them at a profit to their original owners – a practice which only became a felony when Wild's notoriety provoked the government to pass the Act which was popularly known by his name (1719) and under which he was finally hanged (1725). None the less, the fact that the actual official methods for controlling crime were indeed based on the gathering of information and the encouraging of denunciations through the provision of statutory and private rewards and pardons, 'seemed', in Defoe's words, 'to be a kind of authority for Jonathan', who had merely taken the official system to its logical commercial conclusion by organizing it on a professional and public basis.[45] But he of course went further even than the new felony of compounding; he organized a gang which would steal the goods he would then sell back to the owners, and his talent for apprehending criminals was largely restricted to betraying his own employees.

Defoe's 'factual' *True and Genuine Account . . .* (1725) goes a good way towards redeeming both the unrepentant criminal and the society which created and needed him, and for which he served as an ironic metaphor, in that Defoe's greatest moral care is to distinguish not only fact from fiction, but also Wild's public usefulness from his private greed. Even his more extreme abuses merit judicious consideration. His need 'to give up every now and then one or two of his clients to the gallows, to support his rising reputation . . . though the method was in itself wicked in him, yet it certainly brought a great many criminals to just condemnation, who would otherwise have lived to do much more mischief than they did' (p. 240). Society needed someone (like the journalist/novelist?) who was placed on the margins of the two cultures to serve 'The Public Good' by apprehending criminals and restoring property: 'It was allowed that neither of these could be done effectually as Jonathan did them, but by an avowed intimacy and acquaintance among the gangs and societies of thieves of every sort' (pp. 238–9). Like Defoe's own activities in politics and letters, this was both a 'secret service' and a commerce in 'intelligence' (p. 249) in which Wild displayed admirable qualities as a professional business manager: 'If the correspondence he kept was large, if the number of his instruments was very great, his dexterity in managing them was indeed wonderful . . . . He openly kept his compting-house, or office, like a man of business, and had his books to enter everything in with the utmost exactness and regularity' (p. 243). He is the pre-eminent middle-man in a trade which simply conflates the criminal with the civil law, as if in testimony of the former's new role as master-code: 'This part he insisted on as not only very honest, but very serviceable, always insisting that whatever he took on either side was no otherwise than as a solicitor takes his fee, on consideration from both parties for honestly putting an end to a lawsuit, and bringing the contending parties to a friendly accommodation' (p. 239). In conclusion, 'I do not see why he might not have carried on such a commerce as this with the greatest ease, I do not say honesty, in the world, if he had gone no further'. It was not the commerce that was wrong: 'the danger lay on the other side of the question . . . . So that, in a word, Jonathan's avarice hanged him' (p. 245).

According to Defoe, 'The life of Jonathan Wild is a perfectly new scene' (p. 225). In all the versions – Fielding's, Defoe's, and the popular tales – what seems to me to be new about it is the way in which crime and law serve as the central code for economics, politics, and a new form of narrative, through his making of crime/law a business and its use as a metaphor for the new business regime which gave him work. Crime works as a central figure of social representation in the period on two levels; it represented not only the culture of the poor, a mystery created and mastered by the Law which the new property-owning proto-capitalist classes sought to erect as the master code of the modern state, but in its ambiguous use in the 'news/novel' discourse, it also represented the economic bases and contradictions of the new mobile bourgeois society in which the borders between criminality, 'trade', political power and, indeed, in Wild's case, the actual enforcement of the laws protecting property, were highly permeable.

EQUITY

I have so far concentrated exclusively on the 'rule of Law' as a single master code – specifically, the criminal law – governing transformations in the eighteenth century. But in fact the Law itself was also increasingly 'double' at this time. The conceptual and real changes in property in the seventeenth and eighteenth centuries also made themselves felt in the development of civil law and, despite a comparative scarcity of legislation as such, developments relating to intellectual property (patent and copyright, 1709), and to personal property and commercial law. Now the rise of absolute private property is surrounded by a debate over periodization, which in turn raises the entire question of 'the development of capitalism', 'the industrial revolution', 'the rise of the market' and 'the ascent of the bourgeoisie' as explanatory devices for a variety of phenomena – especially for the development of the novel itself. We can however perhaps limit such generalizations by focusing on specific and material historical novelties: for example the use of the press to print money under the aegis of the Bank of England (founded 1694), in its turn another major novel paper creation, the 'joint-stock' company. If capitalism is a new form of production and of social organization, 'capital' is also a new form of production and organization of meaning whose impact is likely to be comparable to that of 'ideal money of account' at the end of the feudal era.

An immediate example is provided by the bill of exchange or discount bill: that peculiar instrument which, through its negotiability, de-personalized debt, transforming it from a relationship effectively of personal patronage into a popular object of commerce. This problematic form of money, increasingly the prime vehicle of the new economy, is itself constituted as a narrative, constructed by two moments of value. In the first place, the original issuing of a bill is a 'creative' act which provides credit (a fiction of wealth), a speculative space to be filled by a 'venture'. But the 'real meaning' of the intermediate space between issue and cancellation (the 'life' of the bill) awaits that final moment when the document, like the criminal, is destroyed as a material signifier and 'redeemed' at its 'true' value. How then did the code of Law deal with the novel mystery of capitalist paper?

Not very easily. The difficulties that the state had in controlling by law the signifiers being created by new forms of trade, ownership and finance is illustrated by the major scandal of the early part of the century, the South Sea Bubble. No sooner did the affair draw attention to a new form of property, the transferable stock, than the government was forced to respond to the financial panic of 1720 by outlawing the trade in stocks (from 1733 until 1825) – a highly retrograde and inhibiting measure in terms of capitalist development.[46] The point is that, however effective it may have been in mastering the population as such with its criminal code, the Common Law, being founded on quasi-feudal concepts, was *ipso facto* limited in its ability to deal with the emerging forms of property. This is then the irony of eighteenth-century attempts to codify the Law: as J. H. Baker puts it, 'Blackstone conveyed to a wide readership . . . the essential beauty and logic of a system of law and constitutional theory about to be submerged by a wave of massive reform. Blackstone was both a final survey of the old common law and the first textbook of a new legal era.'[47] The novelties of property could only be dealt with by the other and hitherto subordinate and incidental system of Equity whose systematization and rise to dominance parallels, in historical terms, that of capitalism, the novel, and, indeed, the mystery/detective story.

As a general rule, it can be said that 'doctrines of an equitable character tend to appear in the development of legal systems when the working of those systems no longer corresponds to the needs of society'.[48] During this period, the codes of the Common Law were increasingly stretched and, in the process, infiltrated by principles of Equity through a traditional recourse to legal 'fictions' ('the pretence . . . of a fact which, if true, would have led to the desired result under established rules of law').[49] Although reforms aimed at extending the principles of Equity were urged as early as 1652 (by Hale), it was not until the great law reform of 1873–5 that they were fully implemented. Resistance was no doubt due to a number of issues; but one of these was certainly that however useful it was, Equity was seen to be, by its nature, subversive of the Law as code.

Equity was founded on the office of the Lord Chancellor, a post traditionally held by clerics until the time of More and Bacon, and is heavily influenced by Roman canon law. The Chancellor's special jurisdiction existed by virtue of his being simultaneously Keeper of the King's Seal (head of the administration) and of the King's Conscience, and hence able to dispense indulgences to petitioners and to execute the sovereign's mercy towards his subjects. For these reasons, his powers were essentially contrary to those of the

Common Law inasmuch as, apart from his traditional ecclesiastical and administrative domains, the Chancellor only intervened where it was felt that the Common Law was not consistent with justice. As a result, 'The essence of equity as a corrective to the rigour of the laws was that it should not be tied by rules.'[50] The problem then resided in the power of discretion and particularly its association with 'the prerogative government of the Stuarts' (as seen in the Test Acts already referred to).[51]

Nevertheless, Equity grew during the period because of its capacity to deal with novel problems: 'Having once begun to remedy the wrongs brought about by the rigidity and technicality of the Common Law system, Equity soon found itself establishing a jurisdiction over matters where the Common Law had failed, and continued to fail, to recognize legal rights and duties.'[52] Such was for example the case of the very ownership and conveyancing of land which was limited under the Common Law by its quasi-feudal literal understanding of land as 'real property'. An alternative existed however in the figure of the 'use' or 'trust' (as we have seen, Locke's model for government). Thus, if a tenant transferred land by common law conveyance to a transferee who undertook to hold that land 'to the use of' the original tenant, under the common law literal perspective on property the beneficiary had transferred his rights along with his lands and thus had no remedy against any violation of that use by the transferee (or trustee). The victims could only have recourse to Chancery, to enforce rights 'against someone who, in the Chancellor's view, had as a matter of conscience to acknowledge them.'[53] For, due to its original status as an ecclesiastical and administrative court, obligations of conscience were the special prerogative of Equity, in which it employed those doctrines of 'uses' and 'trusts' which were derived from its tutelary responsibilities over minors, lunatics and the poor and its jurisdiction over marriage and probate.

The use of the trust as a means for facilitating the transfer and application of land was by no means new, as no more were Chancery's other jurisdictions (such as granting the royal pardon or commutation in the criminal law). What did happen during the seventeenth and eighteenth centuries was that the areas of jurisdiction, the remedies and instruments of Equity gradually became both quantitatively and qualitatively more important in a variety of economic fields, with the result that Equity itself became increasingly codified (at what cost we know from Dickens' *Bleak*

House), moving towards a climax in the 1873–5 reform in which its principles took precedence in all cases in which there was conflict between the two systems. Not only were marriage settlements, wills and the exploitation of and trade in land becoming more complex and important in the accumulation and distribution of wealth, but the new concepts and instruments of property and exchange could not easily be assimilated to the model of 'real' property of the common law, literal possession of material land.

One main difference in modern property 'is probably that many of the most important items today are non-physical movables, rights exercisable against others which are in such a form as to be marketable and so have become assets'.[54] These forms of property, known as 'choses-in-action' ('since the owner cannot assert his ownership by taking possession but only by bringing an action') are precisely those associated with the socio-economic transformations of the period: stocks and shares, intellectual property, negotiable instruments and trust funds. There existed in addition new forms of obligation, that is to say modern forms of contract. Under the Common Law the contract operates by the writ of *assumpsit* or the 'action of trespass upon the case', used when a person who had undertaken to perform something the non-performance of which caused loss to the second party, for which the only remedy was the payment of damages – and this only if it was proven that the contract had been broken in a most literal reading of its terms. In the more complex world of modern business, it very often becomes the case that damages are not a satisfactory compensation; it is more important that the contractor be obliged to fulfill his commitment – and only Equity could oblige someone to do something ('specific performance') or prevent them from doing something ('injunction'). Similarly, the nature of obligations ceases to be capable of being entirely encompassed in literal, detailed written contracts. This gives rise to the concept of 'quasi-contract', the implied promise to perform, a territory unrecognized in Common Law which was particularly fertile for the more subtle forms of fraud which were able to exploit the literal interpretations of statute in an increasingly complex commercial world. *Assumpsit* was an action relating only to fact. The Common Law's dedication to the letter of the contract was thus opposed in Equity by a doctrine of its spirit. In Equity, the essence of a contract is 'consent' and 'consideration' – the concepts which, once again, can be seen as 'the starting-point of technical doctrines such as conversion, joint ownership, assignment

of choses in action, and powers of appointment' which thereby
allowed it to provide 'a liberal substitute for a law about personi-
fied institutions . . . [and] . . . a liberal supplement for a necessarily
meagre law of corporations.'[55] To put it at its crudest, the doctrines
of Equity, founded in absolutist and religious discretion, were,
paradoxically, peculiarly suited to be the law of early capitalism
and its instruments of property, forms of ownership, contract and
remedy.

What I find particularly interesting in the relationship between
the Common Law and Equity in this context is their structure as
rhetorics – the former's similarity to Romance, and the latter's
(what we might call the Law of conscience and intent) to the
modern Novel. The Common Law was a rigid system which justified itself by conceiving justice in terms of uniformity rather than
individuation. Its virtue lay in the defence against discrimination it
afforded to the citizen by its very rigidity and obsessive literalness.
It categorized relations between people in terms of their relation to
the land in a hierarchy of tenancy rights and duties descended from
the sovereign. The sovereign was thus the exclusive initiator and
original author of actions which were undertaken through application of a pre-existing and fixed system of conventional 'writs',
specific claims embodied in precise and unchanging verbal forms
issued under the King's seal. Where circumstances could not be
expressed in the precise traditional verbal convention, there was
no action at law. Cases were judged on the correspondence of the
facts to the textual formulae of the writ expressed in legal Latin, and
judgement was guided by the traditional wisdom of the 'immemo-
rial' past. As a rhetoric the Common Law is a uniform code, like
a classical allegory, based on the authority of tradition and of its
fixed precedent textual expressions, in which the difference of the
subject is subsumed to general extrinsic categories of relationship,
and in which all acts are conceived as absolute and unambiguously
good or evil – a world in many ways rhetorically similar to that of
the Romance.

But if the essence of Law is its strict uniformity, the essence
of Justice is its adaptability to the individual case – the specific
territory of Equity, as defined by Aristotle in the *Ethics*: 'a correction
of law where it is defective owing to its universality.' The rise of
Equity therefore reflects an increasing individuation of the human
subject, a shift from the authority of the letter of the text to that
of its spirit – or, as Aristotle puts it in his *Rhetoric*: 'It is equity to

pardon human failings, and to look to the law-giver and not to the law; to the spirit and not to the letter; to the intention and not to the action; to the whole and not to the part; to the character of the actor in the long run and not in the present moment . . . . to wish to settle a matter by words rather than by deeds; lastly, to prefer arbitration to judgement . . . '

These principles, which, we should recall, were those applied to the new instruments of capitalism, strike me as extremely pertinent to the discursive paradigm of the new fictional prose as opposed to the earlier conventions of authority, classicism and allegory. The procedures of Equity, and particularly their emphasis on what we might call 'self-expression', support this sense: in Chancery, it is the subject, rather than the sovereign, who usually initiated the action; cases were heard orally and in English; there were no prescribed forms of pleading, but the case was decided on the 'novel procedure' of 'examination of the defendant under oath, by which he was compelled to reveal his case'.[56] Finally, the Court arbitrated the case with reference to its actual circumstances, the personal and intrinsic attitudes of the parties and the existential nature of their relationship rather than with reference to fixed extrinsic categories and established conventions. To Common Law concepts based on the morality of uniform general rules and categories, textual authority and the truth of traditional principle, Equity opposed concepts based on the morality of contractual trust, consent, confidence and implied intent, the personal standards and intentions of the subject, and the truth of his own deposition. To the 'reality' of the literal word and physical 'real' property, it counterposed that of individual circumstance, motivation and interpretation and more abstract notions of property. Its watchword is not uniformity but the rigour of the justice of the individual case governed by values of '*civilis et politica*'.

In conclusion, the obsession with crime which is characteristic of society, popular printed literature and the emergent novel during this period of fundamental changes in English society in the eighteenth century is expressive of a concern with Law as the modern social code which masters and harmonizes – or expresses the conflict between – contesting cultures, in which the concept of crime itself operates as a means of representing not only the mysteries of the poor, but those of the new regime itself and the new, highly mobile class thrown up by the commercial capitalist relations of production and exchange. At the same time as, through the gallows confession, the Criminal Law and its rites contributes a tense structural model for a fictional prose narrative with a new 'life-plot' and a new relation between writing, fact, and fiction, we also find that the Law in the eighteenth century is itself in a stage of transition; despite its centrality, it still relies structurally on its pre-capitalist past. Inasmuch as the Novel differs in structure from the criminal confession, it seems to me to be precisely along the rhetorical lines by which Equity differs from the Common Law. The converse would be the charge against detective fiction, condemned by critics such as Franco Moretti precisely for its opposition to the sophistications of the novel: 'detective fiction is radically anti-novelistic: the aim of the narration is no longer the character's development into autonomy, or a change from the initial situation, or the presentation of plot as conflict and an evolutionary spiral . . . . Detective fiction is rooted in a sacrificial rite. For the stereotypes to live, the individual must die, and then die a second time in the guise of the criminal.'[57]

But the question of the novel's eventually more 'equitable' treatment of reality and the subject is not the only difference between popular crime literature and the emergent literary novel. The nineteenth century witnesses a decisive transformation: the replacement of the (reformed) criminal as the narrative authority by the detective – the substitution, in other words, of the first-person confession by the master's solution. This radical displacement forms part of a larger process of reforming the instruments of mastery which will concern us in the next chapter, where we shall analyse the modernizations the Criminal Law was to undergo in the nineteenth century and which lead to the modern social and narrative authority represented by the detective.

3

Police

'Mrs. Pardiggle . . . pulled out a good book, as if it were a constable's staff, and took the whole family into custody. I mean into religious custody, of course; but she really did it as if she were an inexorable moral Policeman carrying them all off to a station-house.'

Charles Dickens, *Bleak House* (1853), ch. VIII.

REFORM

Jonathan Wild and Moll Flanders both announce 'a new scene'. Moll inflects the criminal career, substituting an individualized providential plot of social mobility and respectability for a conventional criminal fate. Moll's new scene was to be the scene of 'Reform': those novel strategies which rewrote the political and economic codes of the nation (the franchise and the tariff) and regulated the culture of the poor during the period from the 1770s to the mid-nineteenth century. And Wild the 'Thief-Taker', in his role within an ambiguous condensation of crime and the new business regime, points towards one of its main contributions: the 'police'. The most important moment of Moll's life occurs in Newgate when, inspired by a visiting minister whose 'way of treating me unlocked all the sluices of my passions', she is persuaded to repent, in effect rewriting her picaresque life as a moral tale. What then is this appeal that can so transform a sinner into a penitent? Alas, 'I am not able to repeat the excellent discourses of this extraordinary man'.[1] Given her expressed concern to provide an example, this absence is most telling. Moll is a scene of reform without, as yet, a reforming discourse.

Whilst Reform has to do with the development of a more humane and democratic society, the impetus behind it had at least as much to do with the legitimation of the new order. In the course of the eighteenth century, the severity of the residually feudal 'sentence' of the Bloody Code, uniformly and symbolically embracing such a wide range of individuals and circumstances, revealed only a limited and transitional capacity to control developing reality. Despite the comprehensive legal apparatus, resistance to socio-economic transformations and general crime rates continued to intensify. Meanwhile, jurors protested with higher acquittal rates and the ritual of execution itself was showing tendencies to disorder (leading to the abolition of the Tyburn procession in 1783); crown commutations were increasing (favouring transportation to execution) as people asked questions of a legal system which made no distinction between larceny and murder. Ineffective on a practical level, the conflict between the exemplary and uniform moral structure of the Bloody Code and the mitigating adjustments patent in its application to real cases was threatening to subvert the rule of Law as the symbolic master code.

Reform thus begins with the movement for repeal of capital statutes, in an attempt to restore the mastery of the Law. Reformers such as William Eden and Samuel Romilly, inspired by Cesare Beccaria's revision of punishment as an instrument of policy (*Dei Delitti e delle Pene* [1764, trans. 1767]), sought to substitute the pragmatic and legitimizing effect of deterrence by 'certainty', 'appropriateness' and 'promptness' for that of universal and symbolic 'severity'. Whereas the doctrine of maximum severity aimed to terrify a threatening culture at a distance, the principle of certainty sought, by making the capture of the criminal within the space of the Law a reality, to establish itself as a deterrent within his or her psychology, *internalizing* the presence of the Law in the consciousness of that culture.

How was this to be done? As Stephen Knight observes in relation to *The Newgate Calendar* stories (1773 *et seq.*), these traditional popular tales still offer the 'sense of an organic model of society. There is no special agent of detection at all. The stories imply that just as society can sometimes suffer from disorderly elements, so it can deal with them by its own integral means . . . . One of the main ideological features of these stories is the basic notion, and hope, that the all-pervasive, inescapable Christian reality provides a protection against crime.'[2] The mastery of criminality through the organic action of the community is traditionally signified by the trope of Providence – as in Henry Fielding's curious text, *Examples of the Interposition of Providence in the Detection and Punishment of Murder* (1752). Here, most of the 'above thirty Cases, in which this dreadful Crime has been brought to Light, in the most extraordinary and miraculous manner' again derive, as Faller observes, from the old tradition of popular tales of crime; but, when he turned to contemporary cases, Fielding found the intervention of Providence distinctly less apparent.[3] Although Fielding may have invoked the omnipresence of the Divine gaze and the marvellous workings of Providence in his propaganda, his practice as a magistrate shows that he was more aware than most that communal mechanisms had broken down and that the failure of organic control opened a space that had to be filled by something that might substitute the ubiquity and omniscience of the Providential eye.

What was to be at issue in the movement for Reform from the 1770s on was the growing awareness that 'the social order . . . could no longer maintain itself by hollow paternalism and ritual displays of terror from the law'.[4] Under the alternative policy of 'certainty' a range of new instruments were required to guarantee the capture of the threatening culture within the governing order of the Law. In the course of the nineteenth century, the organic and communal assumptions and exemplary providential narrative syntax of the Law were to be transformed into an apparently more discriminatory, rational, proportional – in short, realistic and 'equitable' – network of disciplinary controls with their own mysteries – knowledges and rituals – and their own masters. Reform was not merely a question of reorganizing the 'high' political culture of the state, but, in Frank Mort's words, of mounting an 'extensive network of social policing' whose 'strategic aim was . . . the regulation of urban working-class culture.'[5] The secularization of the mysteries of power leads us rapidly from the transitional morality of the Bloody Code to a new model of authority in which mastery by an organic Providence is replaced by mastery by 'police'.

'Police' here does not yet bear its modern sense; rather, at this stage, it refers to a global strategy to control what was perceived as a global problem. If for the first part of the eighteenth century the secret vicious culture of the mysterious poor erupted in terms of crime and riot, in the period of Reform the problem became both more diffused and more deeply embedded in their way of life and the life of society itself. Crime tended to be viewed as an issue transcending the criminal law, as only one element in a new and integrated social fabric, 'a social problem much like disease and poor drainage'.[6] In the minds of figures like Edwin Chadwick, criminal law reformer, inventor of sanitation schemes and author of the 1834 Poor Law, if the problems of crime, disease and poverty were interrelated by class and locality, so then too were their solutions.[7]

The use of the word 'police' in English is thus another of the novelties of the period. Derived originally from the Greek *politea* and the Latin *politia* – state power as it was delegated to the Prefect for issuing 'regulations concerning public order, buildings, fire, religion, assembly, health, morality, prostitutes, beggars and foreigners' and in due course, more generically, 'internal administration, welfare, protection and surveillance' – it passed into English from the French in the eighteenth century: 'For most of the eighteenth century in England, as elsewhere in Europe, the word "police" had the general meaning of the management and government of a particular piece of territory, particularly a town or city.'[8] It was in this sense that the term was first used officially in Britain: the 'Commissioners of Police' appointed by Queen Anne for the general internal administration of Scotland in 1714. This was how Swift used it in 1732 ('what the French call the police'), and Blackstone in 1769 (glossing 'public police and economy' as 'the due regulation and domestic order of the Kingdom'), and how it was defined in the 1799 edition of Johnson's *Dictionary* (a word of French origin referring to 'The regulation and government of a city or country, so far as regards the inhabitants').[9] For Adam Smith, what would correspond to the modern sense of the term is regarded as only a 'low' and minor dimension of what he calls 'police':

> The name is French, and is originally derived from the Greek which properly signified the policy of civil government, but now it only means the regulation of the inferior parts of government, viz: cleanliness, security and cheapness or plenty. Carrying dirt from the streets, and the execution of justice, so far as it regards regulations for preventing crimes or the method of keeping a city guard, though useful, are too mean to be considered in a general discourse of this kind.[10]

Rather, here the term was used as synonymous with 'policy'; by 'police' Smith means the management of the free-enterprise regime itself: history showed that the solution to crime was to have 'so few persons as possible to live upon others. Nothing tends so much to corrupt mankind as dependency, while independency still increases the honesty of the people. The establishment of commerce and manufactures, which brings about this independency, is the best police for preventing crimes.'

However, towards the end of the eighteenth century a more specific sense of 'police' began to emerge within the wider meaning of the term, in large part due to the efforts of Henry and John Fielding, magistrates at Bow Street from 1748 to 1754 and 1754 to 1780 respectively, in drawing attention to the collapse of the communal mechanisms for the discovery and punishment of crime. The Tory Fielding brothers were not 'Reformers' in the sense of the new liberal class of philanthropic industrialists and professionals of the 1770s onwards, except to the extent that for them too the ultimate 'police' consisted in reforming the manners of the poor. However, the Fieldings sought to achieve this not by substituting certainty for severity, but by making the severity of the Bloody Code more certain. The issue for the Fieldings was not a new 'police' of social reform but the more efficient administration of the traditional code through the modernization of its decadent communal mechanisms: the local community administrators, the justices of the peace, their executive arm, the constables, and the community guardians of the parish watch.

Under the organic model the true author of criminal action was the community itself: warrants could only be issued and executed in the name of the monarch on the presentation of cause through the 'laying of information' by a private citizen or organization before the magistrate. However, in cases where the victim or other interested party did not possess the necessary information to obtain and execute a warrant or where a sense of communal responsibility failed to generate the information from those who did, the existence of criminal proceedings was stimulated through what had come to constitute state policy for dealing with crime: a comprehensive system of publically advertised statutory, governmental, *ad hoc* and private rewards, state pardons, commutations and exemptions offered to those bringing information before magistrates – a system which was to continue into the middle of the nineteenth century. The growth of criminal legislation in the new commercial urban economy led to an increasing dependence on what was becoming a quasi-professional group of 'common informers' motivated by private profit, who, like Jonathan Wild, were at least as much part of the criminal community as of the forces of law and order. This mixture of criminality, law and trade in information was, according to Sir Nathaniel Conant, chief magistrate at Bow Street in the early nineteenth century, 'part of the mystery, or of the art, or of the policy' of the administration of the criminal law.[11]

There was hence ample opportunity for corruption, which naturally extended to the unpaid magistrates who administered the system, whose own income derived from fees for specific services. In consequence the Metropolitan magistrates earned a disgraceful reputation as cynical 'traders in justice'. Similarly, the constable and the watch had long ceased to be voluntary community representatives, and most Londoners elected to the post sought to sub-contract the job. The substitute constables and watch (the latter often elderly or poor members of the parish) were as reliant on reward or bribery as the informers. In sum, the communal model of criminal law administration had decayed into a corrupt 'trade' in information and justice. Thus, whilst campaigning for an even more comprehensive and severe criminal legislation, Henry Fielding, successor to the most notorious of the 'trading justices', Sir Thomas de Veil, initiated the modernization of the magistracy in 1748 by proposing the transformation of the unpaid, amateur community servant or the corrupt commercial trader in justice into a professional figure managing a co-ordinated system. His recommendation for a decent salary in place of fees was not systematically implemented until 1792 (and then only on a limited scale), but he himself managed to persuade the government to pay him a salary from the Treasury secret service funds.

The constables and the watch were likewise to be professionalized as agents for the pursuit and arrest of criminals in execution of warrants (not, we should note, for the detection of offences and offenders). In 1750, as London was being terrorized by a gang of robbers, Fielding used his secret service funds to organize the most reliable parish constables under his command into a distinctively dressed task force in which he tried to develop a powerful *esprit de corps*. In 1756 the government authorized John Fielding to maintain a paid force of four constables, ready to pursue criminals throughout the kingdom, plus a clerk to keep records. These constables became known, again like Wild, as 'thief-takers', or 'beak [magistrate]-runners', and, by 1785, as 'the Bow Street Runners'. The system was adopted on a Metropolitan-wide basis under the 1792 Middlesex Justices Act, with seven further 'Public Offices', each under the control of three stipendary magistrates administering six constables per office. Lastly, John Fielding applied similar principles to the watch, establishing small forces to patrol the main highways leading to the Metropolis and its main thoroughfares (1763).[12] Finally, besides the partial professionalization of the magistracy, constabulary and watch, the Fieldings made a significant contribution to what was to prove perhaps the single most important strategy of mastery by 'police', the mechanisms of *information*. Through their efforts, the grounds were laid for a comprehensive and systematized bureaucracy of print: not only inquiries into the causes of crime and tracts containing advice to traders and householders (for example, a first alphabetic guide to the streets of London), but, using the Bow Street Office as a centre for criminal intelligence obtained through systematic correspondence with other magistrates, they organized and published regular bulletins containing information and advertisements for rewards, *The Covent Garden Journal* (1742), the *Register of Robberies* (1753) and the *Quarterly Pursuit of Criminals* and *Weekly or Extraordinary Pursuit* (1772).

The Fieldings hence made an important contribution to the creation and acceptance of an institution and a mythology of a professional and specialized anti-crime force, and it was indeed in large part due to them that Lord Sheridan was able to say in the House in 1781 that, despite the fact that 'it was not an expression of our law, or of our language', 'Gentlemen would understand what he meant by the term police', and that the new 'Public Offices' or stipendary magistrates' courts gradually became known popularly as 'Police Offices' by the turn of the nineteenth century.[13] But the Runners were not yet a Reform 'police'. Despite their move in the direction of professionalization, public resistance to a state force kept pay to the level of a retainer, supplemented by expenses, rewards and shares of fines and by fees for special duties or hire by private citizens. With very little supervision, the system again gave rise to corruption, most outrageously, once more like Wild, in the easy transition from thief-taking to thief-making, as revealed in a number of scandals between 1756 and 1816. More importantly, the constables were agents of certainty within an as yet unreformed criminal law. They were limited in scope, a very small force whose function was to pursue criminals or stolen goods, execute warrants of arrest and enforce licensing regulations. Reform set out to do more than to threaten criminals with a greater likelihood of capture followed by execution or transportation; it sought to intervene directly in the way their culture behaved. What defines the Reform project is the ambition not merely to punish crime but to *prevent* it. But here precisely was the problem. Proposals aimed at converting and expanding the Fieldings' Runners from a specific mechanism of apprehension into a global 'Preventive Police' generated a major irony around Sheridan's observation that 'Gentlemen would understand what he meant by the term police'. For between the recent specific sense being given to the term by the Fieldings' stipendary magistrates' force and the traditional sense of a global social 'policy', interposed another, more recent 'French' connotation: the Ministry of Police established in Paris between 1796 and 1819, particularly under the notorious Fouché (1804–14).

This 'police' was indelibly associated with the tyranny of the *ancien regime* and its resuscitation under the Terror. English tradition was prejudiced against its military structure, but it was even more obsessively repelled by its vast network of state-employed spies. It was in this sense that the concept of 'police' was in fact 'understood' by many 'gentlemen' – and members of the working-classes – in the early nineteenth century, as we see in the response of one writer to proposals for prevention by police in the wake of the panic caused by the 'Ratcliffe Murders' of 1811:

> it is argued . . . [as if] a vigilant magistrate could by means of his agents anticipate and prevent all the robberies that would otherwise be committed. It is not so: all that a good police can do, is to frustrate house-breaking and street robberies, by means of a nightly guard, to prevent the escape of offenders, and infallibly to bring all criminals to public justice. Every other system is a system of tyranny; an organized army of spies and informers, for the destruction of all public liberty, and the disturbance of all private happiness.[14]

According to this author, not even such a total system could prevent crimes like the Ratcliffe Murders: indeed 'The watch that could arrest this man's hand must have the powers of omnipotence, and the attribute of ubiquity.'

Ironically, a 'watch' with 'powers of omnipotence, and the attribute of ubiquity' was of course what was ideally required to fill the gap left by the breakdown of the providential communal model, and indeed these qualities were later to become characteristic of the myth of the police. But, at this point and in these terms, such a 'police' was unacceptable: as the 1818 Select Committee on proposals for a preventive police observed, 'it would be a plan which would make every servant of every house a spy on the actions of his master, and all classes of society spies on each other'.[15] The contradiction between the anxiety of the invasion of privacy and the need for an ubiquitous eye could not be clearer than in the case of Charles Dickens. In the same year as the Detective Department was formed (and remembering the etymology of 'de-tection'), he attacked the New York press for 'pulling off the roofs of private houses, as the Halting Devil did in Spain'; yet by 1848, quite converted to the figure of the detective (as we shall see in Chapter 5), Dickens was calling for an extension of this principle of a benevolent Asmodeus: 'Oh for a good spirit who would take the house-tops off, with a more potent and benignant hand than the lame demon in the tale, and show a Christian people what dark shapes issue from amidst their homes.'[16] How then was this omnipotent ubiquity converted from a sign of tyranny to one of benevolence, in such a way that it became one of the principal heroic qualities which was to characterize the mythical reputation of the Runners, of the 'Bobbie', of the Detective Department in the 1850s, and of so many fictional detectives thereafter?

THE NEW MASTERY OF MANAGEMENT

Despite English horror at his solution, Fouché's sense of the need for 'a good police' to master the mysterious working-classes, as expressed here in a letter to Wellington in 1816, undoubtedly corresponded to English fears and desires:

> In the social order there are invisible strata; things are not always immediately apparent; there is, as it were, a secret world in the midst of the public world; ordinary authority cannot reach it . . . . The peace of the State depends upon the moral attitude of the working classes who compose the greater part of the nation, and who form the foundation of the social edifice, they should therefore be, so to speak, the object of assiduous care and of the vigilance of a good police.[17]

What distinguishes Reform is that it aimed to respond to this threat precisely by bringing the 'secret world' into their 'public world' –

or, as Sir George Onesiphous Paul argued before the 1807 Parliamentary Inquiry on provision for the criminal and pauper insane, to 'unite the police intention with the efforts of humanity and provincial economy, and by that union create a mutual support'.[18] In this sense, in the field of prison reform for example, as Ignatieff writes, 'The reformation ideal had deep appeal for an anxious middle class because it implied that the punisher and the punished could be brought back together in a shared moral universe', forming in this way 'a hopeful allegory for class relations in general.'[19] Mastery of conflicting social and cultural codes had to be achieved within the shared moral universe of the English constitutional and liberal ethos as defined by the Reformers: by consent, not by coercion; by decency and reason, not by spying and betrayal. One model and evidence of this approach, which did so much to make the intrusive eye appear benevolent, was provided by philanthropy.

The most active figures in Reform were thus the evangelical nonconformists of the new industrial, financial and professional classes who, themselves largely responsible for the socio-economic transformations, had partially inherited the social authority of the old oligarchy. These largely self-made men were ideologically equipped with a general programme and faith in their obligation and ability to reform the manners and material conditions of the poor by implanting in them the very values of self-government and self-improvement which informed the bourgeois cultural code of their own material and spiritual success. If the poor were to be encouraged to adopt their philanthropic and evangelical values of personal and social conduct, so too should their governors. In this sense, a major aspect of the Reform project consisted in the conversion of the 'improving' activities of voluntaristic philanthropy into a legislated 'part of government' for the promotion of mass self-improvement. But this implied the penetration of the realm of the private by the state and, just as problematically, major expenditure on the unproductive poor, sick, insane and criminal.

It was this that made the moral energy of philanthropy and the hard-headed accounting of Benthamite utilitarianism mutually reinforcing. Together the two formed a common purpose of replacing the organic mechanisms of authority, identity and fate with a coherent, deliberate and official 'police' through the engineering of a cost-effective institutional environment conducive to reforming both the state and the poor. Just as the social and economic power base of 'the fathers of the factory system and scientific management',[20] such as James Watt, Matthew Boulton, Abraham Darby and Josiah Wedgwood, was to rewrite the franchise, their success placed them in a privileged position to recommend that the state adopt their experience, values and strategies for governing the social conflicts caused by industrialization. Philanthropy extended their managerial techniques to large sections of the non-working population, whilst their economic success demonstrated the cost-effectiveness of utilitarian accounting. At the same time, the equally important involvement of the newly successful and powerful professions – lawyers and physicians – added an ethos of expertise, responsibility and professional discipline. The philanthropic spirit of the evangelists mitigated the coercive and mechanistic tendencies of Bentham's schemes, explicitly modelled on the global French 'Police Machine', whilst benefiting from the latter's utilitarian rationale and technology to translate their charitable intention into political and economic sense. Without transferring the most sinister aspects of Bentham's projects to the evangelists' good intentions, it is still the case that the 'softer' police that emerged provides what is effectively the ideologically acceptable face of a repressive state mastery. The radical Benthamite model presses on the liberal state like its unconscious.[21]

Reform was piecemeal but it was ideologically and, to a large extent technologically, coherent. Strongly informed by the principles of the factory and the professions, and faced with problems of a markedly institutional character, it revealed itself to be crucially administrative in character, a movement for the management of social pathologies through institutional instruments and the professional ethos. In this way it was defined at one level by a fragmentation of mastery: the departmentalization of social terrains of mystery and monstrosity, which were to be governed by correspondingly 'appropriate' social expertises and institutional administration. But, alongside this movement of separation and specialization, the global project of governing the 'morals' of the poor, the interrelatedness of the departmental problems, the common ethos of professionalism and humane improvement, and hence the totality of the requisite 'police', continued to express themselves in the theoretical and metaphorical, and hence technological and ideological, mobility of the analyses and measures produced for the various targets of Reform, based on the dual strategies of prevention/sanitation and reformation/cure. Thus, in considering the question of the substitution of an organic providential model of authority by the construction of a modern state 'police', what is essential to note is the absence of a master-code which would re-assemble these various expertises, a meta-expertise which would correspond to the totality of the contemporary concept of 'police'.

We need not be surprised by the absence of such a totalizing code or meta-discourse at this stage. The preference for appropriate and specific institutional and non-coercive solutions aimed at the alteration of mass behaviour shared by the Reformers in their various fields, seems most of all to prefigure what we nowadays call *management* – the art/science of organizing corporate or institutional populations and governing their behaviour without the use of overt coercion, in such a way as to guarantee the harmony, efficiency and prosperity of the organization and its personnel. Yet, central as it is to our present social and economic organization, 'management' is, significantly, still today, a field of somewhat mysterious and contested mastery whose deontological code and curriculum remains the object of disciplinary and professional debate.[22]

The absence of a meta-code no doubt assisted the acceptance of Reform police by accentuating its problem-solving character rather than its global project. We hence encounter a crucial dialectic in which each field of what became a global system of social *science* and social *administration* reinforced an existing, or, more frequently, gave rise to a new, area of expertise, professionalism and knowledge: in other words, to new codes of mastery. But, despite their common general rationale, these separate codes were no more homogeneous than the various interests and professions which comprised the constituencies of Reform. Indeed, they tended to be organized around what often necessarily became rival models of the law, medicine, and psychology, themselves enfolding conflicting interpretations based on the personal and the social, the material, spiritual or mental, surface and depth. Thus, in what is emerging into a 'management state' without a specified and differentiated 'science of management', the constitution of its meta-expertise and the nature of its master code is, to a considerable extent, a matter of conflict as the various professions, already existing or brought into being by the development of specific expertises, compete to establish their codes as the masters of management. This, I believe, helps explain why it is that in mystery/detective fiction the figure who actually solves the mystery is, as often as not, not a 'detective' in the institutional sense but a lawyer, a doctor, a psychologist, a clergyman, a drawing-master, or a relative, a lover or another private citizen. Rather than being regarded *a priori* as fictions celebrating a particular model of authority, stories of mystery and detection can also be viewed as a critical phantasy of the new 'master of management', putting the question of the constitution of the authorities and the codes of mastery which seek to replace the communal space vacated by Providence.

So, who were the complementary but competing masters of the mysteries of Reform? The master is to a large extent defined by the mystery. The 'secret' population which required a 'good police', as Fouché put it, was perceived to constitute no small number. Patrick Colquhon maintained in 1814 that one in seven of the population was a member of the 'dangerous classes', whilst in 1832 Chadwick estimated the number of paupers as around 10 per cent of the total population.[23] Most – clearly the most dangerous – were to be found on the streets, living in cellars and in new urban slums, surviving on outdoor relief or petty crime. But it was those already framed within existing institutions of confinement, who, by presenting a more obviously acceptable target for intervention than the population at large, provided the laboratory for generating social technologies of management. By the late eighteenth century, these traditional establishments were in a state of institutional crisis. As the Reformers brought their philanthropic impulses, professional ethics, administrative talents and cost-accounting to bear on the increasingly chaotic, subversive and ineffective institutions, the dialectic between the mobility of strategies of managerial mastery and the fragmentation of specific expertise within it was reinforced by the fact that they aimed to apply an expertise of specialized administration to establishments as yet largely undifferentiated in terms of their nature, purpose, populations and problems.

The most important were the houses of correction and the work-houses, created to implement the Elizabethan Vagrancy Acts and the Poor Laws as receptacles for those who had no place, work or communal source of support, an undiscriminated population made up of criminals, quasi-criminals, and the sick – vagrants, idlers, thieves, petty offenders, prostitutes, orphans, the unemployed and unemployable, the aged, the sick, the insane and the destitute. But a similar population was also to be found in the 'hospital' which, since Tudor times, was primarily a charitable rather than a medical establishment, administering 'comfort to the prisoners, shelter to the poor, visitation to the sick, food to the hungry, drink to the thirsty, clothes to the naked, and sepulture to the dead'.[24] Such

places, like their predecessors, the monastic infirmaries and the
Lazar houses (leprosy being governed by a criminal statute of
the thirteenth century), were designed, like the workhouse, as
places of segregation and confinement, with little or no medical
or curative purposes, run by an 'administrator and disciplinarian'
rather than by doctors.[25] Related to the hospitals were the private madhouses, generally small domestic institutions organized
on commercial grounds which received fee-paying clients and/or
Poor Law lunatics boarded out by the parish. Many were owned
by doctors but their dramatic claims for cure were a cover for what
was in fact a 'trade in lunacy', offering a safe receptacle for insane
members of the family and disruptive elements of the workhouse
or outdoor population. This trade provoked more concern with
questions of confinement than of cure, of law than of medicine as,
throughout the eighteenth century, it was associated with a long
series of scandals over wrongful detention (an anxiety which survived into the nineteenth century and its mystery stories as a major
theme).[26] Whilst hospitals and asylums were not yet truly medical
establishments, the gaols and debtors' prisons which complemented
the houses of correction were, in their turn, not yet penitentiaries.
According to John Howard's 1776 survey, less than 16 per cent of
the prison population consisted of petty offenders undergoing brief
periods of punishment; the rest consisted mainly of debtors being
held pending the discharge of their debt or official bankruptcy,
defendants awaiting trial, and felons awaiting execution of their
sentence.

Instead then of being classified by appropriate medical or legal
criteria, the pauper population in these various overlapping institutions of confinement were differentiated by administrative and
managerial considerations: cost (capacity for work and length of
stay) and degree of disturbance to the good functioning of the
institution. They were hence grouped and treated in effect according
to four administrative categories: the able-bodied, the chronic, the
'guiltless' (orphans and pregnant women, intimately linked by the
child-bearing mortality rate), and those who were dangerous to
others and/or institutionally disruptive – the criminal, the insane,
epileptics, and those suffering from infectious and venereal diseases. The history of the Reform of these institutions and their
populations, the creation of the differentiated and 'appropriate'
division of legal, medical, psychological, punitive and welfare terrains, can thus be read in terms of the segregation of these various

categories, in which fundamentally economic and administrative criteria of management are translated into legal, medical and moral terms.

As Ignatieff points out, it was the disruption caused by the unruly and noisome populations of these institutions which gave rise to an urgent and convincing need for reform.[27] Before embarking on their transformation into respectable citizens, the first task was simply to render the population manageable. This was a matter of breaching the 'mystery' of the classes involved, entering the institutions, houses and streets where they were to be found and bringing the secret into the sphere of knowledge. It is here then that we find the first major change wrought by Reform in the relation between the dominant and the dominated cultures and an explanation of the first major characteristic of the popular mystery fiction which accompanies it. The first 'detectives', the first to play the role of Dickens' benevolent Asmodeus and lift the roof on Fouché's 'secret world', were the philanthropists themselves, whose founding and most lasting strategy was a 'police' of *information*: 'to make the inquiry of all that concerns the poor and the promotion of their happiness a science.'[28] Well before Sherlock Holmes made such a thing of the same principle, their watchword might well have been that of the influential Lunar Society (1765) to which many of them belonged: *Observare*. Whereas Fielding sought to capture the criminal and then dispatch him, under Reform the mysterious poor, diseased, mad and criminal were first captured by the penetrating eye of philanthropy as the object of knowledges which reformed their *discours sauvage* within a frame of scientific mastery, 'quite literally putting [the populations] into discourse to gain some control over them'.[29] Whereas the voice of the eighteenth-century criminal, like that of the lunatic at large, was still effectively their own, in the course of the nineteenth century, they will be notoriously *silenced*. In their place, it will be the 'detective', master of observation and information, who has the last word, the word which masters the mystery and the monster and provides the retrospective meaning of the narrative. Confession will be replaced by his explanation, as the disconnected discourse of lunacy will be translated into a scientific aetiology, spoken by the psychopathologist rather than the lunatic, and the vulgar noise of the masses will be rendered into coherence and truth by the philanthropic social researcher whose founding achievement was thus to transform the disruptive clamour of the poor into a silent and passive presence as a statistical event. All the major reforms of this period, themselves often based on observation and quiet (such as the penal 'silent system' itself), were instigated by this 'police' of statistics, the organization of massive and comprehensive inventories of the problem populations and their administration, a series of, at first, private initiatives which the Reformers campaigned successfully to transform into a prime instrument of governmental management itself.[30]

The first of these private reports was John Howard's survey of prisons in 1777 which described in great statistical detail a disorganized, inefficient, overcrowded, diseased, corrupt and corrupting semi-commercial system similar to that which Fielding was combating elsewhere. Regulations varied from institution to institution; keepers and turnkeys, like constables and nurses, relied on fees (for linen, food, etc.) paid by the inmates, their families, or charitable organizations. Corruption was hence endemic. In addition, given the low level of state provision, the prisons permitted an easy commerce with the outside world. In this context, many were effectively run by the inmates as aids or rivals to the guards.

The lack of regulations and order was represented in terms of an organizational *promiscuity* which found its moral corollary in the indiscriminate mixing of debtors, their innocent families, young first offenders and hardened felons, men and women, and, amidst them all, the sub-culture of drink, depravity and prostitution. Crucially, this internal administrative promiscuity was translated into the world as a problem of *disease*. Howard's statistics showed that more died in prison from disease than were executed. Expressing a crisis in the administration of an institution of the Criminal Law as a crisis of health furnished an acceptable discourse and technology for centralized and professional intervention in a cause that concerned all, not just the inmates, whilst simultaneously providing the base for theoretical and technological mobility by proposing a common, feasible and cost-effective solution for various institutions and its extension to society as a whole. In this way, Howard's proposals for the penitentiary were intimately linked with those of his co-researcher, John Fothergill, the leading physician of his time and doctor to the leading Nonconformist industrialists and bankers, and an ardent campaigner for improving institutional hygiene and management in hospitals, dispensaries and workhouses and in the metropolis as a whole. The highly influential G. O. Paul also combined penal reform with the management of hospitals and, from 1807, specifically the campaign for a system of county pauper insane asylums. Reform here was encouraged by scandals at state asylums such as Bethlem and York (1792, 1807, 1813–14) which lead to a series of reports drawing attention to the unhealthy conditions and the parallels in organization, non-regulation and indeed treatment in the asylum and the prison. The addition of the asylum problem to the parallels thus established between workhouses, prisons and hospitals also had a crucial effect in establishing the link between organizational promiscuity, disease, and spiritual disorder.

This link was underwritten by the medical and philosophical theory of the Reformers. In the first place, the focus on disease drew attention to the threat these institutions presented to the outside world through the figure of *infection*, as had been made graphically clear in 1750 when two Newgate prisoners suffering from typhoid (symptomatically itself known contemporaneously as both 'jail fever' and 'hospital fever') fatally infected fifty people, including the judge, jury and lawyers at the Old Bailey. The primary medium for ideological and technological transfers between the various institutions and out into the world was the preferred modern medical response to the social terror of disease: the theory of 'miasmic' or 'atmospheric' infection first put forward in the early eighteenth century, but given new scientific currency by the gas theories of Joseph Black, Priestly and Humphrey Davy and by the series of yellow fever and cholera, smallpox and typhoid epidemics of the early nineteenth century, especially the 1830s. Whilst traditional general medical theory located disease in the organs and bodily fluids, leading to the treatments based on purgation (blood-letting, vomiting, etc.) preferred by the conservative physicians attached to asylums and non-infectious hospitals, infection was held to be caused by invisible and palpable gases given off by dirt, effluvia and putrefaction. It could therefore be cured or, more important, *prevented* by an expertise which consisted in a technology of institutional and personal *hygiene*.

This all-important concept did not imply the dominance of medical codes over the institutions; rather it suggested a new and complex expertise which, whilst it certainly went beyond mere legal expertise, in fact challenged established medical control over health and its institutions. The medical profession had been compromised by the very existence of the diseases in the institutions whose health conditions were the official responsibility of physicians attached to the establishment. Similarly, as has been suggested, the orthodox organic model of disease was unsuccessful in accounting for, preventing or treating infectious diseases. Further, the technology of hygiene necessarily implied a focus on the social organism, rather than on the individual body of traditional medicine. Finally, the evolving science of hygiene was, as we have seen, an expertise in discipline and regulation. At best para-medical, it embraced a personal discipline of regularity, moderation and cleanliness, and technologies related to ventilation, sanitation, whitewash, housing and other aspects of civic organization, which also drew on architecture, engineering, local government administration and on skills to be found in military, philanthropic and factory management and religious (self-) government.

As is already implied by the parallels between the various institutions, the rhetoric of disease applied to all of them was crucially not limited to the care or cure of the body. After all, the physically, mentally and morally diseased (the infectious, insane, and the venereal [syphilis being known as 'general paralysis of the insane']) had already been identified by the administrative economy of the institutions as a related problem population. The Reformers' use of the strategy of disciplinary hygiene was reinforced and transformed into an ideology and technique of *moral reform* by their endorsement of a scientific theory based on Locke's associationism and David Hartley's theory of the reciprocal influence between mind and body which presented an 'equation between physical deterioration and a depressed moral condition'.[31] This 'equation' worked both ways: filth was simultaneously a source of disease and immorality, but, equally, 'immorality . . . was also cited as one of the principal *causes* of disease'.[32] Here, once more, the word 'morals' itself 'condensed a plethora of meanings all jostling for attention. The term served as a synonym for culture, or cultural lack, and to impute blame.'[33] In this way, the language of infectious disease related the administrative reform of institutional hygiene to the reform of the inmates' culture by presenting its rituals as an exemplary moral discipline based simultaneously on the figures of bodily and spiritual prevention and cure.

At the same time, this language finally extended reform within the institution out into the streets and houses of the urban poor. Indeed, one of the major problems recognized in the lack of regulation in the prisons, the continued existence of the promiscuous and unhygienic sub-culture of the poor and its easy commerce with the outside world, was cognate with the growing social problems of crime-and-disease which arose from the development of working-class ghettos within the cities. The incidence of infectious diseases amongst the institutionalized populations and in the domestic environment of the class from which they came was linked through their vicious life-style, which contemporary philanthropic reports also frequently focussed in terms of their general habits of promiscuity in the home: the number of family members sharing the same bed or performing a variety of functions in the same space, their drinking habits, unrestrained language and general 'idleness'. As a bridge between institutional reform and the reform of the population, the model of infection located the source of the danger within the culture and environment of the poor at the same time as it made the poor themselves the link between disease and moral corruption. It further permitted the various objects of specific intervention – the conscience of the criminal, the health of the sick, the reason and passions of the lunatic and the environment, 'morals' and culture of the poor – to be approached by a uniform 'police' of hygienic discipline and environmental management.

Casting the problem in terms of promiscuity automatically made the second phase of the social science of the Reformers, the translation of social observation into scientific *classification*, itself a moral strategy, the guarantee of a rational and just system of 'appropriate' treatment. At the same time it predicated a corresponding institutional *segregation* as the best 'police': a specific architecture of quarantine, separate and 'appropriate' provision for the insane, the correct classification of mental disorders and differential therapies, of criminal offences and corresponding punishments, the development of disease-specific ward systems, the 'separate system' and the imposition of internal silence in the prisons, and differential treatment for the 'deserving' and 'undeserving' poor in the workhouse – and hence the *specialization* of the respective expertises for each class and technique of management. Having been classified and segregated, the populations were to be *regulated* by the Reformers' hygienic discipline of body and mind the therapeutic value of which applied as much to the reform of the institution itself as to the recuperation of its inmates. Just as the cure for disease and moral corruption in the latter was the introduction of a regular collective discipline, so the Reformers' solution to the other major administrative problem, the incompetence and corruption of the staff, was the *professionalization* of the custodians. 'Gaolers' and 'turnkeys' became 'governors' and 'wardens', fees were abolished and a standard and regulamented code of discipline introduced. A second change is thus wrought in the relationship between the disruptive and their custodians: given the Reformers' Lockean model of educability, the latter, reformed by a new professional discipline, are themselves transformed into reformers who were to initiate the disorderly into the ways of order by presenting themselves as an example to be followed by themselves following the regulations laid down by their superiors.

Thus when we try to pinpoint the constitution of the profession of institutional management, we find that it consisted in effect of the new expertise the Reformers had established for themselves as institutional managers, and was conducted under regulations dictated by them. Externally, their 'police' of institutional reform through classification, specialization and professionalization provided the Reformers with an exclusive authority by characterizing their social research, administrative and hygienic technology and discipline as novel and effective areas of professional expertise for the improving management of bodies and morals, whilst internally, the practical example they gave as managers of the reformed institutions served as the model to be followed by their subordinates and the inmates. In short, a hierarchy is established, whose apex is the philanthropic Reform governor, the exemplary personification of professional management of self and of the community, bodily taking the place of the absent meta-code of management. In other words, it is the figure of the reforming Master himself that constitutes the master-code of Reform 'police'.

4

Detectives

THE INSPECTOR

For the Reformers and their claims to professional authority, standardized rules would only be effective if their enforcement were centralized, passing from the part-time responsibility of inexpert local magistrates to national bureaucracies, such as the Commissioners in Lunacy, the Prison Commissioners, the Poor Law Guardians and the General Medical Council. But it was precisely this centralization that caused most resistance. Opposition to Reform derived not only from the reluctance of tax- and rate-payers to finance the 'idle' and the inertia of vested interests in the local power structures. The insistence on centralized control by a state bureaucracy continually threatened to compromise the philanthropic rhetoric of the Reformers by raising the spectre of the French-style 'police' so feared by the English. Yet, it seems to me, behind their rhetoric of humane concern, the principle of *surveillance* was absolutely central to the Reform project. Through their strategy of statistical reports, the philanthropic social researchers had already established the principle that mastery comes from a police of information: one finds out (dis-covers) by lifting the roof of the institutional or private space (de-tecting) and looking in (in-specting). In the second place, their principal administrative technique for reforming the recalcitrant inmates of the institutions was to ensure that they conformed to the rules by keeping them under the systematic and constant invigilation of the wardens. And the same principle had to apply to the discipline of the institution itself, ensuring that the regulations were being carried out in order to prevent disease, stamp out corruption in the staff, control costs and reform or cure the inmates.

The theory and technology of what amounts to management by invigilation and surveillance were made quite explicit by Jeremy

Bentham. In *Panopticon; or, the Inspection House* (1791), he proposed a new model of a total social institution, a circular, tiered honeycomb of open cells built not around the traditional centre of institutional design, the chapel, but a new secular site of omniscience: a central tower from which the inmates would be under permanent invigilation but into which they themselves could not see. The genius of his scheme resided precisely in 'the *centrality* of the Inspector's situation, combined with the well-known and most effectual contrivances for [his] *seeing without being seen*', a strategy which guarantees 'the *apparent omnipresence* of the inspector.' Bentham promoted his Panopticon as the key not only to the management of the penitentiary but also for asylums, hospitals, workhouses, schools and factories; indeed, it was presented as a universal 'police': 'Morals reformed – health preserved – industry invigorated – instruction diffused – public burthens lightened – economy seated as it were upon a rock – the gordian knot of the Poor Laws not cut but untied – all by a simple Idea in Architecture!' [1] And in fact the architecture of the penitentiary and to a large extent the asylum was to be founded on Bentham's 'idea'. But Bentham himself had made his source of inspiration quite clear by including a 'Preventive Police Ministry', on the French model, in his Panopticon project. His model brought Reform dangerously close to a tyranny in the style of Deioces the Mede, builder of the seven-walled city of Ecbatan, who made himself invisible to his subjects but ensured that they remained visible to him 'by establishing one of the first great bureaucracies in Western civilization'. [2]

How then to liberate the Reform project from fears of tyrannical centralization? One of the secrets of the Reformers' success may be found in Bentham's proposal that objections to his 'police' were, after all, mainly linguistic: 'To the word espionage a stigma is attached: let us substitute the word *inspection*, which is unconnected with the same prejudices.' [3] 'Inspection' was, after all, a traditional and entirely accepted instrument of the magistrates in the unreformed system and had been enhanced by the philanthropists' surveys of suffering and injustice; furthermore, it implied a largely non-interventionist posture by someone outside the institution (as opposed of course to the spy, who is secreted within the community). This is hence the figure – as we have seen, itself absolutely central to the Reform project at all levels, but, for Bentham, an explicit euphemism for spying – which lies at the heart of Reform's crucial inversion of the perception of invigilation both within the institutions and, later, on the streets, from the threat of totalitarian tyranny to that of humane moral discipline, beneficial care and the promotion of public health, guided by professionalism and managerial efficiency.[4]

The inspector finally calls. But who should invigilate? What sort of inspector would reform and/or cure the morals of the poor, under what knowledge and authority? Adopting Bentham's concealed inspector as the model for an extension of the principle from the institutions on to the streets would destroy the effect of his euphemism and collapse 'inspection' back into 'espionage'. In seeking a substitute for organic, paternalistic community control and the Providential eye, what was needed was a master who embodied an acceptable *image of surveillance*, ideologically as rigorous but also as *benign* as the eye of God.

This was to be found in the complementary area of reform which came to serve as an emblem of the ambition and success of the movement, the asylums. The early 1790s saw not only Bentham's project and Paul's model penitentiary in Gloucestershire, but also the reforms of lunatic asylums by Pinel in France, William Tuke in York and Benjamin Rush in Philadelphia. In what Donnelly rightly calls 'the most dramatic single sign of reform and the reforming "spirit"', they rejected the dominant medical 'treatment' which complemented what had hitherto been the basically custodial nature of the mental institution, and unchained the madmen.[5] They did so in the name of a novel view of the nature of madness, based on Lockean philosophy and the evangelical temperament, and articulated in Pinel and Esquirol's theory of 'moral insanity'. The theory dislocated insanity from its former roots in organic disorder in the direction of a yet undeveloped mental science. In the words of one of its English propagandists, James Prichard, physician to St. Peter's Asylum in Bristol, moral insanity was a 'morbid perversion of the natural feelings, affections, inclinations, temper, habits, moral dispositions, and natural impulses'.[6] Despite the fact that the category blurred the distinction between insanity and criminality (as Lord Shaftesbury testified ironically in 1844 when he claimed that this new category of mental disorder was '"scarcely distinguishable" from ordinary crime'),[7] by defining such attitudes and behaviours as a disease, the theory of 'moral insanity' proposed that they could be cured, necessarily, only by a 'moral treatment'.

Like Howard in relation to prisoners, Tuke viewed the mad not as 'furious beasts' but as capable of address and recuperation as human beings – albeit confused or childish beings – through their surviving 'desire for esteem', the desire, in fact, to be part of the community. The excitement of Tuke's project was that it 'demonstrated, to the reformers' satisfaction as least, that the supposedly continuous danger and frenzy to be anticipated from maniacs were the consequence of, rather than the justification for, harsh and misguided methods of management and restraint.'[8] A reformist alternative to severity was possible; rather than chain him Tuke 'actively sought to *transform* the lunatic, to remodel him into something approximating the bourgeois ideal of the rational individual'. What the defenders of moral treatment proposed to take the place of physical restraint offers a concise summary of Reform 'police':

> But it may be demanded, what mode of treatment do you adopt in place of restraint? . . . In short, what is the substitute for coercion? The answer may be summed up in a few words, viz. – classification – watchfulness – vigilant and unceasing attendance by day and by night – kindness, occupation and attention to health, cleanliness and comfort and the total absence of every disruption of other occupation by the attendants.[9]

The removal of the chains returned the inmate to his own responsibility for his behaviour, replacing mechanical restraint with *self-restraint*, the very heart of the philanthropists' culture: 'Treatment consisted, therefore, in providing an environment that would facilitate this struggle for self-control, an environment that was itself well regulated and disciplined and governed by moral principles and moral authority. The power of physical coercion was to be replaced by the power of moral authority.'[10]

In the asylum, as in the prison, much could be done towards generating an environment of self-control through an architectural technology and an institutional discipline which simultaneously controlled and, theoretically, cured the lunatic. The patient received more freedom and responsibility to the degree to which he or she rejected the ways of recalcitrance, confusion and idleness and responded to the moral appeal for cleanliness, industriousness, order and quietness. But the real key to the system was the example and intervention of the guardians. According to Tuke, the insane were morbidly influenced by the promiscuous imbalance of their ideas and passions; they could thus equally be benignly influenced back into order: 'Classifying and separating inmates afforded . . . means of interdicting certain influences of inmates over each other, and of opening them more to the contact and sanative influence of the alienist.'[11] Even more than in the prison, behind the new architecture and the therapeutic discipline of hygiene, order, work and self-improvement, it is the figure at the top of the administrative hierarchy who embodies its expertise: 'The absent cause . . . was the enlightened "governor" himself, who co-ordinated the whole and represented its rational design.'[12]

Thus, if the 'inspector' provides the functional profile of the modern master and his omnipresent eye, still seeking to subdue associations with spying, the *'moral manager'*, as the 'governor' of an asylum dedicated to moral treatment was known, furnishes his ideological profile of acceptability, indeed, his heroism. If the inmate's disorder is defined in moral terms, then it follows that his reformer need not necessarily be medically qualified. Indeed, it was the physicians who were responsible for the 'ills' of the institutions – the regime of mechanical restraint, the low level of cure and the prevalence of physical disease. Under this order of moral influence and example, the essential qualification was *intrinsic, personal moral authority*. The asylum governor was a 'moral manager' in both senses: a manager of morals because he himself was, most of all, moral. Many governors were indeed physicians; many were clerics; but, in the absence of any genuine science of 'mind', 'moral management', as a forerunner of a non-medical psychiatry, was a new speciality for which neither qualification was essential. The manager had rather to *embody* those values of esteem which the lunatic was to emulate, emanating an authority which informed all aspects of institutional life: an exemplary self-control and dignity, an evident moral excellence and humanity, a spirit of self-sacrifice and Christian charity, perseverance and optimism, discretion and impartiality, inexhaustible attentiveness and vigilance, paternalistic care and authority. In short, as Donnelly points out, 'it is . . . striking how much a philanthropic temper came to be the principal recommendation in an individual working with the insane.'[13] This was the Reform speciality *par excellence*; in turning the moral manager into a moral hero, the early Victorian philanthropists were thus most of all celebrating themselves and the mystery of their managerial mastery. In sum, in the absence of an explicit scientific theory for the cure, the mystery of Reform is here, perhaps more than anywhere, found in the personality of the Reformer.

The celebration of the power of non-coercive moral influence was focused precisely on the moral manager's charismatic gaze. But whereas the power of the eye of the penal administrator raised fears because it depended on its invisibility, the power of the curative moral manager reassured since it depended most of all on the *visibility of his stare*. As an anonymous French observer reported in 1796, the moral manager Francis Willis 'suddenly became a different figure commanding the respect even of maniacs. His piercing eye seemed to read their hearts and divine their thoughts as they formed and before they were even uttered. In this way he gained control over them which he used as a means of cure.'[14] The very presence of the manager's penetrating and powerful eye was the source of his power. As Donnelly comments: 'The "power of the eye" was a widely evoked and admired symbol of the alienists' power over maniacs. It was an image which easily recalled the taming of wild beasts, or the "fascination" of the snake-charmer.' In constructing the proto-image of what was slowly to become the psychopathologist, its symbolism recalls, secularizes and rationalizes the mystery of the traditional 'healer'; at the same time, it harnesses the more recent power of the 'mesmerist', suspected of mystification and political and moral subversiveness, to a rational and moral cause which vindicates the bourgeois values of the philanthropists. Repairing suspicions of the intrusive and tyrannical eye of the 'inspector', the reforming stare of the moral manager, whose power is a function only of the presence of his moral force, stands as an acceptable and humane image for the influence of mind over mind through *visible invigilation*, the ultimate model for a civil 'police' of social mastery.

THE POLICEMAN

'Ways have to be found, he believes, for the police service to renegotiate its contract with the public. This should include a demonstration by senior officers that they are running economic, efficient organisations of high integrity and professionalism, taking the public's wishes into consideration.'

Interview with Sir John Dellow, Deputy Commissioner of the Metropolitan Police, *Financial Times*, July 23 1990.

And so on the streets; bringing the population at large within the reforming regime without collapsing back into the totalitarian fears of state surveillance was to be achieved once more through information, classification, specialization, professionalism, philanthropy but, most of all, by the invigilation of a *visible* eye.

It was one of the stipendary magistrates appointed under the Fielding-inspired 1792 Act, Patrick Colquhon, who brought the Reform ethos into this field by establishing what he significantly referred to as a 'new science in political economy, not yet perfectly understood'.[15] In his exhaustive and systematic surveys and classification of the causes and costs of poverty, wealth and crime, Colquhon distinguished administratively and morally – on grounds of social cost and degrees of culpability and reformability – between categories of what he called the poor, and the irremediably, the remediably, and the culpably 'indigent'. 'Indigence' was both an economic and a moral condition, characterized by a wide range of personality defects of a criminal nature. The social danger derived from the permeability between the empirical populations of his taxonomic classes in the 'new era in the world' he saw as inaugurated by the French Revolution, in which 'The evil propensities incident to human nature appear no longer restrained by the force of religion, or the influence of the moral principle.'[16]

Armed with information and classification, Colquhon's next and perhaps most important step, in a decisive departure from the Fieldings' model, was to separate the constabulary and the watch from the magistracy. What he called 'Police' was to be a new and distinct area of specialized expertise: 'Police in this country may be considered as a *new Science*, the properties of which consist not in the Judicial Powers which lead to *Punishment*, and which belong to Magistrates alone, but in the *Prevention and Detection of Crimes*, and in those other Functions which relate to Internal Regulations for the well ordering and comfort of Civil Society.'[17] The key was once again inspection: according to Radzinowicz, for Colquhon, a supporter of the Panopticon, 'a police system and organized invigilation were interchangeable terms.'[18] This was to be achieved through the correct identification and classification of the areas where the criminals live, their division into beats, and the institution of regular patrols of the designated areas. The proposal of a new science in political economy translated the science of social observation into the support for a literal and continuous scrutiny of society.

Similarly, the proposal for an autonomous science predicated an autonomous administrative solution: 'The rigid and searching control over more than 40,000 people whose occupations were looked upon as "dangerous", the close supervision of vast areas which were breeding grounds of crime, the systematic invigilation of the mode of life of 115,000 criminal or partly criminal individuals; and a methodical watch over a mass of socially unreliable poor, required a chain of co-ordinated operations of great magnitude and complexity.'[19] Although Colquhon's proposal for a Benthamite 'General Police Machine', was, as it stood, too totalitarian to be acceptable, his economic argument that the criminal justice system was financed from the wrong end was substantiated by his statistical investigation of crime in the Port of London, in which he showed that of the 25 per cent of goods passing through the Port lost in crime, 90 per cent was stolen by dock workers, and could hence be cheaply controlled. This report persuaded the government to permit him in 1798 to implement the preventive plans of the like-minded reformer John Harriot for managing the social microcosm of the London docks on behalf of the West India Merchants.

The Marine Police Establishment was a complete management system made up of four specialized departments: one conducting the usual activity of the Public Office, a second devoted to accounts, another, the 'Establishment for Protection and Labour', responsible for selecting, registering, paying and discharging the 'lumpers' employed by the Company, and the last and most innovative, the Marine Police or 'Preventive Department', committed to supervising the entire area on a permanent basis. Released in this way from executive and administrative duties, the members of this department, numbering more than the total establishment of the Metropolitan Offices at the time, and able to call on a further 200 'ship constables' for special duties, were charged with regular and routine patrols and the daily and quarterly presentation of reports, under the superintendence of 'surveyors'. Specialization was again complemented by the professionalization of the patrols through the use of regulations and inspection which operated not only as a safeguard against corruption, but as a means of giving the new force a specific collective identity. A written code for dealing with the public was issued, in which duties, penalties and rules of conduct were laid out in extreme detail and solemn language. In short, 'every effort was made to build up a force proud of its vocation and fortified by an honourable tradition of public service'.[20] But most importantly, this code established what was to be the main principle of policing: that *the very fact of their visible vigilant presence should determine their preventive efficacy* – or, as the written instructions put it: 'The Authority you are invested with ought to be sufficient.'

The Establishment was a notable success, and despite the reluctance of the local City authorities, in 1800 the Thames River Police Act was passed, integrating a moderated version of the scheme – without the 'Establishment for Protection and Labour' – into the network of stipendary offices. Having proved its worth in defending the centre of English trade, prevention through a systematic and professional supervision of the streets was adopted by the government as a public responsibility. Yet it took thirty years for these principles to be adopted for the entire Metropolis (and another twenty-five or so to be extended nationwide). The problem with Colquhon's scheme was still its proximity to the French 'machine' and its association with the defence of the Port merchants as a particular class. What was needed to extend the dock police to the rest of society, apart from the pressure of a continuing decline in social order, was precisely that mixture of cost-effective economic pragmatism and good intentions that had been articulated by the prison and asylum philanthropists. According to Radzinowicz, this was in large part to be provided by the architect of the new Poor Laws, Edwin Chadwick, precisely through his articulation of the specialized 'police' within the global Reform 'police' of poverty, disease and crime.

Although he had served as Bentham's loyal secretary and endorsed most of his projects, Chadwick was careful to remain strategically silent on questions of central control. Instead, he focused his campaign on prevention as a general principle within the developing fabric of urban *public services* designed 'to unloose not to restrict', within which policing was just one department.[21] Thus, in his first article on the matter in 1828, Chadwick 'insisted that preventive measures should be adopted with regard to all matters adversely affecting public health. Crime was merely another form of socially undesirable occurrence, for which also the best cure was prevention.'[22] Chadwick explained in great statistical detail the economic waste of criminality, idleness and disease. To this careful calculus he adduced the unimpeachable moral theory of 'less eligibility' he had used in his proposals for the reform of the Poor Law. In short, the state could reduce its expense on the relief of pauperism by fighting the defining idleness of the poor through convincing them that it was less unpleasant to work than not to.

By the same token, then, since criminals took to crime because they believed it was easier than working, they could be persuaded otherwise by placing obstacles in their way, such as the presence of a police force on the streets.

The passing of Sir Robert Peel's Metropolitan Police Improvement Bill in 1829 was no doubt in part due to the fact that it did not attempt to impose itself nationwide or to abolish all parochial forces, and in part to the reigning climate of social disturbance. But what most of all guaranteed ideological acceptance was simply that he was by now able to present preventive policing as neither a military nor a secret machine, but as a public service, professional, specialized, morally benign, independent, universal and impartial – the translation of philanthropic institutional principles onto the streets. None the less, there was still much very real hostility to overcome. The actual shape which made the force not only an acceptable but in due course a celebrated institution was determined by the sensitivity to this hostility manifested by the first two Commissioners of Police, Charles Rowan and Richard Mayne. The image of policing they imposed was in effect an inverse reflection of the reasons invoked against the establishment of a police force.

Crime would be controlled by two forms of vigilance: information gathered through 'an unremitting watch' over the poor and centralized, bureaucratized and circulated to the police stations on a daily basis would enable the police to make known criminals realize that they are known, whilst unknown criminals would be deterred through the conspicuous and regular presence of the patrol. Thus the most important decision related to visibility; like the moral manager rather than the prison inspector, the stare of the policeman had to be visible and benign. Hence the Commissioners' rejection of civilian clothes disarmed the very real association with spying; and their choice of a distinctive but distinctly non-military uniform and weaponry (the truncheon, reminiscent above all of the staff of office of the ancient constabulary), enabled them to avoid falling into the fears of an internal standing army. The Commissioners had also learned the importance of the new managerial culture: the need for a sense of professional identity and *esprit de corps*. This was particularly important to the extent that the new force was drawn largely from the class it was to police. The personal and divisional number displayed on his uniform depersonalized the constable and re-identified him as a professional public servant, answerable to the institution. The regular morning meeting of the patrol, where information was circulated and the constables were brought up to date on standing orders and current problems, reinforced their integration into the corporate culture.[23] Finally, the officers were subject to an extremely detailed written code containing strict and superintended regulations, the *General Instructions*. This marked their considerable distance from the Runners by insisting on the absolute priority of prevention over arrest: 'The absence of crime will be considered the best proof of the complete efficiency of the Police.'[24] Emphasis was particularly laid on prevention being a matter of example and influence, as the reformed member of the observed class himself became a reformer. As a professional civil servant, he was to present an exemplary image of high moral standards of behaviour, politeness, sobriety and self-control.[25] The police had to know their powers and duties thoroughly, and to exercise those powers with impartiality, fairness and discretion and, most of all, with great caution – in sum, in the words of the *Instructions*, 'as a public servant performing a necessary and disagreeable duty'. This was the crucial inversion and the purpose behind the all-important decision on visibility and the rigorously imposed code of behaviour – as Radzinowicz summarizes it: 'the ideal set before them remained steady: in all their dealings they must behave as the servants, not the masters, of the public.'[26] The state's masterly eye was to be everywhere but, unlike Bentham's inspector in the tower, the vigilance was to be efficient, benevolent and influential by being itself conspicuously visible and visibly philanthropic.

The Commissioners' success in inverting popular prejudices may be exemplified by the recognition anyone brought up on *Dixon of Dock Green* will give to this remark from the *London Quarterly Review* in 1856: 'P.C.X. 59 stalks along, an institution rather than a man', and to another from *Chamber's Magazine* in 1864: 'they know nothing of politics; the man in blue preserves his neutral tint . . . the good old cause of order is the only side the policeman supports.'[27] The reassuring image won by the new police was the measure and source of their success, as, perhaps because of the very resistance the idea had previously provoked in this field, they became the epitome of the Reform ethos, translating the high personal ideals of the moral manager into an institution, itself a model for the very society the Reformers had sought to promote, 'kept in complete control without any extraordinary coercive power.'[28] The mastery of police established itself as a decisively new narrative principle:

'How complete the power of the police! The arm of the law has bent [criminals'] strong and obstinate wills . . . . For the law, in the records of the police, hold their biographies in its iron grasp.'[29] According to an *Edinburgh Review* of 1852, the Metropolitan Police had grown so successful that 'people began to think it quite as a matter of course, or one of the ordinary operations of Providence, that they sleep and wake in safety in the midst of hordes of starving plunderers.'[30]

THE DETECTIVE

'But we have to recognize that many of the more routine matters cannot be dealt with by the police alone but must involve society using all the agencies at its disposal . . . '

Sir John Dellow, loc. cit.

But this image and power meant something else to the working-class radicals in the industrial north for whom the 'Blue Devils' were a 'plague of blue locusts': 'The other side of the coin of middle-class voluntaristic moral "Domestic missionaries" and social reform (even when sheathed) was the policeman's truncheon.'[31] For the working classes the police were brought in by the philanthropist owners to repress their political and economic demands and to enforce a new code of industrial discipline and a 'bureaucracy of official morality' not only by acting directly against industrial revolt but by taking patrols into working-class areas to enforce the new Poor Law, to watch and control their private and communal life and to regulate their intimacy and leisure (drinking, sexuality and sports).

After a mixed and, on one important occasion, highly unpopular response following clashes at Cold Bath Fields in May 1832, the most conspicuous success of the new police lay in convincing the middle-classes of their usefulness in the explicitly political area of direct action against working-class disturbances, initially in riot control in London and subsequently in policing industrial disputes. Eloquent testimony to their achievement was expressed by Mayne in 1863 when he pointed out to Palmerston that 'It has been stated by a high financial authority, that the quiet decisive suppression of the [Chartist] meeting of April 10, 1848, was of greater importance than the victory of Waterloo.'[32] This was not however the ostensible argument for policing. Its success as a reforming force depended on winning the consent of all classes. Policing could only be popularly justified by its ability to safeguard private persons and their property. However, despite the testimonials cited above, its real, as opposed to perceived, success in this field is more debatable: as Clive Emsley says, 'in spite of an apparent levelling out of crime in the second half of the century the overall and long-term impact of the police on crime levels remains problematic'.[33] According to George Rudé, the police were probably most effective in targeting the prostitutes, youths, servants and employees responsible for by far the most characteristic, common and visible crimes in the nineteenth century: petty thefts in public places and workplace pilfering. He thus endorses the 'tentative judgement' offered by David Jones in 1982, that, in addition to their effectiveness in controlling popular disturbances, 'the new police may be credited with having made three major contributions to the prevention and mitigation of crime': their visible presence on the streets had an important effect on larceny from the person; their surveillance of 'those most likely to commit crimes' inhibited the action of vagrants, prostitutes and unemployed juveniles; and, lastly, 'in the longer term, the police . . . began to exercise a restraining effect as well on those far wider numbers of ordinary men and women whose involvement in crime was occasional and who, even after the 1850s, were frequently faced with economic distress and long or short periods of casual labour or unemployment.'[34] In short, apart from helping to suppress industrial and popular unrest and reducing more visible petty crimes, the principal area of police intervention appears to have been the managerial function. In liaison with parallel initiatives in social reform and control, enforcing campaigns against drunkenness and prostitution, the Vagrancy Acts and the Poor Law, the Contagious Diseases Act, the Sunday Observance Act, legislation against cruel sports, compulsory education laws and the factory acts, etc., their major achievement was in indirectly influencing and recodifying the moral behaviour of the dangerous population under urban industrial discipline.[35]

The point however is that even here their effectiveness was still limited. Certainly, the visible presence of the police eye, along with the reputation of the penitentiary and the introduction of summary conviction for many lesser offences, produced considerable success in combating petty pilfering and influencing behaviour. But it was this same visibility that imposed strict limits on police effectiveness in the wider fight against crime, unrest and immorality. It was for example of dubious value in preventing political threats (as opposed to suppressing riots) and in dealing with less visible crimes, such as burglary and the growing field of 'white-collar crimes' like forgery, embezzlement and fraud. But even their effectiveness in enforcing moral legislation was limited by the uniform which served as a warning to delinquents to desist until the patrol had passed. In sum, because of their visibility the new police were not equipped to deal with the crimes they did not prevent or to prevent the political unrest they were to control.

The dramatic extent of the limitations of visibility were swiftly revealed when, in 1831, Superintendent Andrew M'Lean ordered one of his constables to infiltrate the National Political Union, which, according to police information, was planning violent insurrection. When it was revealed that Popay had maintained his cover as an active member of the Union for two years, a major scandal blew up, reviving the fear that a preventive police was a spy service which, moreover, like the thief-takers and -makers of old, actively participated in crime. Peel and the Commissioners condemned the use of *agents provocateurs*, but, in their testimony before a House Committee, they were obliged to acknowledge the extremely important fact that 'for the apprehension of beggars and felons, three to one are taken by men in plain clothes'.[36] Charles Reith argues that Popay 'deserves historical recognition not as Popay the Spy, but as the founder and originator of the detective system'. Radzinowicz disagrees, maintaining the difference between detectives and *agents provocateurs*, but it seems to me that the ambiguity exists.[37] In any case, the Popay scandal clearly demonstrated to the authorities the limits of prevention by visible vigilance and the need for *invisible invigilation* by plain-clothes or disguised officers – the need, in short, for what Palmerston was later said to have admitted, in telling terms, in the case of continental refugees: that they 'were subject to that which could not be expressed in English – a system of police surveillance.'[38]

When a popular outcry arose in 1842 because of the inefficiency of the police in apprehending the notorious murderer, Daniel Good, and in preventing an assassination attempt on Queen Victoria, the Commissioners suggested the formation of a Detective Office under their direct control. Given continuing fears, only two inspectors and six sergeants were appointed. It had taken forty years for the Fielding-inspired pursuit officers funded by the secret service to develop into Peel's public service preventive police; and it took almost a further fifty years for detection to be fully instituted, along the lines of the French Sûreté, by Howard Vincent's reform of the Criminal Investigation Division, following a major scandal involving the bribery of Scotland Yard officers in 1877. The uniformed force had only proved acceptable because it subdued associations with spying and thief-making by presenting its authority as visible. 'Detection' was instituted – very quietly, one might add – because, after all, visible surveillance was not enough to fulfill the police function of controlling the poor.[39] Despite the uniformed bobby's ideological value as an image of a benign 'police', the formation of the Detective Office was, to a large extent, a sign of the functional failure of the Reform ideal of the visible eye. What was rejected in the promotion of the model new police resurfaces in the Detective Department as the political repressed of the public service police system.

The collapse of the Reform ideal so soon after it was finally instituted was not limited to preventive policing. The failure of Chadwick's Poor Law was made clear by the new round of reports initiated by Mayhew in the 1860s. Indeed, Chadwick himself was forced out of office in 1854. Although the national penitentiary at Pentonville was completed in the same year as the Detective Department was founded, in the field of prisons too 'Faith in the reformative promise . . . barely survived the 1840s.'[40] The practical impossibility of creating a suitable staff, severe overcrowding, impatience with the excessive 'softness' of the reforming prison, combined with the evidence of chronic recidivism (the 'ticket-of-leave-man', or probationer, of popular melodrama) to intensify the failure of the Reformers in the light of their earlier highly optimistic claims. Asylum reform suffered a similar fate. The moral propaganda of the managers, even as it achieved its climax in the implementation of a nationwide asylum programme under the 1845 Acts, failed, for a variety of reasons, from deficient provision and difficulties in staffing to the inadequacy of their psychiatric theory, to live up to their dramatic claims to cure. In face of the perceived failure to reform, cure and prevent, all that was left was the institutional frame itself: the civilizing discourse, the architecture, imagery, discipline and principles of management of what again came to be viewed as incorrigible disorderly populations. If Reform sought to change the mechanisms and aims of institutional and urban 'police' from containment to cure, from repression to care, what remained by the half-century were the mechanisms, but not the aims: a technology dedicated to the invisible invigilation and simple confinement of the poor. The modern conflict of cultures could not, it appeared, be influenced into harmony; it could only be at best safely contained.

As might be expected, the asylum constituted an important battleground for the heroic place vacated by the failure of the moral manager and for control over the meaning of the science of managing 'mind' (the word 'psychiatry' first being used in English in 1873). The managers had established their own particular moral expertise as an emblem of mastery against the traditional expertise of the physicians. Tuke had in fact explicitly rejected a medical qualification for asylum managers and the term 'hospital' for his institution. In the early nineteenth century, excepting perhaps the fashionable London physicians of the Royal College, the medical professions still possessed a relatively low status, especially those involved in care of or attendance on the insane, above all the pauper insane. This was of course not helped by the lack of professionalism – the inefficiency and uncaringness of the physicians attached to public asylums and the 'trade in lunacy' in the private sector. However, during the period surrounding the 1845 Lunacy Act, physicians as a whole and those doctors who had been involved in the asylums as managers and as medical ancillaries began to form themselves into professional bodies.[41] From this base they launched an attack on the non-medical moral managers. The latter, lacking a scientific theory for the efficacy of moral treatment, but already reliant on a moralized use of medical terms (like 'insanity' itself), were particularly vulnerable to the attempts of the medical professions to reclaim their expertise in the asylums. The physicians reversed the tables by translating moral treatment back into a medical discourse, through the synthetic physiologico-moral concept of the invisible but organically sounding 'moral lesion' – 'a functional injury, an often temporary physiological condition leaving no trace of its presence.'[42] Furthermore, unlike the moral managers, the medical psychopathologists of the later part of the nineteenth century were now capable of offering an explanation for the failure of moral treatment by availing themselves of the theory of hereditary degeneracy to account for the incurability of the insane – a condition which, given their model of reformability, the moral managers were particularly unable to explain. Lastly, their biological vision was underwritten by the decline of the miasma theory in favour of the cell theory, developed with the help of the microscope (invented in 1830). The body became a 'cell-state in which every cell is a citizen'[43] and disease the result of the abnormal growth of particular, naturally harmful cells or, later, the corruption of the healthy body by foreign 'germs'.

As the moralization of medicine was replaced by the medicalization of morals, the new model of the psychopathologist was extended to cover the rethinking of the prison, through a more positivistic science of biologically-based pathology which provided a similar naturalization of working-class criminality. Already in 1851 Thomas Plint deflated the Reforming penologists by observing that 'in fact little was known about criminals': the criminal poor were not only a product of their environment but 'a large majority of the class is so by descent and stands as completely isolated from the other classes, in blood, in sympathies, in its domestic and social organization . . . as it is hostile to them in the whole ways and means of its temporal existence'.[44] Plint's early intuition was to develop, in the wake of Darwin and developments in cell hystology and neuropsychology, into an autonomous post-Reform science of moral class eugenics which provided a new discourse for describing social pathologies, culminating in Cesare Lomboroso's physiologico-hereditary discipline of 'criminology'. Through the 1860s and 1870s, this model, equally applied to character and intelligence by Francis Galton, to sexuality by William Acton, and to insanity, most notably by Henry Maudsley, reunited criminality and insanity as joint pathologies with a common biological class basis, thus bringing the medicine of the psychiatrist again closer to the legalistic function of the police inspector as guardians of the incorrigible poor. As Maudsley's disciple, Furneaux Jordan, put it in 1886, 'to organization, in other words to inheritance, is mainly due the existence of criminals, paupers, drunkards, lunatics and suicides'.[45] In this way, the moral corruption of the culture of the poor was understood as a biological condition from which society needed to be simply protected, and these writers, reappropriating the moral discourse evacuated of its reforming purposes for medicine, staked their claim to manage the recalcitrant and dangerous mysteries of modern society.

In short, the failure of Reform opened a space for the return of its repressed on the back of its acceptability. The detective department, the punitive penitentiary and the custodial asylum now possessed an institutional and technological frame and an accepted legitimacy as models for modern management – despite the fact that they had ceased even to seek to achieve the aims which had provided their moral and political justification. The rhetoric of prevention and cure served its purpose in rendering acceptable, indeed heroic, an image of state institutional mastery, a 'police' in short, for the social mystery of the poor, under the guise of the creation of a shared and benevolent moral universe, a new social providence. Thanks to the ideological success of Reform, its practical failure in all fields did not however destroy its consoling mystique but merely translated the professions, disciplines and institutions into a system for controlling social threats derived from an incorrigible natural predisposition communicated by hereditary transmission.

The police detective, like the penitentiary governor and the medical psychopathologist, is a true creature of the era of repression; and, like them, despite representing an inversion of the principles which informed his Reform predecessors, he enjoyed the benefit of their reputation. This might seem to imply that detective fiction also necessarily shares the post-Reform model of repression. But, as I have already pointed out, since it is far from always the detective who solves the mystery, his representation in fiction permits the interrogation of his model of mastery. That is not to say that some species of mystery/detective fiction do not endorse the repressive model – indeed, this is, at least in one body of popular literature, which we shall be looking at in the next chapter, very much the case – although not, as we shall see, according to the accepted formal model. But in what follows I propose to show that, contrary to those retrospective formalist accounts extrapolated from Sherlock Holmes, such an endorsement is not a fatality of stories of mystery and detection. There are other sorts of stories which question the authorities the detective, police or 'amateur', may represent, and that open, rather than foreclose, the question of the management of modern mystery, particularly by operating within the gaps created by its conflicting codes. In dealing with varieties of literary mystery and detection in the nineteenth century, and particularly the place of Poe and Collins, we shall hence be analysing the ways fictional detectives and mysterious narratives confirm, condition, explore or subvert the constitution of the mastery of modern mysteries.

Part III

Writing Wrongs and Wrong Writing

5

The Romance
of the Detective

'I don't think I like mysteries. If I did I wouldn't have become
a detective.'
Detective Sergeant Dick Bloodworth, in Loren D. Estleman,
The Glass Highway (1984)

'DETECTIVE LITERATURE'

In the emergence of new forms out of the popular confession a major
difference is marked, as has already been observed, by the change
in the voice which gives meaningful form to the narrative. The
substitution of the criminal by the detective would seem to resolve
the tension found in the confession by unequivocally celebrating
the capture of the subversive adventure within the detective story's
'official' moralizing syntax. On the other hand, it might be argued,
the insistence on crime in the early novel indicates the survival of
the vitality of the adventure as a resistance to official ideologies,
marking the novel, as in D. H. Lawrence's much later statement of
the case, as itself a form of subversive adventure:

> Philosophy, religion, science, they are all of them busy nailing
> things down, to get a stable equilibrium. Religion, with its
> nailed-down One God, who says *Thou shalt, Thou shan't,* and
> hammers home every time; philosophy, with its fixed ideas;
> science with its 'laws': they, all of them, all the time, want to
> nail us on to some tree or other.
> The novel is the highest example of subtle inter-relatedness
> that man has discovered. Everything is true in its own time,
> place, circumstance, and untrue outside of its own place, time,

circumstance. If you try to nail anything down, in the novel, either it kills the novel, or the novel gets up and walks away with the nail.[1]

Again, as in the opposition between Equity and the Common Law, a 'natural justice', adjudicated ostensibly on the internal, existential circumstances of the 'case', asserts itself against the pre-determined categories and formulae of an external and artificial code. In contrast to the intrusive detective, the master of the narrative in the classic novel is proposed as transparent, if not invisible; the voice that frames and rewrites the *discours sauvage* presents itself as the self-evidence of a complex existential universe. In short, the subversive capacity of the Novel derives from its characteristic commitment to and strategies of *realism*. However, as Lennard Davis argues in *Resisting Novels*, it is precisely this strategy, the attempt 'to destroy the veil of its own artifice and to appear as natural common sense', which also makes the realist novel cognate with ideology as a form of social control.[2]

In this sense, as I have been implying, the Novel is the major literary product of Reform, and, like Reform, its concern with crime in fact bespeaks not only a humane existentialism but also a project for a new 'police'. It differs from detective fiction not by an inevitable resistance to rigid ideologies, but by its distinctive strategy for enforcing its own discipline. As D. A. Miller observes, the strikingly negative manner in which the police are characteristically treated in the novel, whilst it helps ensure the latter's anti-repressive reputation, in fact conceals a deep congruence between the discipline of police and the discipline of the novel itself. In the realist novel 'omniscient narration assumes a fully panoptic view of the world it places under surveillance';[3] the author, like the detective-spy, seeks, invisibly, to penetrate social and personal surfaces and to register, examine, know, re-form and narrate his or her characters. Indeed, Flaubert's classic phrase of 1852, quoted by Miller – 'l'auteur, dans son oeuvre, doit être comme Dieu dans l'univers, présent partout et visible nulle part' – could serve as a slogan for the repressive Benthamite side of the Reform project for the substitution of Providence by a mastery by police. So, as Reform police overcame English common law fears by denying and inverting the image of spying, the novel's criticism of the police itself as conspicuously incompetent, intrusive and tyrannical serves mainly to divert attention from its own discipline in favour of what it thereby advertises as its more humane discretion. In short, what is at issue here is 'a strategy of *disavowing the police*: acknowledging its affinity with police practices *by way of* insisting on the fantasy of its otherness. Rendered discreet by disavowal, discipline is also thereby rendered more effective – including among its effects that "freedom" or "lawlessness" for which critics of the novel . . . have often mistaken it.'[4]

This disavowal forms an integral part of the Novel's ideological and mimetic system of realism, positing, like Reform, a more effective mode of ideological discipline by which coercive functions are assumed, as it were transparently and naturally, by 'the world' or 'the social order'. Whereas, as we saw in Chapter 2, in the pre-Reform world the realism of the new writing was a potential source of tension in relation to a moral law still close to the fixed universe of Romance, according to Terry Lovell, from the 1840s on these strategies became central to the establishment of the 'novel's respectability regarding both its literary status and bourgeois values'.[5] Bearing in mind Jameson's notion of the Novel as a negotiation of inherited codes, we can see its form of realism as an attempt to conciliate the popular and aristocratic cultures by expelling their extremes and re-assembling the conflict of codes into a new, reformed, 'organic' reality. Since the most important register of those extremes was the presence of the 'marvellous', a principal difference between the novel and its antecedents is hence registered by the status of that which disrupts the natural order: the monster. When recaptured in the realist novel, 'the monster is one which may be educated, tamed, accepted and loved, in spite of its fearful mien'[6] – in short, integrated into a universe of Reform. But the realist novel had not only to reform the monster; it had also to reform its own monstrous origins. Realism becomes instrumental in guaranteeing literary status and social acceptability for the novel because it marks the novel's generic disavowal of its popular antecedents: 'To become [the dominant literary form] it had to show that it could rise above its dubious origins in the literary market-place, above its function as "mere entertainment" to claim a legitimate place as literature.'[7] As the trade in print gained importance through the eighteenth-century it was accompanied by the elaboration of an ideology of 'Literature' based on disclaiming its own commercial dependence. Writers of 'Literature' – the natural product of disinterested and independent 'men of genius' – distinguished themselves from writers of entertainment and propaganda by characterizing the latter as 'verbal mechanics' or 'hacks' (a word borrowed from contemporary 'cant').[8] In addition then to the disavowal of overt coercion and control and of the 'monstrous' past of popular writing, the realist option in the novel, with its regime of mass printing, standardization of form (the 'three-decker'), circulating libraries, series publication, etc., is overdetermined by the disavowal of the mechanical conditions in which it is itself produced. As a survivor of the popular, commercial and 'monstrous' past, the mystery/detective story was clearly a privileged target for such disavowal.

I have hitherto avoided any strict literary definition of the 'genre' (if such it be). The popularity of mystery/detective fiction is only matched by the popularity of received ideas about what it is and what it does. But the literary disavowal continues. Even the sympathetic (the entertained or the theoretically-inclined), who find personal, theological, metaphysical, anthropological, narratological or socio-political justifications for the fascination of detective fiction, all tend to deny its status as literature by underlining its conservative structure as a mechanical, formulaic genre. But, as I observed at the beginning, theoretical accounts depend on historical perspectives. What these received ideas have in common is that they virtually all extrapolate their model from Conan Doyle, rewriting the antecedent history from this retrospective. For example, whereas many critics find the way science is used in detective fiction to be evidence of its anti-literary and mystifying repressiveness, Ian Ousby points out that 'science and scientism did not become relevant to the English portrayal of the detective until the advent of Sherlock Holmes.'[9] Similarly, when Julian Symons summarizes what appears to be the traditional formula ('it should present a problem, and . . . the problem should be solved by an amateur or professional detective through processes of deduction'), he is immediately obliged to observe that 'When one looks at the attempts at definition more closely, they can be seen to apply only to the detective stories written in what is often called the Golden Age'[10] – that age, indeed, in which detective writers themselves set down genre rules. Most of these writers and (when they were not themselves, like Dorothy Sayers, doubling as historians and critics) the critics who supported them, saw Conan Doyle as the model and read Poe and Collins through him. But, in fact, Edmund Wilson may well be right in the discriminations he introduces: 'the detective story proper had borne all its finest fruits by the end of the nineteenth century, having only declined from the point where Edgar Allan Poe had been able to communicate to M. Dupin something of his own ratiocinative intensity and where Dickens had invested his plots with a social and moral significance that made the final solution of the mystery a revelatory symbol of something the author wanted seriously to say.'[11]

Anachronistic analysis is dangerous because it collapses and rewrites the period prior to Holmes as a mere anticipation whose significance is valued only through the retrospective teleology. Much of the blame apparently lies with poor old Watson: 'You remind me of Edgar Allan Poe's Dupin. I had no idea that such individuals did exist outside of stories.'[12] By looking backwards, Holmes recaptures Dupin as his 'very inferior' ancestor, makes him the first, but very 'showy and superficial', detective, and places himself in an intellectual tradition of his own manufacture. At the same time as he denigrates Dupin he disavows his own fictionality – a gesture of some significance, for reasons that will soon become apparent. But even if we were to take Holmes at his word, how are we to explain that it took forty years for Dupin to find his inheritor? What was happening in the meantime, merely inadequate attempts to develop the genre 'invented' by Poe, which, barring a largely isolated attempt by Wilkie Collins some twenty years later, had to await the genius of Conan Doyle to get it right? Poe apparently offers himself as the 'founder' of the genre inasmuch as Dupin is 'invented' at the same time as the detective himself. But it is much less clear that Dupin is a 'detective' in the line of what became the dominant literary tradition, or that Poe generated a form of writing which can be properly described as 'detective fiction' in the sense of Conan Doyle's stories, until his Dupin tales were re-read as such by Sherlock Holmes. Rather, as I shall seek to show, not only is Poe concerned with quite different social, epistemological and literary issues, but also, and despite his reference to Poe, Sherlock Holmes' more pertinent antecedents are to be found in a quite different corpus.

What strikes me as most relevant to this problem is that, despite the writings of Poe, Collins and others, as R. F. Stewart has shown, there is no evidence of the existence or emergence of a recognized genre of 'detective fiction' between the 1840s and 1880s. The first literary application of the epithet 'detective' (and note the inverted commas) occurs in 1850 with Dickens' '"Detective" Anecdotes', one of a series of journalistic articles *reporting the 'real' personalities and activities of the Detective Department.* There is no suggestion here of using the detective and his activities to generate a new fictional hero or form. Indeed, Dickens is scathing about the commercial literary exploitation of the earlier force, the Runners, who, with the help of 'the penny-a-liners of that time . . . never lost a public occasion of jobbing and trading in mystery and making the most of themselves'.[13] According to Philip Collins, the real novelty of the articles written by Dickens and his co-editor W. H. Wills lay strictly in the realm of factual journalism: the reporter's accompanying the subject on patrol, and the use of the interview.[14] Rather than 'trading in mystery', the articles pursue authenticity in an attempt to contrast the Detective Department with its predecessors and, in the face of their failure, to promote the former as the new mythical model of the Reform ideal.

We have already seen briefly how Rowan and Mayne's police created a reputation for itself as the epitome of Reform which has survived at least until very recently in figures like Dixon of Dock Green; and we have also seen how the limitations of this force became apparent, most of all in terms of the continuing need for invisible invigilation. Notwithstanding the recognized virtues of the new force, this was to give rise to another popular myth of the policeman, in the guise of P. C. Plod. As the detective comes to substitute the uniformed policeman as the embodiment of the new discipline, the Peelers' image of steady restraint and institutional identity becomes converted into a reputation for *stupidity* – as Wills puts it, 'Had the whole matter remained in the hands of X49, it is possible that your troubles would have lasted you till now.'[15] This disavowal of the uniformed police would be most strange, were it not that it represents a crucial shift in issues in order to account for the failure of uniformed policing and the need for an invisible force – a shift that was to be almost universally endorsed by later writers of detective stories and, when the private detective finally appeared, eventually attained the plainclothes force itself and made it the caricature of officious stupidity.

Reform 'police' was, as we have seen, institutional in character; the uniform overcame fears of corruption by depersonalizing the officer and transforming him into a civil servant, with all the virtues that this had come to imply; but it also threatened to reduce him to an agent of an impersonal bureaucracy. The policeman may act with exemplary restraint and fairness, but he still requires detailed written instructions to guide him – 'doing things by the book'.

As behaviour becomes increasingly institutionalized and regulated by Reform, the power of mastery needs to be re-personalized by invoking that sphere most dear to English liberalism as an expression of its opposition to impersonal, machine-like tyrannies: the individual mind and moral will. However decent and admirable the policeman may be, his professionalism, moral correctness and conformity, and his very effectiveness, are not virtues if they are only a result of bureaucratic regulation; they have to be the consequence of an independent intelligence and moral choice. As we know very well, what characterizes the later fictional detective hero is precisely this: the personal and voluntary commitment of his individual intelligence and distinctive knowledge to the service of justice.

Disavowing the uniformed police by thus shifting the issue allows Dickens and Wills to accrue and transfer the virtues claimed for Reform to the institution which might otherwise be seen as the return of precisely what Rowan and Mayne had sought to repress in the image of policing. In this sense, the detective here is not new, but a re-formed version of the Reform police. The same terms are used, but, crucially, the detective's very invisibility becomes a sign of his greater proximity to the humane ideals of Reform: the Detective Department 'is so well chosen and trained, proceeds so systematically and quietly, does its business in such a workmanlike manner, and is always so calmly and steadily engaged in the service of the public, that the public do not know enough of it, to know a tithe of its usefulness'.[16] By being less conspicuous, the detectives, an 'important social branch of the public service',[17] can exercise their discipline humanely and discreetly, warning off rather than arresting potential offenders. This allows them to succeed where, as we have seen, the uniformed branch had only limited effect, in the main police ideal of dissuading quietly and efficiently by their presence: 'This is an excellent characteristic of the Detectives, for they thus become as well a Preventive Police.'[18] Here then the preventive presence becomes an effect not of visibility but of the ubiquity that invisibility permits. As Inspector Field takes the author through the London underworld, he is 'equally at home wherever we go' since, like the good angel Dickens had called for in *Dombey and Son*, all houses are 'open to him'.[19] The uniform not only limited the penetration of policing, it also made the nature of its threat explicit. The detective may not be visible in the same sense as the policeman, but one knows he is there. Like the boats of the Marine Police, which 'go about so silently, and lie in wait in such dark places, and so seem to be nowhere, and so may be anywhere',[20] his power derives from the imaginative visibility of his invisibility, just as the moral manager's spiritual, rather than physical, presence informs every corner of the asylum. This is, as I observed in Chapter 3, the Reform ideal *par excellence*, to make the presence of the Law a reality within the imagination and culture of the poor.

The virtue of intelligence and that of ubiquity come together in what is probably the main characteristic of Dickens' mythology and which clearly draws on the image of the moral manager: the detective's eye. The eye is both the focus of his personalized power, moral authority, knowledge, experience and intelligence, and the means by which he penetrates, like the philanthropic social researcher, into every part of the 'secret world': 'Inspector Field's eye is the roving eye that searches every corner of the cellar as he talks.'[21] It is the eye of a master of mysteries, which sees what cannot be seen: 'Every clue seems cut off; but the experience of a Detective guides him into tracks quite invisible to other eyes.'[22] It is the source of a fund of knowledge, for the eye sees and remembers everything: 'Every man of them, in a glance, immediately takes an inventory of the furniture and an accurate sketch of the editorial presence. The Editor feels that any gentleman in the company could take him up, if need should be, without the smallest hesitation, twenty years hence.'[23] The power of this eye resembles nothing so much as that of the moral manager taking control of an unreformed madhouse, as Field goes 'through a labyrinth of airless rooms, each man responding, like a wild beast, to the keeper who has tamed him, and who goes into his cage.'[24] Thus, from the criminal's point of view, 'If it's the accursed glaring eye that fixes me, go where I will, I am helpless.'[25] Its photographic and transfixing qualities provide an encyclopedic knowledge of the identity of criminals: 'In order to counter-act the plans of the swell-mob, two of the sergeants of the Detective Police make it their business to know every one of them personally.'[26] Finally, and perhaps most of all, the power of this eye is, according to Wills, its ability to read the eyes of others: '"The eye," said our informant, "is the great detector. We can tell in a crowd what a swell-mobsman is about by the expression of his eye."'[27]

However, when we look at the 'anecdotes' themselves, we find that the theme of intelligence and knowledge and the iconography of the eye in fact represent little more than a mystification of the traditional practices of thief-takers and spies, raising those practices to an almost magical level of mastery and providential intervention. Dickens' own keen 'eye' for character humanizes the skills of intelligent detection by individuating his detectives, men of 'superior sense . . . [and] . . . a perfect mastery of their character', in terms of their personal talents and expertise: Dornton is 'famous for steadily pursuing the inductive process', Witchem is particularly knowledgeable about the swell-mob, Mith's expertise is housebreakers, Fendall's is 'private inquiries of a delicate nature', and Straw's is disguise.[28] But in the examples Dickens gives us, the success of these detectives is due not so much to the charismatic penetrating eye, personal talent, knowledge and intelligent analysis as to more vulgar and traditional police skills of simple pursuit, infiltration and entrapment, interfering with the mail, confidence tricks and pocket-picking, and spying on thieves, plus a series of what Dickens himself calls 'curious coincidences'.[29] In fact, little has changed since Wild's time: as Wills points out, all the thief's qualities and skills are needed for thief-taking; the difference is 'If thieving be an Art . . . thief-taking is a Science.'[30] The methods remain the same; but what characterizes the detective as he distances himself from both the Peeler and the thief is the way he claims to himself exceptional and 'scientific' qualities of intelligence and knowledge. However, despite Poe's contemporary invention of Dupin, no real intellectual or methodological content is offered to substantiate the detective's claims to intellectual heroism; what makes the traditional quasi-criminal methods described by the magistrate Nathaniel Conant as the 'mystery', 'art' or 'policy' of catching thieves 'scientific' is nothing more than the fact that it is a detective who employs them on behalf of the law.

The same was to be true in the sort of narrative which was first described as '"Detective" Literature'. The expression occurs in 1862 in the preface to the volume publication of the purportedly *factual* memoirs of Inspector F., *The Experiences of a Real Detective*. However bogus its authenticity, this was a hugely popular form of narrative in the 1850s in which, twenty years after the Detective Department and Dupin, the adjective 'detective' continued to be used as Dickens had used it to designate a supposedly 'real' social institution and its members, rather than a new literary form or genre; it did not mean 'like the narrative form or hero of Poe's stories', but 'what real-life detectives do'. In brief, as we shall see, rather than

inspiring a new genre of fictional writing, the invention of the
police detective merely gave further life to the popular tradition of
the undifferentiated 'news/novel' discourse that Davis indicates as
the immediate antecedent of the eighteenth-century novel: what the
Saturday Review characterized in 1863 as *'the romance of the detective'*,
the appeal of which survives in the twentieth century in the popular
taste for magazines, newspapers and books that purport to recount
true, remarkable and horrific cases.[31] It is to this that we now turn.

ADVENTURES, MEMOIRS AND RECOLLECTIONS

In considering the impact of policing and detection, and of Poe's
invention, on narrative, it is useful to look first at a text of this sort
which pre-dates not only the Detective Department and Dupin, but
the Metropolitan Police itself. Although the expensive three-volume
anonymous *Richmond: Scenes in the Life of a Bow Street Runner, drawn
up from his private memoranda* (1827) was apparently not a popular
success, it is none the less an interesting transitional collection of
stories.[32] The narrative is not structured by the policeman's life;
rather, the entire first volume consists of a series of unconnected
episodes in which Tom Richmond plays the part of the likable rogue
hero of the traditional, popular adventure story: 'I must certainly
have been born to a stirring random life, – at least, from earliest
remembrance, I have ever been engaged in some bustling scene of
mischief' (p. 1).

In a universe in which 'orchard-robbing is somehow, like poaching
or smuggling, always considered as a kind of pardonable crime'
(p. 3), the 'first fruits of [Tom's] genius' are the apples he steals
to give to his childhood love, Anne. Driven by the desire for
romantic adventure, Tom flees from the contrastingly prosaic fate
in a Liverpool counting-house to which he is destined by his
father, to become an actor. This provides no more than a pretext
for wandering through entertaining interludes populated by stock
characters – rogues, fools, and helpless women – as for example the
series in which the romantic landscape of the Wye valley gives onto a
traditional universe of intersections – of carriages, highwaymen, and
corrupt officers of the law, and of Tom with his own past – furnishing
an almost limitless possibility of providentially coincidental encounters. But the world of mischievous, outlawish adventure holds
dangers. The combination of the romantic heroism Richmond learns

in the theatre and Anne's gothic-novel reading bears out the worst fears of the critics of popular literature by providing the young people with a language of love: 'My late dramatic studies and her romance reading rendered us both much more aware of our situation, and also furnished us with words more expressive of our feelings than when we first met there. It was, in truth, a finished love scene' (p. 15). Not quite finished yet: Anne is, for now, still able to resist Tom's suggestion, when he persuades her to flee with him, that 'It will be better to say at once that we are married, which we really have been, you know, love, ever since we exchanged vows' (p. 30). However, after she disappears mysteriously and is rescued from her wrongful arrest by the 'gypsy gentleman', Wilton, she can no longer resist Tom's proposal not to 'submit to have our warmest feelings chilled and withered by the church ceremony'; now she has 'no remedy: – she must either go with me or return to prison' (p. 54). Shortly after, and as if as a result of, their gypsy wedding, Anne falls sick and dies and Richmond is forced to reconsider and condemn his phantasies, both his life and his narrative: 'She had fallen a victim to my rash romancing; and I was now punished, by her irretrievable loss, for my wild folly' (p. 57).

The result of this crisis is not a reform of personality, but an inflection in plot. Internal experience has no place here as the movement of the story again takes over: 'I cannot dwell on this sad event: it recalls feelings too painful. I shall therefore proceed to subsequent adventures, in which, perhaps, the reader may take greater interest' (p. 58). Tom's world begins to give way to a somewhat more prudent and modern universe. Nevertheless, like his eighteenth-century literary predecessors, he still rejects the careers in service which offer themselves to one of his class, especially those which involve the mark of livery. What he seeks is a compromise between his past and the modern world: 'some settled occupation' which would not frustrate his 'restless habits' and love of liberty (p. 87). Thus when his earlier colleague in adventure, Bucks, suddenly reappears dressed in the 'spruce blue coat and scarlet waistcoat' of 'the establishment at Bow Street', Tom immediately recognizes this as his true vocation. Just as his confession of folly had been directed at both his life and his narrative (his 'romancing'), the attraction of the Runners emerges as an alternative as much in narrative as in personal terms, the possibility of a form for his life: 'This was precisely what accorded with the views I had been forming of a life, partly regular and partly adventurous.' In contrast to the dull and subservient plots traditionally available to one of his class and skills, this new profession involves no loss of narrative continuity and productivity, rather the opposite: the Runners 'exhibited a more varied picture of human life than I had hitherto met with in all my wanderings', and his new duties mean that 'new adventures are always springing up and leading me, as at first, into unforeseen difficulties which must be encountered, or business which must be performed. My desire also for mingling in the bustle of the world and the eccentricities of life, remain unsatiated and insatiable' (note that 'business' is here used in the theatrical, not the commercial sense – p. 89).

In contrast to the aristocratic solution Fielding found for Tom Jones and the mercantile fate of Colonel Jack, the Runners present a petit-bourgeois means of modernizing the life of the rogue by furnishing an institutional context which retrospectively justifies his roguish qualities. They rehabilitate the mischief and romance previously exhibited in what has become a dangerous and marginal setting by providing a new *framework* (a 'regular' life) in which to cast his otherwise still basically traditional adventures – in its 'regularity', indeed, the potential beginnings of a new *formula* for adventure. But since, as we have observed, the Runners are a transitional institution, not yet part of the universe of Reform, they provide little more than a frame for adventure, without significantly affecting the form. Much survives intact from the first, 'criminal', volume. With their activities of pursuit on the margins of respectable society, but now, decisively, in its defense, the Runners are perfectly compatible with the tropes of freedom and travel within a limited universe which permits providential encounters and chance resolutions. The resources required are identical to those of the actors and gypsies: a network of information, skills of cunning, histrionics and disguise, and the capacity for dramatic and heroic deeds. In this way, Richmond is less reformed than, like Fielding's constables, recruited. By the same token, we do not yet have here the structure of the 'case' but a series of five episodes, largely connected by simple temporal or spatial contiguity.

Only three of these stories deal with recognizable crime (gambling fraud, connected either with smuggling or forgery and in a lesser way with seduction, kidnapping and blackmail). The first serves mainly to exculpate his old friends, the gypsies, from the macabre accusation of body snatching and to introduce the master-criminal, Jones, and is loosely linked to two episodes involving characters from the first volume, Lord —— and Sir Bryan, and their gambling fraud. The last episode, forming its own separate and uninterrupted narrative, centres on a decadent society beauty who exercises a mildly prurient fascination on Richmond until she is driven to a romantic suicide (this was to become something of a convention in later examples of the genre). These are interspersed with and enlivened by unrelated comical episodes which owe more to the traditional popular fiction of the broadsheet than to the annals of modern crime. One (Vol. II, Chapters 7–11) concerns a conspiracy by the parish to 'haunt' a disliked rector. Now prevented by his 'oath of office' from joining in the mischief on the side of the parishioners, Tom invents another form of mischief by comically 'exorcising' the evil spirits set up by the local wags. In the other case (Vol. III, Chapters 6–8), Tom is sought out by an old man whose daughter has married a squire who appears to be trying to drive her mad. Although he sympathizes with the husband, Tom accepts the job as, again, one of those opportunities which allows him to discharge his office whilst still having 'fun'. In a clearly comical context, he and Bucks disguise themselves as 'mad doctors' and treat the husband as he had the wife, until he agrees to treat her better. Whilst spending a major part of his time in the comical representation of such 'gothic' mysteries as body snatching, haunting and madness, the only major criminal whom he actually brings to legal justice is Jones, and not only is he not convicted of the crimes for which Tom had pursued him, but Richmond is singularly unconcerned, indeed relieved, at the sentence. As for the elements of the forgery gang in the last episode, 'It will not be of interest . . . to the readers of my narrative, to follow it up with a detail of what occurred . . . at the Old Bailey' (p. 266).

The very credibility and continuity of Tom's passage to the side of the Law derives most of all, even on the eve of the Runners' conversion into the Metropolitan Police, from the transitional reputation of the force: 'At first, I had an indescribable notion that I was now degraded and shut out from all society, as every body has a dislike and horror at the very sight of an officer' (p. 89). Like Rowan and Mayne, Tom has first to confront and transcend social distrust by his own strategies of disavowal, disarming the institution of its perceived threat to liberty. The process begins by Richmond's distinguishing himself from the stupid and corrupt constabulary and the militaristic and anonymous 'marines or preventives' who actually capture Jones' gang. Second, Tom is highly selective in the adventures he recounts and careful in presenting his motives for pursuing them. By taking 'but little interest in the petty routine of the office' (p. 121), he not only guarantees that his adventures will be exciting, but he avoids associating himself with the routine corruption of the force. Third, even in the more strictly criminal cases, rather than acting as an agent of the impersonal state and its laws, Tom resolves problems on a distinctly personal and individualized basis.

This distantiation is assisted by the actual limited functions of the Runners (pursuit and apprehension) and by the dissociation of policing from punishment established by Colquhon: 'All that I had to do, however, was, if possible, to secure the desperado: after that they might either hang him, or make a justice of him for ought I cared' (p. 162). At the same time, this disavowal of the Law allows him to reverse the implications of the semi-freelance status of the Runner by dissociating himself from the blood-money of capital rewards: 'that he was *not* sentenced to execution, however, eased my mind of a very disagreeable feeling connected with the emoluments arising from the capital conviction of criminals' (p. 195). Although Tom works for contract and reward, he is (albeit rather artificially) personally scrupulous about the limits of his honourable activity. He is neither a profiteer, nor a bureaucrat, nor an employee. This is made clear in his first adventure as a Runner: having been contracted by the parents to find their abducted child, suspicions of mercenary motives are disarmed by the behaviour of the ungrateful and miserly father ('I can get as many labourers as I choose for half the money') and Tom's contrasting attitude to the mother: he feels 'well rewarded . . . in the burst of pleasure I had given to this charming lady'; he takes her money reluctantly, so as not to offend her (pp. 119–20). In sum, Tom maintains a highly ambiguous relation to the Law, showing himself less concerned with legality and punishment than with conciliating 'fun' with doing what he sees as his personal duty to himself, his friends, and, within the terms he lays down, to those who contract him; the rest is not his concern. In the meantime, the principle motor behind the succession of the stories is that of Tom's energy and the very momentum of the heroic adventures themselves. Either Tom sets off in a speculative attempt to increase his reputation or, more often, events simply follow on from earlier events through chance encounters. His adventures as a Runner remain linked by principles which survive from the first volume: the excitement of activity ('restless habits') and the convention of a universe in which, wherever he may travel, a limited set of stock characters drawn from the traditional literature reappears – a comical and corrupt magistracy, a lower and upper class criminal fraternity, and attractive women to be served and fallen women to be pursued.

It is important to note that something else that derives intact from the first volume are Tom's methods and skills learnt in his life as an actor and gypsy. Apart from his frequent display of vitality and bravery in pursuit and in a fight, Tom's main skills depend on his histrionic talents which he uses to infiltrate Jones' gang as a disguised spy, whereafter, in celebration of the authority of the police presence, he need only identify himself and make his arrest (e.g., p. 104). In the same context of play-acting, he also employs the strategy of creating false confidences (to catch fraudsters!), that is to say, the talent of knowing how to make people talk in order that they reveal their secrets – something he had learnt 'During the wandering life which I had led . . . tact in getting into the good graces and confidence of all classes of people by talking as much as I could in their way, and by giving them *line*, as a fisher would say, to talk most themselves' (p. 112). But we must not forget that Richmond is now, objectively, an agent of the Law. Thus, if his motives, cases and consequences are distanced from popular prejudicial notions of the role of the police, the particular techniques he now harnesses to his role as Runner, inasmuch as they are recognizable as police practices, are precisely the despised and feared activities of deceit and spying which defined the repressive image of policing. The point however is that if Richmond brings his adventurous skills from the early volume, he also brings with them the providential principles of its universe – indeed, the very appearance of Bucks as a Runner is singularly providential in resolving Tom's own crisis. Thus, Tom is successful in finding the missing child in his first case through nothing more than 'our being accidentally on the spot' (p. 96), and his success in pursuing Jones derives from his fortuitously overhearing conversations – in effect confessions – and being in the right place at the right time to catch the criminal in the act. Although much importance is laid on information, this is always timely and readily obtained; we are still dealing with the common informer, not the investigator with exceptional powers of observation.

So this is how Richmond repays the Runners: just as the office conciliates restless liberty with regular employment, Tom seeks to reconcile police practices and the Law with vitality, adventure and, most of all, with Providence. The feared techniques of policing are here not only disarmed by being dissociated from the venal motives of immoral profit and from the corruption, impersonality and severity of the legal institution, but are positively valued by being employed by the attractive hero, guided by his spontaneous sense of honour, in alliance with the coincidence and good fortune of a beneficial Providence. In other words, Tom's integration into the Runners does not compromise the values which survive from the earlier traditional mode, ensuring that he remains unaffected by the threatening bureaucratization of the new role. He thereby in his turn enhances the reputation of the force, in large part by showing how it takes its place so happily in the former universe.

Little in fact is changed here, beyond the superficial framework. Richmond's conclusion may remind us of Moll's pragmatic moralistic justification, but, the first phrase apart, it is even less convincing: 'My purpose will be answered if what I have recorded in these volumes shall serve to beguile an idle hour, or show to those, who are inexperienced, the innumerable snares which beset the path of life, particularly in this overgrown and bustling metropolis' (p. 266). The story's moralizing purpose is quite secondary to its functions as an adventurous entertainment, a re-framing of the picaresque eighteenth-century hero which gives him a place in the modern landscape and attempts to harness his energies on the side of the Law. But this place, structurally that of a primitive policeman, has little to do subjectively with the system of Law or the new morality. In his discrete use of his powers in support of Providence, it remains dependent on his own, albeit somewhat more prudent, but still unreformed and highly personalized moral judgement. It is only the profession itself and the nature of some of the offences which give the touch of modern realism to the story, which is otherwise concerned with the non-juridical and old-fashioned gothic excitements of body-snatching, sexual seduction, hauntings and madness and still largely propelled by a spirit of healthy mischief and adventure.

Despite the historical and institutional distance between the Runners and the Detective Department and, most importantly, despite the intervening appearance of Dupin, there is little difference between the 'romance of the detective' and what we have observed, before the invention of the New Police, in *Richmond*. These pseudo-factual 'memoirs' – indeed, in their very attempt (itself taken increasingly less seriously) to present themselves as authentic – merely continue the popular, pre-novelistic genre of 'news/novel' adventure stories by reframing them within the new institutions. This attempt at modernization without a genuine reform of writing commits these narratives to a constant search for superficial novelty in order to preserve an outdated form. As in Dickens' journalistic detectives, the main novelty is the premium awarded to intelligence and knowledge as a means of resolving the surviving tension between the adventure and the Law. The adventure becomes increasingly a 'battle of wits', an intellectual distraction which serves as a cover for a repressive recuperation of the Reform ideal. But, as we shall see, despite Poe, although the 'adventure of intelligence' begins to develop a vocabulary it most crucially continues to lack an intellectual *content*. The 'romances of the detective' written after the founding of the Detective Department do not inaugurate a new literary structure of capture – 'detection' as it is later understood, the retrospective rationalistic unpuzzling of a mysterious plot. What we tend to find here, is not, as in Holmes, crime + solution + (retrospective) explanation, but still the simple 'Runner' structure of crime + chase + capture. These are adventure plots, driven forward towards a climax of action. They are reactionary precisely in the sense of being conservative: in their lack of a revision of plot.

The existence of the Police and the Detective Department obviously produce some alterations to the adventure story. In the first place, there is no longer any need to integrate the adventures in a personal biography. This is not to say that the personal dimension disappears entirely, for the first 'real-life' detective narrative, 'Thomas Waters', *The Recollections of a Policeman* (1849, 1853, 1856),[33] begins with a case of gambling fraud in which Waters conciliates personal revenge with official duty: obliged to become a detective after being defrauded of his fortune, his first reported action is to arrest the man who had tricked him. But beyond this we know very little about our hero; the only antecedent he gives is already a mythical detective story, an unreported case in which he apparently established his reputation. Biographical details are, in effect, substituted by the history of the institution in which, like Dickens, Waters transfers the image of the Reform ideal established a generation ago to the discreet sign of its failure by conspicuously conflating the date of the foundation of the Detective Department with that of the New Police: 'The Detective Policeman is in some respects peculiar to England – one of the developments of the last 25 years' (preface to the American edition). With no need for a personal biography Waters is able to organize his narrative immediately around his police activities. We now find a text divided into distinct cases, united only by the figure of the hero and framed by legal process. The stories tend to originate not with the social event of a crime but with the institutional event of official police orders, and they close not with the discovery but with the conviction of the criminal – a 'sentence'. The only exceptions are found in a middle set of cases in which the absence of this closure registers critiques of aspects of police and their narratives. The crimes which appear in the ten cases in this volume also contribute to the air of modernity and realism surrounding the stories. Consistently more contemporary and less bizarre than those confronting Richmond, they are the sort of cases in which the uniformed branch had least success: forgery and gambling fraud, burglary and murder, house-breaking, larceny, embezzlement (this turns into an unrelated case of blackmail), and assault on a police officer (the attempted murder of Waters himself).

However, the use of the institutional context, the legal frame and modern crime is purely superficial. As the case titles indicate, the stories are organized less around particular problems posed by modern crimes or the individuals who commit them than by a series of stock characters or situations of popular melodramatic fiction: 'The Gambler' (Part I), 'X.Y.Z.' (III), 'The Widow' (IV), 'The Twins' (V), 'The Revenge' (VIII), 'Mary Kingsford' (a provincial girl working in a London shop and preyed on by 'swells' – IX), and 'Flint Jackson' (a miserly gang leader – X). Only three titles refer to the legal dimension of police work: 'Guilty or Not Guilty' (II), 'The Pursuit' (VI), and 'Legal Metamorphoses' (VII).[34] Similarly, Waters' relationship to the institution is clearly idiosyncratic. By birth the social equal of his Chief (p. 5), he is often employed precisely when his colleagues have failed and for skills, like his ability to speak French (p. 109), which his colleagues do not possess – he is in short, like Holmes, a detective of last resort. But rather less like Holmes, Waters is useful as a detective precisely because of his *gentlemanly* accomplishments (like the Reformer's philanthropic temperament was the best claim to managerial mastery). He became a detective not through a desire for social respectability or personal enrichment, nor because of any temperamental or methodological peculiarities, be they roguish or scientific, but simply because he sees it as a suitable profession in the modern world for a gentleman who has lost his independence to a new class of social speculators. Whilst this rubs off on the institution itself, we are brought to perceive Waters not so much as a subordinate state functionary than almost as a free agent, a single, moral, intelligent, cultured and honourable man fighting crime.

Finally, the identification with legal process exists only at the level of the narrative frame. Although he is more often in the 'office' than Richmond, it is not necessarily the official order which actually motivates the action. In half his cases he is called in by the Commissioner or Superintendent, but only the fifth case seems at all routine – and whilst this begins with orders, it does not end with a sentence. More to the point, even in those cases initiated by orders, other motives – indeed, other crimes – rapidly take over and remove the action and its hero from the direct and dependent service of the state legal system into a more personal universe. Indeed, the most striking stories are those in which Waters acts independently of the routine or orders of the department. In two cases he is motivated by his own personal interest (the reverse stories of 'The Gambler' and 'The Revenge'), and in four he begins by pursuing a criminal in the course of his normal duties, but only the last of these is a simple and complete operation of routine; of the others, the case either fails or is abandoned in order to help a friend.

Nor do Waters' actual techniques of 'detection' greatly differ from those of Richmond or Dickens' real detectives. Although the suspicious character of the policeman is dismissed with only a slightly apologetic tone, once again he combats crime with precisely the sort of quasi-criminal and spy-like activities which fuelled resistance to modern policing: disguise, infiltration, false confidences and trust, entrapment, intimidation of witnesses, illegal search, and spying on private correspondence and conversations from which he obtains key information or virtual confessions. His lack of operational ethics is brutally clear in 'The Revenge' where he tricks a woman into helping him escape death at the hand of her master by convincing her that her long-lost daughter had been found. He confesses: 'I do not know, by the way, whether the falsehood . . . was strictly justifiable or not' (p. 140); whatever, when she has served her purpose and is 'gently undeceived', she falls into 'positive insanity'. The issue is dismissed with a reference to a fund he philanthropically helped set up for her rehabilitation. If this might be excused by the personal extremity of the case, in the relatively routine episode of

'Flint Jackson', Waters uses the full armoury of illegal and ethically dubious tactics, tricking an imprisoned suspect into writing to her employer, intercepting the letter, and plea-bargaining with her (as in the old informer system). He then disguises himself as Jackson's wife and entraps him by pretending to have heard him confess in his sleep. This being the last story, Waters' book ends with the confession that 'This affair caused considerable hubbub at the time, and much admiration was expressed by the country people at the boldness and dexterity of the London "runner;" whereas, in fact, the successful result was entirely attributable to the opportune revelations of Sarah Purdey' (p. 185). This conclusion may, in fact, serve as the rule for the entire book, the anachronism of his referring to himself as a 'runner' betraying the unchanged nature of his activity.

This is not of course how Waters presents himself. In the first place, he covers his traditional practices with a superficial vocabulary of intellectual excellence, very probably in this case derived from Poe, which makes much of his own 'ingenuity and boldness . . . in hitting upon and unravelling a clue' and his 'patience, as well as acumen' (clearly a term taken from Poe – pp. 5–6). But, more like Dickens' detectives than Dupin, despite ample illustration of his 'patience' in following and waiting and the 'boldness' of his physical courage, we see no real evidence of 'acumen' and 'ingenuity'. Waters is still very much a detective of action – most of all an example of the dictum of the relatively intellectual Mrs. G—— in Andrew Forrester's *The Female Detective* (1864), 'with us detectives action is as nearly simultaneous to act as it can be.'[35] Instead of a new methodology, the superficial claims of perceptivity and intelligence are underwritten by a further mystification of his techniques: for all his claims, the main instrument of his success is the intervention of Providence. Criminals and crimes reveal themselves to Waters in particular: in Part III, for example, he solves the crime by overhearing a conversation between the culprit and his wife which he himself describes as 'a wonderful interposition of Providence' (p. 58) and in Part VII he is put on the trail of the criminals by the chance noticing of an advertisement. Like Dickens' detective heroes, what most characterizes him is a fortuitous capacity to be in the right place and the uncanny certitude of his suspicious detective's eye, its inexhaustible ability to recognize people, and its masterly talent for reading the criminal eye – as, for example in Part IV, where, in consequence of a fortuitous encounter with an attractive widow whilst engaged on another case, the adventure develops from 'a growing conviction, especially on noticing a sudden change in the usual cunning, impudent, leering expression of his eyes . . . that I had somewhere had the honor of a previous introduction' to the blackmailing lawyer Gates (p. 64). In no case is suspicion rationalized by a theory or process of analysis, or the ability to recognize criminals related to a specialized fund of knowledge of criminal records.

The nature of the detective's alliance with Providence here goes beyond the simple survival of an outdated mode by establishing a crucial revision of the police function. The paradigm is established in Part II, 'Guilty or Not Guilty?'. Suspicion has fallen immediately on the murder victim's nephew. The detective is however far from convinced but, having no 'evidence producible in a court of law', he is obliged to arrest the unfortunate Bristowe. The latter tells Waters: 'You of course but perform your duty, mine is not to distrust a just and all-seeing Providence' (p. 30). But this is exactly the key to the detective's novel function, for, as Waters is aware, 'My duty, I knew, was quite as much the vindication of innocence as the detection of guilt' (p. 26). It is of course his independent perseverance in the case that will allow Bristowe's faith in Providence to be vindicated. This situation occurs in no less than half the stories (II, III, VII, IX and X). Part VI – a story of failure – neatly inverts it by having Waters distracted from his duty by playing on his tendency to assume that the apparent culprit has been falsely accused. In other words, Waters overcomes the potential tyranny of his methods and the institution he serves by establishing a central trope of detective fiction: he inverts the police role from that of the agent of a punitive law to that of the public protector of the falsely accused, at the same time as he lays the basis for the future convention of always doubting the obvious and suspecting the 'least likely'. Hence, in the end, the methodological claims cannot help but be superficial. The Criminal Law is based on the primacy of empirical evidence: the incontestability of eye-witness and the materiality of objects. Yet, in many of these stories, were it not for Waters' intervention, the dependence of the legal system and the reader of realism on the evidentiality of the senses would almost certainly have ended up punishing the innocent. Waters functions as the only defence against the tyranny of empirical circumstance. But, without having an alternative epistemology, as Dupin has, with which to combat the empiricist paradigm of Law, Waters is committed to a mystification of his powers.

None the less, Waters' function as the privileged vehicle through which Providence overcomes circumstance is highly important for the reputation of the detective, for here the police detective is distanced from the Law by becoming the agent of a superior form of justice which in fact enhances the police by keeping the Law from error. This is just the sort of supplement that Reform required, an agent who ensures that the legalization/criminalization of behaviour remains consonant with the higher, providential justice it claims to serve, rather than the generalized repression of which it was accused. As a consequence, the reputation of the institution benefits from Waters' intervention. Waters is an exemplary detective – and simultaneously an exemplary social and literary hero – precisely because he has this ability to make his police 'duty' and professional skills coincide not with institutional but with Providential justice, whilst the unethical police techniques he actually employs are redeemed as his particular ability to make Providence work.

A flood of 'real-life' memoirs, in very much the same vein, followed 'Waters'' success in a continuing search for new ingredients to enliven, without reforming, the modern adventure story, of which the most important was the 'Lady' or 'Female' Detective. If, previously, the figure of the detective filled the gap opened by the modernization of the economy and culture for the eighteenth-century rogue and the gentleman reduced by circumstances, here, in a way parallel to but quite different from the figure of the governess, we find it also, in Michèle Slung's words, finding 'a respectable economic, intellectual or spiritual place for the unattached woman.'[36] The first was Mrs. Paschal, in *The Experiences of a Lady Detective* (1861), written by W. S. Hayward, the author of a highly successful series of yellowbacks.[37] The ten independent stories are characterized by a general tone of modernity and fascination with 'progress' – indeed, one tale, 'Stolen Letters', seems to exist merely to allow the suspect to escape down a pneumatic tube in the general post office. Others include such typical gestures as references to the exhilaration of the night mail train ('typical of progress', p. 35), an explanation of how to open that grand novelty, the bottle of soda water, and the praise of such modern heroes of respectability as the 'relieving officer' and 'sanitary inspectors' involved in the reform of St. Giles' – 'the genii of modern civilization and improvement' (p. 298). In all her remarks and information, Mrs. Paschal shows herself to be the spokeswoman of a thoroughly modern institutional common sense. But beneath this fascination with the topically modern, the stories register no development in narrative technique. These are still the sort of stock melodramatic or sensational situations by now well established in the genre. But the text remains important, particularly in relation to Sherlock Holmes, in that it indicates how, as this genre develops in the post-Reform period, the image of policing becomes more aggressive in a clear reinforcement of legal ideologies, and that this process is accompanied by and related to an increased professional autonomy and an intensified pretence of intellectual heroism.

Like Waters before her, Mrs. Paschal declines to discuss her past; her choice of profession seems almost natural: 'It is hardly necessary to refer to the circumstances which led me to embark on a career at once strange, exciting, and mysterious' (p. 3). She only tells us that she was well born and educated, but the death of her husband when she was 'verging on forty' had left her badly off. But her post-Reform aggressiveness can be observed in the institutional past which Mrs. Paschal invents for herself. Rather than seeking, like Waters and Dickens, to claim the Reform reputation of the New Police she actually suppresses it in favour of precisely that despised force which the Police itself was designed to disavow, telling us that 'the much-dreaded, but little-known people called Female Detectives' introduced into the 'London Detective Police' by her Chief, Colonel Warner (some twenty years before women were in fact employed), were modelled on Fouché's 'petticoated police' as employed 'in discovering the various political intrigues which disturbed the peace of the first empire' (p. 2). As for her institutional independence, although subordinate to the impressive and hyper-intelligent Colonel (described, with the author's consistent talent for bathos, as 'a man of spare build, but with keen searching eyes, like those of a ferret' – p. 1), Mrs. Paschal's relationship with the police is by no means at all routine; the Colonel almost always requests, rather than orders, her collaboration (so long as the job is not 'disagreeable' to her – p. 5), and in eight of her cases she works for reward – in half of them, on her own initiative. At the same time, she is remarkably free with her criticism of the regular forces, who are presented as foolish (arresting her by mistake in the first case), officious, insolent, and brutal. One can feel the lingering presence of Reform in the way Waters' partial distantiation from the police relocates his practices in a context in which his moral purpose can itself reflect back on and reform the image of the professional institution. But Mrs. Paschal's increased autonomy is related to a difference which marks this text decisively within post-Reform reaction: in contrast to Waters' representation of earlier Providential values as a corrective to legalistic procedures, Mrs. Paschal's highly autonomous and self-motivated policewoman acts unequivocally beyond legal process *as an agent for the extension of legal discipline.*

The clearest example of the significance of her autonomy is given in the last case, 'Incognita', in which Warner calls her in to tell her of a lady who had appealed to him to help her son who is being fleeced by a mysterious young woman:

> 'What has that to do with us?' I asked, in some surprise.
> 'Nothing whatever,' he replied, calmly.
> 'Why, then, should she have come here?'
> 'Because she wanted some clever person, man or woman, who would in some way help her to reclaim her son. She knows very well that the law cannot assist her.' (p. 267)

And Mrs. Paschal comments:

> It was nothing very unusual for us to have an application of this nature made to us, people always think that the 'police' can help them out of every difficulty. If a man loses his umbrella at his club, or a lady leaves an opera-glass in a cab, the police are applied to, as though they were omniscient and infallible. I rather like a case of the kind in which I was about to embark. There was more money to be made out of it than there was in the legitimate way, and generally less danger and fewer risks. (p. 269)

In short, Mrs. Paschal is a member of the police only inasmuch as she is *not* involved in routine activities or, as it turns out, even with the enforcement of the Law in any statutory sense; she has choice in the cases she undertakes and her explicit and quite shameless motivation is that of reward. Although institutionally still a public servant, she operates like an independent professional working through a privileged relationship with the Chief. Rather than a coincidence between police and providence, Mrs. Paschal generates a coincidence between legal discipline and her own financial advantage.

As the formal relation to the Law becomes even more tenuous, the 'case' reverts to a simply episodic form, dependent entirely on the character of the heroine. Few of her cases are instigated by an indictable offence and only three of the ten result in a formal arrest.[38] Instead, Mrs. Paschal operates independently and in a business-like fashion as an instrument of punishment, a reforming discipline and, occasionally, an arbitrary mercy – in short, as a para-legal extension to legal discipline. Here, the fact that she is a female detective takes on a particular significance, offering a privileged position for an ideological narrative about the role and place of women. Three stories may illustrate this.

Paschal's first investigation, 'My Mysterious Countess', is again, here in an ideological rather than a personal sense, a case of revenge. She is given the curious, not to say sinister, job of investigating the sources of income of the widow of the late Count of Vervaine who is at first sight guilty of no more than spending money. Now reduced to crime by the death of her husband, the Countess is, significantly, a traditional figure of popular fiction, the beautiful former actress who married into the nobility. In short, Mrs. Paschal, the widow in genteel poverty making her own way in the world, pursues a figure who is in many ways the obverse of herself. Mrs. Paschal invokes her pretence at factuality to distinguish herself from the actors of popular melodrama in which crime and detectives now featured so much: in her pseudo-factual role, it is she who is engaged in the 'dramas of real life' and 'it is such as I who really create the incidents upon which their dialogue is based and grounded' (pp. 3–4). In this context, the fact that the stupid uniformed police initially arrest Mrs. Paschal rather than the Countess has a certain irony. None the less, her victory over the decadent actress establishes her superiority as a new professional woman over the earlier popular romantic heroine.

In another story, 'Fifty Pounds Reward', Mrs. Paschal defends the proper relation between husband and wife against the seductions of an excessively independent spouse. She catches a wayward wife who had been encouraged to forge her husband's cheque by the pernicious argument that 'a wife ought to be mistress in her own house' (p. 217), and persuades her to confess and reform. Since Mrs. Wilkinson, the instigator of the forgery, 'who had played a part in this domestic drama more worthy of a fiend than of an educated woman in a civilized portion of the globe' (p. 236), is not actually guilty of a legal crime but merely of an ideological offence, Mrs. Paschal punishes her by using local gossip to humiliate the evil woman until she and her unassertive husband are forced to sell up.

The story ends by telling us that the Wilkinsons opened a pub and drank themselves into abject poverty. Finally, in the case already referred to, 'Incognita', Mrs. Paschal continues her work of domestic discipline. Here she is not only influenced by the easy money; she is also resolved to 'do all I could for the unfortunate mother, who saw her only son doing what was extremely distasteful to her maternal feelings' (p. 268). The mother herself points out how women like 'Incognita' are the enemies of motherhood: 'They dread home influence more than anything else, and therefore they fight it in a most determined manner' (p. 271). The detective balances her sense of duty to her job, motherhood and the home with her feminine sympathy for the 'secret grief gnawing at [Incognita's] heart' by reforming the foolish young man and letting the unfortunate temptress go free (not that she had committed any indictable offence).

Apart from these stories of direct intervention in women's roles (and her similar role in disciplining the noble family of 'The Lost Diamonds'), and the disturbingly significant case of the political secret society ('The Secret Band'), the other five concern more banal cases of larceny, extortion, fraud, and murder. But they are of interest in manifesting one of her most conspicuous characteristics: the high degree of melodrama with which she covers the banality of the processes of discovery. This too follows from the choice of a female heroine. The fact that, as a lady detective, Mrs. Paschal cannot rely on the virile powers of her male predecessors (despite her assertion that, 'owing to frequent acquaintance with peril, I had become unusually hardened for a woman' – p. 65), necessitates the reinforcement of the self-proclaimed methodical and inspired intelligence as the hallmark of the detective. She is obliged by her sex to use subterfuge, for example, to bribe her way into the Countess' household 'to play the spy upon her actions' (p. 6). Because she relies so much on disguise, infiltration, false confidences and, most of all, spying (supplemented by more mechanical activities like following, confronting and fortuitous confession), Mrs. Paschal has to emphasize more than Waters the intellectual brilliance of her methods, insisting that her conclusions are based not on 'random thoughts. I had made minute observations, and deduced . . . the inferences I have stated' (p. 99) and that her lack of ethics is justified by the fact that 'detectives, whether male or female, must not be too nice. The unraveling of crime is always a conflict of wits' (p. 272). As adventure and harmless 'mischief' had generated the narrative interest and justified the social role of Richmond, here the 'conflict of wits' becomes the absolute point of interest and at the same time the transcendent justification behind which Mrs. Paschal goes about her policing.

However in this case, whilst again, almost twenty years after Dupin, these processes are never analysed or explained, the fact that we are dealing with a lady detective means that, by invoking the stereotypical talents of the woman, a rationale can be offered for what looks like simple guesswork: in effect, she 'invariably had an intuition that such and such a thing would happen before it actually took place' (p. 14). Likewise, all her most important skills of spying and deceit are implicitly or explicitly presented as 'feminine' traits: she has access where her colleagues would fail because 'Men are less apt to suspect a woman' (p. 43) and she has an unrivalled capacity for disguise due to her 'histrionic powers' (p. 76) and her 'wardrobe, which was as extensive and as full of disguises as that of a costumer's shop' (p. 9). She boasts that 'gaining access to people's houses in the capacity of a domestic servant was a favourite plan of mine, and one I very frequently had recourse to' (p. 275), in which she has a particular advantage through her 'thorough knowledge of the class' of housekeepers and domestic servants (p. 14). When all else fails, 'marvellous' good fortune again comes to her aid, like the miraculously opportune and accurate bolt of lightning which saves her from death at the hands of 'The Secret Band'.

In lieu of any intellectual content for her brilliance, Mrs. Paschal displays her claim through one more major quality characteristic of many a later detective, including Holmes: an irritating ability for making the simple appear difficult. Those tales, such as the four which form the middle of the book, which do not involve spying as such, reveal how strikingly banal in their false complexity her supposedly remarkable intellectual skills are. Mrs. Paschal shows her experience and cleverness for example in 'Mistaken Identity' by opposing bail for the suspect (a civil engineer engaged on the new sewers for the Muswell Hill Board of Works – a testimony of respectability if ever there was one) because 'I never allow appearances to have any weight with me' (p. 241). Nevertheless, despite having no grounds *except* his appearance, and without any evidence or reasoning, she proposes to the Inspector that it might be a case of mistaken identity. Paradoxically, it is only after Halliday is positively identified by an eye-witness that she offers her services to 'see if I cannot unravel this tangled skein' (p. 246). She begins with a typically uncannily opportune question: does Halliday have a relative who resembles him? As it happens, he had a wastrel twin who had died at sea. '"Oh!" I said, with a prolonged exclamation; I began to see my way a little clearer.' Her slowness is obviously not intended to signify stupidity, but to raise the level of complexity: 'I had a shrewd suspicion that I was about to embark in the investigation of one of the strangest cases of mistaken identity that had ever been heard of; nor was I mistaken, as after events tended to prove' (p. 247). These further events turn out to be no more than the confirmation of the guilt of the lost twin brother. However, even then she is incapable of solving the problem alone. In this case she calls on the quasi-criminal assistance of a colleague, a representative of the Vidocq-style policeman-spy: 'I was acquainted with a man of the name of Pegon – a Frenchman – who had, it was popularly supposed, been a thief in his own country, although he might have left France through political motives. On arriving in England he had taken service in the police-force, and evinced such wonderful dexterity in tracking criminals that he speedily became one of our most valuable detectives' (p. 247). It is the spy and *agent provocateur* Pegon who, on condition that Paschal let a friend of his escape, identifies the skittle-sharping gang.

It is useful here to compare Mrs. Paschal with Andrew Forrester's Mrs. G—— (1864). This is a rare case of a detective who explicitly refers to Poe, but only to invoke the theory of what she calls 'audacity hiding' used by the writer she significantly calls the 'great enigma-novelist' ('Enigma novel' being a term applied to sensation fiction in the 1860s – see Chapter 7).[39] This lady detective, motivated by curiosity (although 'I need not say the general, the chief motive power in the detective is gain'),[40] is considerably more 'scientific' than our other detectives. She makes a good deal of what she calls 'footmark evidence' and the work of the 'microscopic chemist' (two real contemporary developments in police work). She is highly observant and uses a methodological discourse of 'evidence' and 'inference' and even invokes a scientific principle she refers to as a 'detective law'. However, all that this careful theory and attention to fact does is to bring her to a point where 'the theory was at total variance with the ordinary experiences of life'.[41] She gets further in solving the mystery by using traditional and often traditionally 'feminine' talents: her 'corkscrew-like qualities as a detective'[42] – her ability to get women to gossip and to gain the confidence of a suspect in order to infiltrate the house – her generalized suspicious-ness, and the 'tricks of detective police officers', such as the use of a false advertisement to remove an obstacle to the investigation.[43] But, in a moment of honesty which is as typical of Mrs. G—— as it is uncharacteristic of Mrs. Paschal, she tells us that what really and finally solves the case is 'Chance!' This, after all, is the general principle of detection: 'Examine most of the great detected cases on record, and you will find a little accident has generally been the clue to success . . . . So with great discoveries . . . . In the history of crime and its detection chance plays the chief character.'[44] If it is true of the more serious Mrs. G—— that the vocabulary and procedures of method still serve to cover traditional activities of deceit and an ultimate reliance on chance, this is even more the case with Mrs. Paschal.

In sum then, whilst giving the respectability of modern disciplined and stereotyped femininity to the name of the detective, Mrs. Paschal increases the institutional distance between the officer and the state, but, decisively, not from its ideology, granting the police privileged access to areas previously managed, in principle, by non-legal institutions: most importantly, questions of feminine and marital discipline. Waters' ambiguous relation to the institution suggested a detective role in mitigation of the legal order; but what Mrs. Paschal represents is a move towards professional autonomy which is permissible because, at the same time, she guarantees its consonance with an extension of 'police' discipline into the realm of the private and domestic, to investigate non-crimes and punish culprits without the safeguard of legal process. As the narrative structure is again disconnected from the legal frame, with Mrs. Paschal the detective stands virtually alone, ready to take the important step of generic autonomy that will take her or him into the commercial agency where Catherine Louisa Pirkis' Loveday Brooke works or, more importantly, into Sherlock Holmes' private profession: an autonomous agent, not circumscribed by legal process, but using her intelligence and knowledge to preserve the modern discipline where the Law fails to reach and justifying her deceitful practices with the spurious excitements of intellectual activity in itself.

'A DETECTIVE STORY'

Despite the increasing emphasis on intelligence, knowledge and method in these 'romances', significantly one fails to note that their authors were at all inspired or influenced by Poe's Dupin. Although some of his vocabulary does find its way in as an intellectual cover of respectability for spy activities and sheer good fortune, it is clear that the authors of these highly conservative, pseudo-factual adventure stories did not view Poe as the creator of a new hero whose procedures could credibly be imitated in the context of police-work and adventure. On the other hand, detectives did become popular *fictional* elements, particularly in the sort of novel we will be dealing with in Chapter 7. In 1863 Mrs. Oliphant complained about 'detectivism' as the current 'police-court aspect of modern fiction.' Two years earlier, the *Sixpenny Magazine* had complained: 'what a complete *Deus ex machina* a detective now is in a sensation novel!'[45] Yet even the insistent appearance of the detective as a fictional element in sensation novels, many of whom owed something to Inspector Field and his colleagues, did not in itself cause the latter to be transformed into something called 'detective fiction'. In any case, the fact is that the role of official detectives in sensation fiction was usually as secondary and ineffective as in the realist novel. Thus, when, thirty years after the founding of the Detective Department (and immediately following its transformation into the CID), a review of the sensation novel *Poor Miss Finch* in *The Athenaeum* (1872) referred for the first time to 'what may be called the "detective" novel', we find that it is not being used to refer to the presence of a detective but simply as a revision of the earlier term, 'Enigma novel', coined by *The Spectator* in 1861 (and, as we have seen, used by Mrs. G—— to describe Poe) – the sort of novel in which, according to *The Saturday Review* critique of Sheridan LeFanu's *Uncle Silas* in 1865, the reader's role is like that of a detective following the clues to the solution of a mystery.[46] In short, the inverted commas around 'detective' denotes an analogy, and that analogy was restricted to the role of plot and secrets. In Stewart's words, 'it is in the criticism of sensation fiction's emphasis on plot that the word "detective" begins to appear as a critical term . . . . "[D]etective" was used originally as a useful derogatory description for the type of story which rested on the unravelling of a secret – sensation fiction, in other words – the application coming from the activities of real life detectives who were supposed to unravel the cases they met.'[47]

The transition of 'detective' from 'real life' to a category of fiction is then related to the way, as we have noted above, that the novel's claims as serious literature depended on its disavowal of its monstrous ancestors and contemporaries. The period between the 1840s and 1870s saw a particularly fierce debate which set up a series of decisive options through which serious narrative fiction sought to distinguish itself from the commercial sensation novel: instruction was opposed to entertainment, realism to romance, nature to melodrama, and 'character' to 'plot'. And, whatever the pleasures of the sensation novel, according to *The Quarterly Review* of April 1863, 'Deep knowledge of human nature, graphic delineation of individual character, vivid representations of the aspects of Nature or the workings of the soul – all the higher features of the creative art – would be a hindrance rather than a help to work of this kind.'[48] It is clearly not the presence of the detective or of a crime which is determinant here; rather it is an option taken in the debate on the nature of the novel.

The sensation novel gradually lost the battle and entered its own decline. And this is where '"detective" fiction' emerges, inheriting the criticisms used against the earlier 'enigma' novel's promotion of plot against character, entertainment against improvement.[49] Even when the expression '"detective" fiction' itself appears in a *Saturday Review* article in 1886, Stewart draws our attention to the fact that the author is still 'diffident' about using the term; he maintains the inverted commas and indicates his preference for the expression, 'the modern Gaboriau novel, to adopt the generic, but by no means exact, expression by which this kind of literature is now generally known.'[50] Three years later, Anne K. Green published a text with the subtitle 'a Detective Story' (or, as the English edition significantly has it: 'A Story Told by a Detective'). But, in contrast to her earlier sensation novel, *The Leavenworth Case*, 1878, which, despite more closely resembling a modern 'detective novel', was still subtitled 'A Lawyer's Story', *X.Y.Z.* (1883) is very much in the tradition we have been studying in this chapter.[51] The story also clearly draws on the 'real-life' memoir's more natively American parallel, the 'Dime Novel'. This is a complicated genre which owed a good deal to the first important real-life private detective, Allan Pinkerton, whose ghost-written and sensationalized cases were published during the 1870s and hold a similar place in relation to the genre in America as Dickens' anecdotes in England. Like Pinkerton's own activities, the genre is made up of action-based tales of the frontier (responsible for the myths of Buffalo Bill and the James gang) and of the 'secret service' which gradually became urbanized into action-based 'detective' serials.[52] Indeed, *X.Y.Z.* can serve as an exemplum of the convention, and of its exhaustion – to the point where, in Green's hands, the story appears to turn back on itself as its own critique.

The tale begins with the anonymous narrator engaged unsuccessfully in the pursuit of a gang of counterfeiters when he is sent out of town to investigate a number of suspicious-looking letters addressed to 'X.Y.Z., Brandon, Mass.'. He spies on the post office, and sees a young man call for X.Y.Z.'s letters and, having opened them, hand some back, saying 'There must be another X.Y.Z.'. Demanding the letters from the clerk, our detective discovers that they are part of a 'common fraud' (a betting information scam). But, as so often happens, Providence operates, though the figure of the detective, on the random syntax of adventure: 'Sometimes in the course of his experience, a detective, while engaged in ferreting out the mystery of one crime, runs inadvertently upon the clue to another' (p. 3). There is one more letter, unconnected with the above, which calls the recipient to a rendezvous and gives the password 'counterfeit'. The detective alters the meeting-place and returns the letter.

Without this having any apparent bearing on the case, he begins to gather information concerning the family of the mysterious Mr. Benson, 'the richest man in these parts and the least liked as I take it', his suspicions aroused by the fact that, although a very busy man, 'no one ever sees anything he does' or knows where his money comes from (p. 11). Benson lives with his son and daughter, but there is also, conventionally enough, an estranged son (Joe) somewhere. When the respectable son, Hartley Benson, appears, the same suspiciousness makes the detective take an immediate and professional dislike to his face: 'I did not like it . . . . It was too impenetrable perhaps; and to a detective anxious to probe a man for his motives, this is ever a fatal defect' (p. 17). In the meantime, he also overhears that there is to be a masked ball at the Benson's, and recognizes that this renders the password innocent. Nevertheless, he remains convinced, without any explicit evidence or reason, that something criminal is afoot, and to support this he displays his methodical intelligence, like Mrs. G——, by making a list of 'facts' – in themselves innocent enough – and draws his suspicious conclusion, not necessarily of an indictable offence, but of a *family mystery* which demands the intervention of the policeman.

He reconnoiters the grounds and infiltrates the household through the 'daring' scheme of contacting the owner. Whilst waiting to be received, he overhears a man and a woman conversing 'in smothered tones' but, since 'my senses are very acute', he is able to give us verbatim the entire conversation. He is favourably impressed by Mr. Benson Snr and, in order to justify his presence, he pretends to have heard that uninvited guests were planning to gatecrash, and offers his services as a guard. Both son and daughter try to dissuade him. He insists, but he tells Miss Carrie that if she wants him to ignore someone at the ball, she need only give him a description of the person in question. Here arises the first major fortuitous coincidence: 'Look in the glass when you get home and you will see the *fac-simile* of his form, though not of his face' (p. 34). The detective draws his conclusion: 'A love-letter of course; and I had been a fool to suppose it anything else' (p. 36). However, the password (although already explained) and Hartley's tone keep his suspicions alive.

That night he takes his place in the garden, ready to implement his 'daring plan' (p. 39). A man appears in a black domino, gives the password, and instructs the disguised detective to leave a certain window open. When the former refers to 'your father', the detective realizes that the party he is impersonating must be the lost son and begins to have doubts about 'my recklessness . . . folly . . . impertinence' in interfering in a family affair'. Similarly, back at the party, when Carrie addresses him as 'Joe', he again reproaches himself for his 'perfidious duplicity'. Before he can return the disguise to its rightful owner he is interrupted by his contact from the garden who whispers, as if a criticism of the detective's strategies: 'To counterfeit wrong when one is right, necessarily opens one to misunderstanding' (p. 46). In a conversation with Joe's uncle and cousin/lover, Edith, the disguised detective discovers that young Joe had been accused of stealing from his father. The black domino returns and leads him to the library. On entering the library he sees Mr. Benson poisoned by his wine. Hartley and Carrie arrive and the detective hides behind a curtain. A doctor pronounces suicide, but a servant testifies that he saw a man in a yellow domino enter from the balcony with a glass in his hand. Hartley immediately identifies this man as Joe. At this moment the detective reveals himself as the yellow domino.

Hartley accuses him of being his brother or, if not, 'some reckless buffoon' engaged in 'criminal jests'. The narrator removes the mask, declaring: 'now look at me, one and all, and say if you think I am likely to be a person to destroy Mr. Benson' (p. 85). There then occurs a fascinating dialogue. Hartley accuses him of being a 'Villain! . . . spy! informer!' set on by his brother. The detective replies:

> You call me a spy; so I am; but a spy backed by the U.S. Government is not a man to be put lightly in prison. I am a detective, sir, connected at present with the Secret Service at Washington. My business is to ferret out crime and recognize a rogue under any disguise and in the exercise of any vile or deceptive practices. (p. 86)

He proves that Mr. Benson was poisoned but, strangely for one who initiated his investigation before there was any reason to suspect a crime, he now discharges himself from any responsibility: 'Who put [the poison] there, it is for you to determine; my duty is done for to-night.'

All now is explained: Joe appears, declares his innocence and is supported by his uncle in proving Hartley's guilt. The latter goes conveniently mad, runs out and shoots himself, and the detective, baffled by the culprit's motives, can only invoke the conventional theory that 'the solution be found in his undoubted passion for the beautiful Edith, and in the accumulated pressure of certain secret debts' (p. 94). The story ends with the marriage of Joe and Edith and with the capture of the counterfeiters he was originally after – 'but not by me.' As to the present story, he never revealed to the family 'the true nature of the motives which actuated me', since, as if to bear out Hartley's accusations, he 'was too much ashamed of the curiosity which was the mainspring of my action'.

In sum then our detective here is little more than a self-assumed spy, motivated by a 'curiosity' which is in no way intellectual but rather the fruit of the generalized suspiciousness of his professional eye, animated by the simple presence of mysterious sources of income, a family secret, and a face and tone of voice he dislikes. Under this personal curiosity and his professional brief to suspect all men with 'impenetrable' faces and, by all accounts, all family secrets on behalf of the state, he deceives his hosts, disguises himself, and becomes the confidante of family and sexual intimacies destined for another. His procedures are the standard illegalities and coincidences, for which he repeatedly congratulates himself as evidence of his daring, intelligence, method and cunning. Yet he exhibits little control over the narrative. His meddling in a private affair providentially 'saves' an innocent party from accusation and discovers the culprit, largely through the latter's confession, but it singularly fails to save the victim (the person who had employed him for guard-duty). Lastly, at no point, not even in face of the murder, is the Law involved.

Be it the dying breath of an exhausted convention (although, as any devotee of current television detective series will recognize, the genre is quite alive and healthy), or an implicit critique of that very convention, the first pre-Holmesian 'Detective Story' is, despite the superficial intellectual vocabulary, still an entire genre away from Edgar Allan Poe. What was needed to transform the 'romance of the detective' into a new genre of 'detective fiction' (without the inverted commas) was of course Sherlock Holmes, not so much the culmination as the patriarchal source of a tradition – as he himself says, 'I have chosen my own particular profession, or rather created it, for I am the only one in the world.'[53] This new figure will turn out to be a combination of the traditional pseudo-factual 'romance of the detective' we have been studying in this chapter, with a revised reading of Dupin and the detective(s) found in sensation fiction. It is hence well time we turned to the Chevalier Dupin.

6

Monsters

If we go deeper into the human heart, we shall find in it a
secret disposition to believe the marvellous . . . These are the
causes, which have established the belief in spectres, ghosts,
possessed persons, devils, vampires, magicians, sorcerers – all
those frightful beings, who have ceased to play a part in courts,
but still appear in the cottage.

Jeremy Bentham, *Rationale of Judicial Evidence*
(London, 1827), p. 28.

AN IDIOSYNCRATIC ARTICLE

'If now, in addition to all these things, you have properly reflected
upon the odd disorder of the chamber, we have gone so far as to
combine the ideas of an agility astounding, a strength superhuman, a ferocity brutal, a butchery without motive, a *grotesquerie*
in horror absolutely alien from humanity, and a voice foreign in
tone to the ears of men of many nations, and devoid of all distinct
or intelligible syllabification. What result, then, has ensued? What
impression have I made upon your fancy?'

I felt a creeping of the flesh as Dupin asked me the question.
'A madman,' I said, 'has done this deed – some raving maniac,
escaped from a neighbouring *Maison de Santé.*' [1]

Close – as Dupin sketches the perimeters of the cage of signifiers in
which he will capture the inhuman culprit, all that saves the maniac
is the physical evidence of the hair and the handprint, plus the fact
that 'Madmen are of some nation, and their language, however incoherent in its words, has always the coherence of syllabification.' By
the 1840s, madmen were no longer considered to be in a condition
of absolute animality; they had been deemed reformable. The flesh
is made to creep not so much by maniacs, as by *monsters*.

136

'The Murders in the Rue Morgue' continues to be regarded as the founding document in the detective story genre. Yet, if we compare this tale with those discussed in Chapter 5, we can see that this is to take a lot for granted. In the first place, it is no wonder that the Dupin stories did not generate a genre, in that, unlike the 'romance of the detective', they present no framework of regularity which would permit such a development, beyond their idiosyncratic hero, who has conspicuously little interest in crime as such. Drawn into this case by his personal debt to LeBon, as soon as he has solved the mystery and vindicated his friend, 'the Chevalier dismissed the affair at once from his attention, and relapsed into his old habits of moody reverie' ('The Mystery of Marie Rogêt', III, p. 724). Although these reveries were occasionally interrupted ('It thus happened that he found himself the cynosure of the policial eyes; and the cases were not few in which attempt was made to engage his services at the Prefecture'), crucially, as the first published version of this story (in the *Ladies' Companion*, Nov./Dec. 1842) made explicit, 'The only instance, nevertheless, in which such attempt proved successful was the instance to which I have already alluded.' Dupin is moved to take on a second case only by the particularly 'liberal proposition' made to him by the Prefect (III, p. 728), after which 'several years' pass before he is again called on ('The Purloined Letter', III, p. 974). Once more, it is only the offer of reward, again combined with personal motives and, on this occasion, political loyalty to the Queen, which rouses Dupin. In short, it would not be easy to make a detective-story series out of a socially unconcerned recluse with no real interest in crime as such and no professional or institutional relationship with the police.

It is as if the very concepts of law and crime, so central to the modernization of society, are almost out of place here. We are perhaps misled in the first case by the term 'murders'. Yet, in its crass sensationalism, the press ironically introduces a significant hesitation: 'A murder so mysterious, and so perplexing in all its particulars, was never before committed in Paris – if indeed a murder has been committed at all' (II, p. 544). What actually makes the case equally atrocious and mysterious is the lack of the *mens rea* essential to a criminal offence – 'The police are confounded by the seeming absence of motive' (II, p. 547). The error of the police, and the reader, is to search for a human agent for events which, as it turns out, could not, by definition, have been committed by a human being and hence cannot accurately be said to be a 'crime'.

Given that the question of crime is equally moot in the last case, it is only 'The Mystery of Marie Rogêt', the *least* quoted of all, which deals with the solution to a recognizable criminal offence – and even here, as we shall see below, he got the wrong crime.[2] Whereas the 'romance of the detective', especially as it reaches outside the strict interpretation of the Law, enforces the new discipline by supporting the generalized criminalization of certain forms of behaviour, Dupin deals with mysteries beyond the reach of both legal process and the legal discipline.

In consequence, the structure of these tales is quite different from those in which crime provides the occasion, pursuit the dynamic, and the police institution or legal process the frame. Indeed, in order to make 'The Murders in the Rue Morgue' serve, as we are often told, as the first story 'deliberately' written as a 'detective story',[3] it is almost necessary to rewrite it – in one typical appreciation: 'The first thousand or so words of "The Murders in the Rue Morgue" are devoted to an introductory essay on analysis . . . . This preliminary essay . . . is unusual for Poe . . . . Having read it with care, I can assure you that today's reader does not need it at all.'[4] But this 'essay' and the continuing reflections on truth and method, are no mere pseudo-scientific gestures; rather, in place of the institutional frame found in the detective romances, Poe provides his story with a *theoretical frame*. If 'detective fiction' is characterized by its emphasis on the intricacies of plot, it has to be recognized that the story of 'The Murders in the Rue Morgue' is quite undistinguished, especially in the light of its surrounding theory. Dupin maintains that his intelligence is not just greater than that of the police, but qualitatively different. Yet, in terms of the supposed crime, what he actually *does* is no more than apply police procedures more thoroughly than the police: he inspects the room with greater care, finding the broken 'clew' and the rather self-evident details of the ape's hair and the handprint – next to which the business about language is quite redundant. Finally, he entraps the ape's owner with an advertisement. Nothing could be more banal, and 'The Purloined Letter' will make clear that traditional police methodology is normally perfectly adequate. It cannot be the action that makes this story what it is – in Poe's own words, 'something in a new key'[5] – but the theoretical essays and reflections in which it is enfolded, precisely that methodological discourse lacking in the detective romance.

Poe's stories are incorrectly associated with 'plot' because, despite their being a 'character' portrait, like the other detectives we have seen, Dupin is not a 'character' in the novelistic sense. However, in contrast to the detective romances, the idiosyncratic absence of a personal life, history or relations is replaced here not by an institution but by a body of theory. The narrator is explicit about the importance of the theory and, simultaneously, about the equation of Dupin's very personality with its theoretical content. The first indication to the reader – 'The narrative which follows will appear to the reader somewhat in the light of a commentary upon the propositions just advanced' (II, p. 531) – is revised in 'The Mystery of Marie Rogêt': 'In an article entitled "The Murders in the Rue Morgue," I endeavoured, about a year ago, to depict some very remarkable features in the mental character of my friend . . . This depicting of character constituted my design; and this design was fulfilled in the train of circumstances brought to instance Dupin's idiosyncrasy' (III, p. 724). Rather than a 'character' or a simple agent of action, Dupin is fundamentally a theoretical site, an embodiment of a synthetic – or contradictory – set of 'propositions'.

If, as seems clear, some writers of detective romances, such as Forrester and Russell ('Waters'), drew some of their superficial vocabulary of intelligence from Poe, why did they not adopt the corresponding theories? It is my sense that Dupin's theories militate against the conservative form and functions of the detective romance; they imply an authentic reform of writing – something which the romances do their very best to avoid. However, it does not seem to me that Dupin's reform of writing can be identified with that of the realist novel. What I shall be arguing – particularly in the last section of this chapter – is that what prevents Dupin from being available to writers of detective romances – but *also* problematic in relation to the realist novel – is the way his reform of writing puts radical questions to some of the basic tenets of and relations between contemporary literary, scientific, and legal realism.

In this context, one of the most important ways in which Dupin distances himself from the police and its discipline is that, in this first tale at least, his methodology is designed to deal with precisely that which disrupts the surface of realism: the extra-ordinary. As he repeatedly tells us, normal disruptions of the social order are quite capably dealt with by the police (as, one might argue, normal states of reality are dealt with by the novel or ordinary crimes by the adventure story). But for this mystery by the author of the 'Tales of the Grotesque and Arabesque', what is needed is not a detective of crimes, but someone who possesses a *different* mastery, capable of capturing what, despite the totalizing project of Reform, cannot be captured within its normal and normalizing discourses and institutions: the monster.

What then is the significance of monstrosity? In Hobbes' *Leviathan* – in a sense, where our story of modern crime and detection began – society itself is presented as intrinsically monstrous, needing Law to keep it in order. As Chris Baldick shows, the French Revolution gave renewed currency to the metaphor, which was used by both left and right to describe either the *ancien regime* (Paine and the 'Jacobin novels' of Godwin and Wollstonecraft) or the new Republic (Burke).[6] This was the spectre that haunted the movement for Reform more than any other. The threat of the breakdown of English society into a Hobbesian state of monstrous civil strife had to be avoided without falling into either of the French forms of monstrosity – in other words, as we have seen, by 'humanizing' both the state and the poor into a newly organic 'body politic'. At the same time, as we have also remarked, the supernatures of the romance and the folk tale and their modern entertainment-commodity form, gothic fiction, were gradually replaced by the art-form of the realist novel as a 'natural' and 'organic' fictional mode. Nevertheless, as the violence of social conflict continues to threaten despite the efforts of Reform, so too the fascination with the monstrous – the horror story – affirms itself as a popular sub-genre, intertwined with the mystery, sensation, and detective story. The substitution of the framing voice of the *discours sauvage* was not as straightforward as the literary transition from criminal hero to detective might suggest. One thing was to silence the disruptive culture; to make it learn to speak the language of polite society was to turn out to be quite another. The mysterious which in this way escapes or resists the humanizing efforts of Reform by refusing or being denied articulation in its totalizing language of Law, Science and secular reason becomes reified as the monstrous.

Hence, for example, the ape. As we have seen, the failure of Reform in the second half of the century was to be explained by re-interpreting the condition of the mad, criminal and chronically poor as a form of atavistic or degenerate animality. Here, as in so much else, with his solution to a superhuman violence only a syllable away from a human maniac, Dupin stands on a crossroads, the site of a conflict of codes, in this case between Reform and its reaction. Through the nineteenth-century, we find that as the claims of Reform prove unsustainable and the effort of repression increases, we watch a crescendo of vengeful contact of the monster with the human, until Poe's destructive ape and LeFanu's demonic monkey (by which the former may have been influenced) are revealed as living within the master himself, in the guise of Mr. Hyde.[7]

A 'monster' may be of one of three types: supernatural, unnatural (also in the sense of a physically or morally misshapen being, a traitor to its species), or simply 'giant'. In describing the characteristics of the agent responsible for the violence in the Rue Morgue, Dupin describes a space which can only be filled by a monster. Which monster? As a solution, the ape may appear to come as a relief, but only to the extent that it saves us from having to choose between two other types of monster: the human maniac or the supernatural. But, however 'natural' this animal may be in its far-off habitat, in the Rue Morgue it is still a monster in at least two senses: firstly, by being gigantic and grotesque, and secondly because it tries to behave like a human (imitating the sailor in shaving the women), a misshapen and savage parody of a man. It thus fills the gap of agency opened by the singular and monstrous crime, but only as a stopgap. Just as we cannot say what is in the purloined letter, Poe's ape does not 'stand for' any one thing in particular.[8] Fixing its meaning in relation to any one specific referent only serves ultimately to diminish and domesticate the monster; and the impossibility of doing so was what the Maltese sailor learned to his cost. Indeed, the ape remains at large and may strike again (although this is something which, curiously, seems not to bother Dupin). For this 'criminal', there is neither reformation nor execution. Despite its identification by Dupin and Cuvier, its refusal, *qua* monster, to be imprisoned and exhausted in a single rational or historical category holds it close to the alternatives, keeping its horror alive and making its story too unstable to be allegorical.

It is clear that this instability is, to some extent, valid for all writing. But I am not taking a globally deconstructionist position to deny historical contexts and the existence of meaning; rather I am seeking to distinguish a sort of writing which specifically exploits the instability intrinsic to signification by using the historically specific category of monstrosity. In this sense, the figure of the monster generates an anxiety similar to the 'hesitation' between natural and supernatural explanations which Todorov identifies as the defining characteristic of the genre of the 'fantastic'.[9] What in grand part terrifies us in horror fiction is that we can never quite know, and every indecision puts in question the limits of the known and the speakable. Poe's ape presents a form of monstrosity which saves us (just about) from the anxious hesitation in the mind of the narrator, but not from the anxiety that monsters are about and can strike within our domestic spaces. Generally speaking then, the monster, by definition, defying both language and nature, focuses both the semiotic and the narrative mystery of language: through its own referential irreducibility, it disturbs the given system of signs as an exhaustive reproduction of the world; at the same time its existence threatens the 'naturalness' of the plots of realist fiction by attacking what Fielding had shown to be one of its most important empiricist guarantees, the accepted rules of possibility and probability.

Since, according to David Hume, the terms of existence result not from *a priori* or innate ideas or entities but from experience, then 'there is no species of reasoning more common, more useful, and even necessary to human life, than that which is derived from the testimony of men, and the reports of eye-witnesses and spectators.'[10] This is, as we know, the major criterion in the empiricist paradigm of realism – legal, scientific, and literary. However, 'Suppose, for instance, that the fact, which the testimony endeavours to establish, partakes of the extraordinary and the marvellous' (p. 128). The problem with the miraculous ('a violation of the laws of nature' – p. 129) is that it is the very *reductio* of empiricist reality; it relies *only* on testimony: 'No means of detection remain, but those which must be drawn from the very testimony itself of the reporters' (p. 143). In the case of the extraordinary, the very basis of knowledge becomes its potential source of error. Since Hume obviously cannot invoke *a priori* laws to disprove testimony which violates natural law, he does so by emphasizing the fallibility of individual testimony in relation to the mass testimony on which the 'laws of nature' are based:

> Upon the whole, then, it appears, that no testimony for any kind of miracle, has ever amounted to a probability, much less to a proof . . . It is experience only which gives authority to human testimony; and it is the same experience which assures us of the laws of nature. When, therefore, these two kinds of experience are contrary, we have nothing to do but subtract the one from the other, and embrace an opinion, either on one side or the

other, with that assurance which arises from the remainder. (p. 143)

In the empiricist paradigm of realism then, the characteristic hesitation of the 'fantastic' is experienced in terms of narrative reliability. A tension is set up between the person *qua* universal subject of the experience of the 'laws of nature' and the person *qua* individual site of difference.

Thus, if the narrator is to obtain the sense of authenticity and credibility offered to the empiricist by personal witness he or she must persuade us that what is recounted is an event which would be valid for everyone, and not an imagined event or figment, created by and valid only for himself or herself. In short, the individual subject of empirically realist narration has to present itself as a universal, natural subject. Three conventional devices commonly assist in underwriting narrative testimony: a natural history, an external paternity, is provided for the narrator and his or her characters; the reader is positioned so as to identify with the narrator's point-of-view (be it actual or implied); and this is supported (or qualified) by the collaborative testimony of independent third-parties within the text, which, in the case of the reliable narrator, confirms that reality is available to a narrative subject whose universality is underwritten by its identity with our own and those of our fellow human beings (and in the other case, provides us with a universal position from which to judge). A narrative becomes credible by emanating from a site in which we – or anyone else – can eventually place ourselves.

The question of reliability is obviously focused most clearly in first-person narration, where the empiricist paradigm of direct, personal experience is foregrounded. This is very probably the reason why it is the most common form for stories of mystery and detection. In any case, the fascination of mystery and horror stories with narrative experimentation, most often with multiple and/or embedded points of view, is not mere gimickery. It seeks to use empiricist techniques to promote credibility for the innately incredible or extra-ordinary, but, at the same time, like the presence of the entities and events it recounts, it paradoxically draws attention to the contradictions of such realism by introducing the Other which is elided in the latter's creation of a unifying point of subjectivity with which to universalize its meanings.

CREATION AND SEXUALITY

This is one of the major 'fantastic' effects of the textual monster *par excellence*, Mary Shelley's *Frankenstein* (1817/1831). Victor's 'madness' does not explain away the monster, since the latter's existence is sufficient cause for his creator's insanity. Rather, the primary hesitation is reproduced in the mortal struggle between Frankenstein and his creation for both physical and narrative authority. As Victor Sage points out, above all in this text 'reading is a process of directly apprehending and judging testimony'.[11] Here, the same epistemological and ontological values which work to support the narrators' witness to the existence of the monster bring us to a point of contradiction when we encounter the latter's own testimony. The emergence of the monster's voice, from deep within the hierarchy of authoritative testimony which guarantees its existence, unbalances our identifications, our 'sympathies' (it almost does the same for Frankenstein himself), and invites us to rewrite the story. Herein lies the main 'hesitation' of this tale. We cannot simply 'change sides', for to do so is to simplify the terrible story into a moral tract. The text has as much to do with the tragedy of the master, the 'modern Prometheus', as it does with that of his creature. *Frankenstein* is a horror because it obliges us to identify and 'sympathize' with two irreconcilable subjects. The contradiction of points of view is made even more radical by the unique relation between the two. Nothing, of course, could be more 'literary', for this is the story of the struggle between a creator and the simulacrum of a man he creates.

Attention is all the more acutely drawn to the relation between creator and creature, author and simulacrum when the creation is monstrous; or at least Mary Shelley seems to have thought so in the parallels established by the 1831 preface between herself and Frankenstein as creative beings. She wrote the preface, she tells us, 'because I shall thus give a general answer to the question so very frequently asked me – how I, then a young girl, came to think of and to dilate upon so very hideous an idea.'[12] There is a horror here: how such a monstrous piece of writing could be created by an 'innocent' girl. She explains this by establishing a fundamental distinction between dreaming and writing. Since childhood, 'indulging in waking dreams' had been the privileged realm of her own independent subjectivity in which she could escape from the empirical universe into a Frankenstein-like creation of other beings: 'I was not confined to my own identity, and I could people the hours with creations far more interesting to me at that age than my own sensations' (pp. vii–viii). But her 'literary' parents also encouraged her from an early age 'to "write stories"'. Whereas 'my dreams were all my own; I accounted for them to nobody', writing implies a social dialectic; stories are always intended 'at least for one other eye', particularly 'my childhood's companion and friend' (probably her future husband).

The tale originates then from a transgression of the barrier between 'dreaming' and 'writing'. The men get together and Byron declares that they shall each write a ghost story. Mary is somewhat at a loss *to think of a story* (p. ix). However, in bed that night, she is terrified by a 'mental vision' from which she flees by trying to write: 'I must try to think of something else. I recurred to my ghost story' (p. xi). The socialized discourse of story-writing offers relief from the terror of her isolated subjectivity through the decisive insight that 'What terrified me will terrify others; and I need only describe the spectre which had haunted my midnight pillow.' The monstrous tale of *Frankenstein* is thus the result of crossing the line between the solipsistic creation of a subject *qua* isolated and self-sufficient individual ('all my own') and the subject as social subject (directed at some 'other eye').

This takes us back to Victor's 'madness'. Victor is not 'mad' in the sense that he imagines things which are not. Although he is subject to fits of nervous hysteria, his 'madness' reveals itself firstly as an obsession with the fear of madness, expressed in his repeated justification for not telling his tale on the grounds that people will think him mad. But it might have been worthwhile, for example, to make an attempt to save Justine; after all, he could merely have told the court that he had seen what Walton first sees – 'a being which had the shape of a man, but apparently of gigantic stature' (p. 23) – near the place of the crime. However, his consciousness that he is the creator of this monster prevents him from being an ordinary witness. He clearly feels obliged to furnish the improbable creature with a paternity, and his reason for not telling his tale is that to do so would reveal the being as *an artificial creation produced solely by himself*. Frankenstein's tragedy is the heroic yearning to literalize the modern ideological figure of the autonomous individual as the source of all things: to become a *master of creation*, one who seeks to transform 'the deepest mysteries of creation' into 'One secret which I alone possessed' (pp. 47, 53) and produce a 'new species' which 'would bless me as its creator and its source'

(p. 52). For this a specific curriculum is required: Frankenstein dedicates himself to natural philosophy, chemistry, and anatomy, and deliberately rejects 'the structure of languages . . . the code of governments . . . the politics of various states' (p. 37), and the science of 'natural history' which, to his mind, is 'a deformed and abortive creature' (p. 41) – a monster, in short. This then is his 'madness' and the monstrosity of his creation, as it is of Mary's: that the creature let loose upon the world originates exclusively within the solipsistic universe of the isolated subject, rather than being the consequence of a socialized dialectic with an 'other eye'. Frankenstein's desire is for a creativity without language and politics but, most of all, without sexual dialectics.

This is no wonder, given his own 'family plot'. As has been observed, the creative subject may aim to overcome suspicions of solipsism by the convention of presenting himself in terms of his own paternity. But what a 'natural history' is Victor's! He is, he tells us, the first-born son of a nobleman, the key to whose character was his marriage to the daughter of his best friend – young enough, in other words, to be his own daughter. His mother however wants her own daughter, so one day his parents in effect purchase one. The unnatural arrival is announced by his mother as 'a pretty present for my Victor' (p. 33), and the latter comments: 'when, on the morrow, she presented Elizabeth to me as her promised gift, I, with childish seriousness, interpreted her words literally and looked upon Elizabeth as mine – mine to protect, love, and cherish' (p. 35). But, presented first like a bridal gift, Carolyn's dying words – 'Elizabeth, my love, you must supply my place to my younger children' – makes her the mother to his father's children. In short, Elizabeth holds the place of *all* female relations: 'We called each other familiarly by the name of cousin. No word, no expression could body forth the kind of relation in which she stood to me – my more than sister, since till death she was to be mine only.' Any such embodying word would be sure to be a monster. The monster's threat, 'I shall be with you on your wedding-night', could not be otherwise: the unnatural creation of the monster as his 'child' (p. 52) clearly substitutes the impossibility of his sexual relations with Elizabeth.

By rejecting the difference implicit in social and sexual reproduction, Frankenstein is committed to reducing the world to a function of his own subjectivity. This is made clear in the second aspect of his 'madness', the disavowal which he substitutes for telling his story: as he declares to his own father, "'I am not mad," I cried energetically, " . . . I am the assassin of those most innocent victims; they died by my machinations. A thousand times would I have shed my own blood, drop by drop, to have saved their lives; but I could not, my father, indeed I could not sacrifice the whole human race"' (p. 177). It is not surprising that his father is convinced of his insanity; rather than telling the tale, Victor has, after all, revealed the nature of his creative subjectivity: Frankenstein is 'mad' not so much because he creates a monster, but because he expands this act into one which heroically conflates the fate of his subjectivity with that of 'the whole human race'. The entire world comes to revolve around his self and its self-sufficient creative act. Overreaching the limits of creation by transforming his autonomous subjective desire and fear into objective reality, his madness becomes the *reductio ad absurdum* of the realist writer: whilst disavowing his role as creator, he inflates his creation into a universe and demands that everyone believe in it.

Our defence against this demand is the scepticism permitted by the conventions of realism in relation to the reliability of the witness. Here however, in order to avoid our falling back on an explanation of the tale in terms of Victor's deranged imagination, his narrative is embedded in a more natural frame, provided by Walton as apparently independent witness. Representing himself not as a creator but, as in Defoe's classic disavowal tactic, as an editor, Walton corroborates Frankenstein's testimony, serving as a bridge for the identifications of the sceptical reader, our surrogate 'other eye' – to such an extent that he has usually been deemed unnecessary for subsequent versions of the story, especially in film, where his role has been taken by the universal realist eye of the camera himself. But the question which he focuses is precisely that of the relationship between the 'I' and the 'other eye', between the narrator and his reader.

The first thing that Walton does in his letters to his mother-substitute, his sister, is to reveal that 'ardent curiosity' is *not* the story's unique driving force. In Walton, the search for knowledge covers a more central *affective* lack:

I have one want which I have never yet been able to satisfy, and the absence of the object of which I now feel as a most severe evil. I have no friend, Margaret . . . . I desire the company of a man who could sympathize with me, whose eyes would reply to

mine. You may deem me romantic, my dear sister, but I bitterly
feel the want of a friend. (p. 18)

The language of love he uses is disturbed by the word 'man'. Walton
wants 'sympathy'; but for him this means a total identification
between subjects who are *both symmetrical and the same*. Walton
explains that his shipmates will not serve because they are too
brutally masculine, especially for one, like Walton, brought up
under his sister's 'gentle and feminine fosterage'. On the other
hand, a more apparently suitable 'friend', the ship's master, is
'silent as a Turk' (p. 20), too self-sacrificing and, in any case, he is in
love with a woman. The 'other eye' that Walton seeks is a reflection,
a figure who will confirm his subjectivity by reduplicating it. The
lack is no sooner announced than it is filled by Frankenstein, the
subject who seeks to reproduce without difference. Indeed, Walton
'creates' Frankenstein in similar language to that in which the latter
created his monster: he 'restored him to animation' by imbuing
Victor with 'vital warmth'; and, as he gets better, 'a new spirit of
life animated the decaying frame of the stranger' (p. 25). When
Victor speaks, Walton recognizes that he has found that romantic
other to whom he can use 'the language of my heart'. What he
has re-created is a being whose 'eyes have generally an expression
of wildness, and even madness'. And Frankenstein's first reply to
Walton's account of himself confirms the encounter of sympathetic
subjectivities of reflecting eyes: 'Unhappy man! Do you share my
madness?' (p. 26). But it is this 'sympathy' which makes the deeply
homophone Walton the ideal reader of Frankenstein's story. It is
not just the epiphenomenal character traits they have in common,
it is the fact that they both elide difference, insisting that their
interlocuteurs – the 'eyes [that] would reply to mine' – take the
position of symmetrical identity: not an 'other eye', but an eye that
replicates their own subjectivity.

   This does not turn the monster into a mere figment of a *folie à deux*,
since his existence is, ironically, the only element which allows us to
escape our imprisonment in the autistic universe of the sympathetic,
'homogeneous' pair. For this reason Mary Shelley draws him as a
site of pure subjectivity, a Lockean *tabula rasa* on which to inscribe
a theory of the natural subject. From the differentiation of primary
sense experiences, the monster, in an uncanny parable of Lacan's
stade du miroir, simultaneously enters into language and recognizes
his image in the pool through his encounter with a family structured

by the insight that 'the youth and his companion had each of them several names, but the old man had only one, which was "father"' (p. 107). In contrast, the monster has no name at all (making life particularly difficult for us, who often fall into the symptomatic slip of referring to him by the name of his creator): no place in language from which he can speak to others. This driving lack develops into a desire: specifically, once more, a desire for 'sympathy'. This is the minimal condition for escaping the status of monster: the existence of a subject who can identify with him and thus provide him with an identity – in short, an other 'with whom I can live in the interchange of those sympathies necessary for my being' (p. 138). But it is precisely here that we find the difference between the monster and Frankenstein and Walton: for, in contrast to these, what the monster demands is a responding subject who is symmetrical – 'as deformed and hideous as myself . . . . of the same species and . . . [with] the same defects' – *but different*: 'You must create a female for me' (pp. 137–8).

Both Frankenstein and Walton recognize this desire as a moving sign of humanity, but Victor's project to manufacture such a creature becomes fatally caught up with what is repressed in his own impending marriage, as, reflecting again his self-referential and transgressive desire for self-generation, he quickly translates sexual difference into sexual reproduction: 'one of the first results of those sympathies for which the demon thirsted would be children, and a race of devils would be propagated upon the earth' (p. 158). Of course, nothing the monster had said would lead to such a conclusion, and, in any case, Victor is not obliged to make a fertile creature. If, for Frankenstein, the monster's desire raises the spectre of the natural history he seeks to repress, for Walton, his power to arouse sympathy is merely an effect of language, the 'powers of eloquence and persuasion' Victor had warned him against. Both condemn the monster to be a monster: that is to say, the subject for whom no sympathetic subject exists: 'no sympathy may I ever find' (p. 209).

The creature is condemned to monstrosity because it is encased in a discourse whose mutually-supporting creators/narrators/witnesses elide the difference between the creating subject and the eye that is in a position to witness that creation. So too in empiricist fictional realism, a world where individual subjects reproduce their reality in artifice and present it as a natural world in which we are to believe. In order to guarantee the trustworthiness of this testimony, it has to deny the individual partiality at the source of the discourse by positioning the reader in such a way as to replicate the 'natural' point of view of the narration. This is the position in which Walton locates himself on our behalf. We cannot forget, then, the parallels Mary Shelley drew between herself as author and her protagonist (who, in his turn, therefore appears as her own simulacrum). She employs realist techniques to bring us to this point of readerly schizophrenia, of simultaneous identification with different and mortally opposed subjects – the master and the monster. By literalizing the figure of 'creation', she pushes the realist paradigm to the crisis of its logic, at the heart of which is revealed a monster for which it has no place and no interlocutor, and which has to die, along with the creator whose existence as a creator its own existence denounces.

But, after all, the creature does have a 'sympathetic' listener, a listener who can occupy its position, rather than that of its creator. We, modern readers as we are, were certainly moved and convinced by his discourse and identify with his oppression. But such a kind solution misses a final irony, for it is the monster's most human-like speech which is Frankenstein's last and most Frankenstein-like creation: 'Since you have preserved my narration,' he says to his witness, Walton, 'I would not that a mutilated one should go down to posterity', so he revises the latter's notes, 'principally in giving the life and spirit to the conversations he held with his enemy' (p. 199). What we read is the paternal authority's life-giving version of his creature's desire, enclosing the latter's *discours sauvage* in the former's masterly and homogeneous discourse which, in order to gain our 'sympathy', denies, to the end, its creation's right to a desire marked by difference. So too, of course, was Mary's 'story' revised by her husband.

THE CONFESSION REVISITED

"How can I be a character in fiction," he demanded, "if I am here talking to you?"'
Brian Nolan [Flann O'Brien], 'A Bash in the Tunnel'.

Tales of monstrosity are themselves monstrous in that, as is clearly the case in *Frankenstein*, they denounce the homogeneity of the discourse of mastery by splitting the subject. In this way, they figure the conflict of codes which Reform sought to pacify within its new social order. On the other hand, the virtue of the sort of 'Literature' which replaced the old tales as respectable reading matter for the young was seen to derive in large part precisely from its intrinsic capacity for creating sympathetic identification – as, for example, in the stated aims of F. C. Cook's anthology *Poetry for Schools*, 1849, whose 'broadest hope . . . was that the "children of the peasantry and artisans" would come to understand and "sympathise with sentiments and principles by which well educated persons are influenced" and "to understand and sympathise with the views of their superiors".' [13] 'The Purloined Letter' is a story of our 'superiors'. The monster here is unnatural in a political, rather than a biological sense, a traitor to the body politic, striking at its intimate heart – the private relation between the King and Queen. Notably, the Minister D—— escapes the totalitarian control of the French police, despite its exhaustive methodical eye. No doubt under the influence of Sherlock Holmes, we tend to assume that Dupin has contempt for the Prefect, but in fact he is careful to give credit to the police and their methods: 'They are right in this much – that their own ingenuity is a faithful representation of that of the *mass*' (III, p. 985). Where the danger derives from the ordinary, positivistic police methods, ordinary in themselves, are perfectly adequate, but when it arises from the extraordinary – in the Minister's case, the genius – a similarly extraordinary theoretical position is required to vanquish it. In short, the crux of police is precisely 'sympathy' – that is to say *the assumption of a symmetrical position* in relation to the threat: 'an identification of the reasoner's intellect with that of his opponent', as illustrated in the schoolboys' 'odds and evens' guessing game (p. 984). In mastering this particular monster by placing himself in a 'sympathetic' position, Dupin suggests the presence of another traditional literary image of the unnatural, one singularly preferred by Poe himself: the all-too-human 'double'.

This particular form of monster pulls in a variety of themes. In the first place, its presence clearly upsets the fundamental bourgeois model of the subject as a unique individual with a distinctive and essential 'character'. At the same time, it invokes the quintessential 'same-but-different' of realist fiction – the imagined presenting itself with the gesture or texture of factuality as a 'portrait of life' or of nature – in short, a simulacrum of reality. As we have already observed in our discussion of *sjuzet* and *fabula*, it is precisely the simulacrum that is foregrounded in the classic detective story as it mirrors the mystery with its corresponding explanation. And finally, the issue of the simulacrum is, of course, most clear in what we have seen to be one of the principal historical sources of both the novel and the detective story: the confession, in which the simulacrum in question is that of the narrating subject itself.

In James Hogg's *The Private Memoirs and Confessions of a Justified Sinner* (1824), the paternity of the extraordinary confession – 'an original document of a most singular nature, and preserved for [the reader's] perusal in a still more singular manner'[14] – is vouchsafed by a pair of 'Editor's Narratives': the first recounting the story of the Colwan brothers as handed down from 'history' and 'justiciary records', but mainly from 'tradition'; the second recounting the discovery of the original text and the undecayed corpse of its author – 'a thing so extraordinary, so unprecedented, and so far out of the common course of human events, that if there were not hundreds of living witnesses to attest the truth of it, I would not bid any rational being believe it' (p. 203). Two other versions of the discovery are included: a letter to *Blackwood's Magazine* from someone called James Hogg, a man renowned for his 'ingenious lies' (p. 235), and a correction to the former by an old shepherd (remembering Hogg's journalistic character as 'the Ettrick Shepherd').

The Editor holds the contents, 'marvellous' as they are, to be less incredible than the very existence of the material text and its author in defiance of the 'laws of nature'; yet, paradoxically, only this event, explicitly the most extraordinary of all, is given the status of truth – for the overriding reason that the Editor can himself vouchsafe it, in the company of other witnesses. If this is the criterion of credibility (and the safeguard against any suggestion that the Editor is no editor at all, but a 'creative' author), then it brings us immediately to the central crisis in the text. When Mrs. Calvert and Mrs. Logan first observe the total likeness of Robert Wringham's companion to his late half-brother, Mrs. Calvert observes: 'We have nothing on earth but our senses to depend upon: if these deceive us, what are we to do' (p. 95). In true Humean vein, she goes on: 'The thing cannot be, Mrs. Logan. It is a phantasy of our disturbed imaginations', and the latter replies:

It cannot be in nature, that is quite clear . . . yet how it should be that I should *think* so – I who knew him and nursed him from his infancy – there lies the paradox. As you said before, we have nothing but our senses to depend on, and if you and I believe that we see a person, why, we do see him. Whose word, or whose reasoning can convince us against our own senses? (p. 99)

It is the existence of a simulacrum that provokes this 'chaos of mystery' in the ladies: something which, though not alive according to the general experience of nature, is so convincingly 'like' living reality as to appear to be so. In a literary sense, the text itself suffers from a similar paradox: it looks like what it seems to be, a 'true confession' of actual events; but to the empirically-minded Editor the presence of a monster makes its veracity unlikely. The text is itself monstrous, unclassifiable: 'What can this work be? . . . I cannot tell' (p. 230). Once more the Editor's hesitation takes the form of a question of narrative reliability: even if the actual fratricide is true, the rest is either *discours sauvage* or a twisted Romance – 'I account all the rest either dreaming or madness; or, as he says to Mr. Watson, a religious parable' (p. 241). Since it is a confession, a necessarily double text in which the hero of the parable is an image of the author himself, it is, in the end, probably *both* a parable *and* a deranged vision. The Editor concludes that it is a parable written 'by a religious maniac, who wrote and wrote about a deluded creature, till he arrived at the height of madness, that he believed himself the very object whom he had been all along describing' (p. 241). The word that Mrs. Logan fears can 'convince us against our own senses' is 'writing'; in the hands of a madman, it can turn fictions into realities.

However, Mrs. Logan is a normally constituted subject, not a maniac. But Hume had warned us that 'Nothing is more free than the imagination of man . . . It can feign a train of events with all the appearance of reality, ascribe to them a particular time and place, conceive them as existent, or paint them out to itself with every circumstance that belongs to any historical fact, which it believes with the greatest certainty' (*Inquiry* . . . , II, p. 61). Furthermore, we have a tendency to be credulous which, according to Hume's earlier *Treatise of Human Nature*, derives 'from the influence of resemblance'[15] – for the very good reason that resemblance is the basis of all our reasoning:

In reality, all arguments from experience are founded on the similarity which we discover among natural objects, and by which we are induced to expect effects similar to those which we have found to follow from such objects . . . From causes that appear similar, we expect similar effects. This is the sum of all our experimental conclusions. (*Inquiry* . . . , II, p. 50)

In this context, how are we to tell a simulacrum from the real thing? This is the question of 'belief': 'something felt by the mind, which distinguishes the ideas of judgment from the fictions of the imagination' (p. 64). But Hume has major problems in defining this 'sentiment or feeling' which distinguishes belief from fiction, and his text turns quite repetitious and dogmatic around the issue. Belief is only 'a more vivid, lively, forcible, firm, steady conception of an object, than what the imagination alone is ever able to attain'. Beyond this feeling of solidity and life-likeness, 'I confess . . . it is impossible perfectly to explain' (pp. 62–3). We must remember here that, at the time Hume was writing, the term 'fiction' was highly unstable, being used to a large extent – as we saw in Defoe's use of the word – as a way of denigrating Romance in favour of the new emerging novel. The qualities which Hume ascribes to the feeling of belief – particularly 'vivid' and 'lively' – are precisely those which the new realism seeks to capture for its 'firmer' fictions. The distinction, so difficult to define, becomes less easily felt in a fiction which specifically tries to create the sensation of belief. In the end, as Hume had argued more forcefully in his earlier, more sceptical text:

> It is difficult for us to withhold our assent from what is painted out to us in all the colours of eloquence; and the vivacity pro-duced by the fancy is in many cases greater than that which arises from custom and experience. We are hurried away by the lively imagination of our author or companion; and even he himself is often a victim to his own fire and genius. (*Treatise* . . . , p. 123)

So, holds the Editor, the author of these confessions writing himself into the insanity or the parable he was imagining. But it is not so much the madness of the writer as the 'eloquence' which provides 'vivacity' to the imagination, that is responsible for destroying the distinction between parable and reality, imagination and belief, fiction and fact.

This fiction so vivid that it commands belief reintroduces the issue of ideology. Now, clearly, *The Private Memoirs and Confessions* . . . is no more a simple tract against Calvinism than *Frankenstein* is a

polemic against technology. That is not to say that it is not a satire
on Calvinism or that it is unconcerned with religious questions;
the point is that its 'family plot' casts religion from the start in
the context of politics and ideology. The origin of the fratricidal
violence can be traced to the parents' wedding-night, when the
original and legal father, the country Laird, a supporter of the 'free
principles cherished by the court *party*', upbraids his city-bred Lady,
a supporter of the 'stern doctrines of the *reformers*', for disappearing
into her bedroom to pray instead of going to bed with him (pp. 30,
32 – my italics). The split celebrated on that night and pursued in
Lady Dalcastle's relationship with the Rev. Wringham is ideological
in the sense that not only is it caused by ideological difference
but because that difference has, at bottom, to do with the very
place given to ideology, specifically in relation to sexuality.[16] The
antagonism between the two brothers is a direct consequence of this
split which places them not in a simple opposition, but, significantly,
as the 'same-but-different'. George and Robert are, and are not,
brothers; they have, and have not, the same name (of the Father);
and though related through their natural mother, they are unlike
in their natures. This conflict of the like and unlike is articulated
in the text at the level of religious ideology and is played out
against a background of party politics (as the Editor notes, 'party
spirit was the order of the day' – p. 50). Robert's prosecution of
his half-brother provokes political riots in the city, which illustrate,
this time comically, how the splitting of ideology again divides and
turns, in this case, the collective subject against its own likeness:
'[A]t length [the court] began to perceive that they were examining
gentlemen of both parties, and that they had been doing so from
the beginning, almost alternately, so equally had the prisoners been
taken from both parties. Finally, it turned out, that a few gentlemen,
two-thirds of whom were strenuous Whigs themselves, had joined
in mauling the whole Whig population of Edinburgh' (p. 54). As
the first meeting in Edinburgh had shown (when Robert attempts
to occupy the space in which George stands on the tennis court),
the 'same-but-different' cannot be in the same place simultaneously
without violence.

Robert 'justifies' his behaviour on ideological grounds, but his
half-brother, not being an ideologue, finds it quite incomprehen-
sible: both his antagonism and his ubiquitous contiguity – the fact
that, like the victim of a spy, 'he had never sat or stood many
minutes till there was the self-same being, always in the same

position with regard to himself, as regularly as the shadow is cast from the substance, or the ray of light from the opposing denser medium' (p. 59). The notion of the double is invented by George, after his 'vision' at Arthur's Seat, as a somewhat desperate metaphor to express this mystery. What the metaphor does is to redouble the earlier 'self-same' being: George speculates that 'he was haunted by some evil genius in the shape of his brother, as well as by that dark and mysterious wretch himself.' In sum, as he tells old Dalcastle, Robert 'seemed to have some demon for a familiar' (pp. 66–7). This is a nice irony: the breakdown of family relations is explained by a strange being which we call a 'familiar', a creature physically 'like' the original and inevitably contiguous to it – like a family relative; even more ironic then when applied to a brother who rejects his paternity and seeks to destroy its source and its collateral evidence, his father and his sibling. The 'familiar' replaces the family; as such, in literary terms, it fills the break introduced into natural history by artificial, created plots, offering another paternity, a new beginning and a reformed life, like that of the author of the confession which renounces its own history and initiates a new one by its willing endorsement of the reformed cultural code. As Karl Miller tells us, 'Where the double is, the orphan is never far away, with secrecy and terror over all.'[17] Robert's ideological and physical patricide parallels the orphaned nature of the text: 'What can this work be?'

It is, at least, a text constituted by doublings: of subjects and of characters (Robert the author of one version and a protagonist in both), of readings (madness or parable), of sources (tradition etc., personal testimony) and of authors (the anonymous authors of 'tradition', the courts, Robert, the Editor, plus the literal Hogg as the empirical author of the text) and, finally of course, a doubling of versions.[18] Tradition and court records can only provide a partial, incomplete account of events; the mystery of Robert is filled only by a stopgap, the hyperbolic fiction of a 'familiar'. It has to be told again, now in the literary and epistemologically privileged first-person form of the criminal confession. But all the second version will do is insist on the literality of George's monstrous conception.

Gil first appears, like an autobiographical character or, as we have seen, an ideal reader, as the symmetrical reflection of the narrator. The story is generated by the first meeting between Robert and this 'young man of mysterious appearance':

our eyes met, and I can never describe the strange sensations that thrilled through my whole frame at that impressive moment; a moment to me fraught with the most tremendous consequences; the beginning of a series of adventures which has puzzled myself, and will puzzle the world when I am no more in it. (p. 125)

What is mysterious, thrilling and decisive about Gil's appearance is that he so resembles Robert as to elide the difference in metaphor between the similar and the same: 'What was my astonishment, on perceiving that he was the same being as myself!' In other words, Gil, the master of eloquence ('though I cannot from memory repeat his words, his eloquence was of that overpowering nature that the subtility of other men sunk before it' – p. 140), raises Hume's imaginary 'resemblance' to the level of a belief. He is so convincing that he appears to be able totally to annihilate the difference between the real and its image.

The primacy of ideology over 'nature' which causes the violence of *The Private Memoirs and Confessions* . . . literalizes both similarity and difference. As it is, most importantly, Robert's endorsement of Gil's argument of the superiority of ideological relations to natural ones which overcomes his spontaneous reluctance to kill his father and brother ('The feeling is natural, and amiable,' Gil tells him, 'but you *must* think again. Whether are the bonds of carnal nature, or the bonds and vows of the Lord, strongest?' – p. 150), similarly, it is Gil's *ideological* resemblance to Robert which makes them physically both alike and contiguous, just as Robert's ideological difference made natural likeness and physical contiguity with his brother impossible. Gil reassures Robert: '"You think I am your brother," said he, "or that I am your second self. I am indeed your brother, not according to the flesh, but in my belief of the same truths, and my assurance in the same mode of redemption"' (p. 126). If two materially 'like' beings can be ideologically antithetical, by the monstrous logic of the primacy of ideology over materiality, two ideologically identical beings should be able to be physically 'like'.

Gil-Martin, and the story itself, are a monstrous literalization and inversion of the principles of Humean empiricist realism. According to Hume perceptions may be divided into 'impressions' (the senses) and 'ideas' (memory and imagination), the latter being 'derived' from the former, to which they correspond and which they 'represent' (*Treatise* . . . , pp. 11–14). These impressions are indivisible; but not so ideas. The capacity of the imagination 'to transpose and change its ideas' is what allows us to create the notions of continuity, universality and totality out of our discrete sensual experiences of reality. Experience is organized by ideas through three basic imaginary principles: 'resemblance, contiguity in time or place, and cause and effect'. These principles constitute an interconnected hierarchy, based in resemblance, passing through contiguity – 'when we find, that any particular objects are constantly conjoined with each other' – and 'succession' (the priority in time of the one perception over the other) to the *inference* of cause and effect (*Inquiry . . .* , II, p. 40). But with Gil and his monstrous tale, as we have seen, ideas are given primacy over the perceptions of the senses, and in this way ideological resemblance and contiguity take physical form, transcending material difference and dissolving individual identity: Robert's statement – 'we were incorporated together – identified with one another' (p. 182) – is echoed by Gil himself: 'Our beings are amalgamated, as it were, and consociated in one' (p. 187). Ultimately, by the same order, resemblance and contiguity are built up by their 'succession' and 'constant conjunction' ('I am drawn towards you as by magnetism, and wherever you are, there must my presence be with you' – p. 200) into a literalized relationship of cause-and-effect in which Gil becomes the compelling agent of Robert's actions – indeed, Robert tells us that, since meeting Gil, in writing his own memoirs and confessions, 'I have written about him only, and I must continue to do so to the end of this memoir, as I have performed no great or interesting action in which he had not a principal share' (p. 142). The simulacrum ceases to be an idea or fiction, and takes on *all* the qualities of a reality – resemblance, contiguity, *and* causation. Not only do ideas and fictions become indistinguishable from impressions and reality, but the latter become the effect of the former, as Robert loses his will to Gil's eloquent influence over his story.

If Robert, as a 'justified sinner', functions as the figure of the author of the confession, then Gil-Martin's monstrosity, even more than that of Frankenstein's creature, resides in his being, not just a simulacrum, an artifice of a particular subject, but the literal embodiment of the principle of the simulacrum. Gil's monstrously protean ability to imitate others convinces George that he sees Robert, Mrs. Logan that she sees George; and a number of witnesses that they saw George murder Drummond – and Robert that he sees himself. This strange talent is, in the first place, a literalization of the principle that ideas arise as copies of impressions (as Robert correctly speculates: 'it struck me, that by setting his features to the mould of other people's, he entered at once into their conceptions and feelings' – p. 127). But what is even more monstrous about Gil than his Dupin-like capacity for 'sympathy' in that sense (cf. the guessing game in 'The Purloined Letter') is the inverse: his ability to resemble others physically by imitating their ideas: 'My countenance changes with my studies and sensations' (p. 132).

In sum, what Hume says, sceptically, about ideas and their fictions, Hogg's *Private Memoirs and Confessions* . . . takes literally, like the deranged allegorist favoured as author by the Editor. If, for Hume, belief is the feeling provoked by reality, then here it becomes the cause of the real. What permits this is, on the one hand, the dominant and divisive role attributed by the tale to ideology, and, on the other hand, the presence of the monster who embodies that role, Gil, the phantasy of the reality of the simulacrum. What is played out here is the literal force of ideology (an 'operation of the imagination on like bodies'), as determinant of material reality, and, at the same time, its relation to the realist fiction of the world as simulacrum. The fictional monstrosity of the double reveals that it is ideology, like realism, creating simulacra by transforming the tropes of the imagination into principles of the real, that is responsible for eliding or, in Robert's extreme case, annihilating difference.

But is the confession 'true'? That's a difficult question. Under common law, a death-bed testimony has to be accepted as evidence; but under Scottish law, no one may be convicted solely on the evidence of his personal confession. These are questions to do with the admissibility of evidence . . . .

THE LAW OF FICTION

The coroner smiled.

'The account that you posted to your newspaper', he said, 'differs, probably, from that which you will give here under oath.'

'That', replied the other, rather hotly and with a visible flush, 'is as you please. I used manifold paper and have a copy of what I sent. It was not written as news, for it is incredible, but as fiction. It may go as part of my testimony under oath.'

'But you say it is incredible.'

'That is nothing to you, sir, if I also swear it is true.'

Ambrose Beirce, 'The Damned Thing', 1926.

I have tried to suggest how monstrosity is the consequence of realism in the sense that it is the ironic and literal receptacle of its principles of the simulacrum, whose difference has therefore to be disavowed or annihilated to protect the sexual and ideological site of its artificial creation from being denounced. This then is the ideological force of the realist novel as it uses the tropes of resemblance, contiguity, succession and inferred cause-and-effect to produce the illusion of a simulacrum of reality: 'As the first powerful, broad, and hegemonic literary form, the novel served to blur, in a way never before experienced, the distinction between illusion and reality, between fact and fiction, between symbol and what it represented.'[19] Before the classic detective story as defined by Sherlock Holmes endorses this as its very *raison d'être*, the sort of mystery story we have been discussing denounces those very tropes, reifying them into monstrous objects and events whose very impossibility wreaks a vengeful violence against realism and puts in question the limits of fact and fiction.

This is where the Dupin stories return, since it is precisely the question of the simulacrum as the locus of the relation between fact and fiction that is posed by 'The Mystery of Marie Rogêt' (1845). Indeed, this journal 'article', as the narrator calls his writings, was published in the same year as Poe's notorious 'Facts in the Case of Monsieur Valdemar' – a story of the survival of bodily death through mesmerism, which, significantly like Defoe's 'news/novel' piece, *The True Relation of the Apparition of Mrs. Veal* (1705), deliberately and successfully perplexed its readers as to its authenticity.[20] Although apparently the most banal, Poe's only genuinely crime-based story is in fact the strangest of the Dupin tales, whose relative unpopularity with traditional historians is, to my mind, largely due to its monstrous character. By its very existence as an attempt to solve a real contemporary crime by recounting it in a story (very much the reverse of the pseudo-factual pretence of the detective 'romance'), it takes realism literally, transgressing the unspoken difference between reality and its representation in narrative.

The epigraph establishes that 'There are ideal series of events which run parallel with the real ones. They rarely coincide.' Here however, as a footnote tells us, 'the author has followed, in minute detail, the essential . . . facts of the real murder of Mary Rogers. Thus all argument founded upon the fiction is applicable to the truth: and the investigation of the truth was the object' (III, p. 723).

The provocative object of the story is thus to make two parallel levels of probability – that of the narrative and that of its referent – 'co-incide'. This is a gigantic, a mythic ambition. Poe's play with the word 'coincidence' relates the outcome of narrative to the successful articulation of both the levels which we saw in Brooks constitute the mystery of narrative: the mystery of metonymy (the matching of agent [cause] to action [effect]) and the semiotic mystery of the matching of signifier to signified (ideal/real). Dupin is explicit about the secondary importance of questions of criminal justice: 'If, dating our inquiries from the body found, and then tracing a murderer, we yet discover this body to be that of some other individual than Marie; or if, starting with the living Marie, we find her, yet find her unassassinated – in either case we lose our labour' (III, p. 737). Either case would be fair work for a detective, but what Dupin requires is a double solution which consists in the 'co-incidence' of a *matched pair* of signifiers and signifieds. It is this testing of the relation between the ideal and the real, the fictional and reality, and their two laws of probability, which justifies Poe's statement in regard to this story that 'I have . . . handled my design in a manner altogether *novel* in literature.'[21]

This 'novelty' is defined by its difference from conventional adjacent discourses. As in 'The Murders in the Rue Morgue', newspaper reports play an essential part as the witnesses of the modern city. But, for Dupin, newspapers are guilty of a pernicious, almost mesmeric, power of 'suggestion' over public opinion; they are essentially ideological: 'it is the object of our newspapers rather to create a sensation – to make a point – than to further the cause of truth' (III, p. 738). So too in certain forms of *bellelettrist* philosophizing: 'In ratiocination, not less than in literature, it is the *epigram* which is the most immediately and the most universally appreciated. In both, it is of the lowest order of merit.' By epigram, Dupin explains, he means '*pungent contradictions* of the general idea', and he argues that 'it is the mingled epigram and melodrama of the idea, that Marie Rogêt still lives, rather than any true plausibility in this idea, which has suggested it to L'Etoile, and secured it a favourable reception with the public.' The, again provocative, implication is clearly that the present text is not, as readers of Poe might be led to expect, a species of melodramatic fiction and paradoxical theorizing, but a new discourse in 'philosophy', dedicated to that 'truth' which was defined at the beginning as the coincidence of the 'ideal' and the 'real'.

Most importantly, conventional forms of writing are seen as cognate with the discourse of police and law. The problem with the newspaper editor is that he

> has thought it sagacious to echo the small talk of the lawyers, who, for the most part, content themselves with echoing the rectangular precepts of the courts. I would here observe that very much of what is rejected as evidence by a court is the best of evidence to the intellect. For the court, guided itself by the general principles of evidence – the recognised and *booked* principles – is averse to swerving at particular instances. And this steadfast adherence to principle, with rigorous disregard of the conflicting exception, is a sure mode of attaining the *maximum* of attainable truth, in any long sequence of time. The practice, *en masse*, is therefore philosophical; but it is not the less certain that it engenders vast individual error. (III, p. 747)

As we have observed, in terms of the 'sympathetic' theory of mastery, to the extent that most crime is banal, the courts, the newspapers, and the sort of fiction and philosophizing cognate with them, are as adequate as the police methodology of the ordinary.[22] But for the mystery of what lies beyond the 'mass' or the 'ordinary', another discourse is necessary: 'You will say, no doubt, using the language of the law, that "to make my case," I should rather undervalue than insist upon a full estimation of the activity required in this matter. This may be the practice in law, but it is not the usage of reason. My ultimate object is only the truth' (II, p. 555).[23]

The centre of the question lies in Dupin's attack on the 'booked' principles of law. 'It is,' he says, 'the malpractice of the courts to confine evidence and discussion to the bounds of apparent relevancy' (III, p. 752). In drawing attention to this, Poe is responding to yet another novelty of the eighteenth century, the systematization of the laws of evidence.[24] Curiously, it was Jeremy Bentham, in his *Rationale of Judicial Evidence* (1827), who undertook the most thorough-going critique of what he called the 'Technical System' of restrictive rules, developed in the common law tradition of precedent, which overlaid the empiricist assumptions of evidence theory. In place of what he presented as the consequence of 'the sinister interests of "Judge and Co." and their delusions of ideology (religious, political and professional)', Bentham proposed a 'Natural' model of open admissibility.[25] What William Twining characterizes as Bentham's 'anti-nomianism'[26] is not only a political argument against the power of the legal profession. The rules of evidence are legal conventions aimed at safeguarding personal liberties and establishing criteria by which various types of evidence should be judged. By arguing against rules of admissibility, Bentham necessarily raises the very novelistic question – which is equally a pertinent question for Equity – of how to judge and weigh evidence other than by *a priori* or external criteria. Without agreed conventions, how are we to distinguish between a fiction and a belief – or, for that matter, a lie?

Once more the question of the reliability of witness is expressed in terms of the probability of what is narrated. The limiting case is, as we have seen, that of the 'miraculous'. But here Bentham, notwithstanding his empiricist assumptions, argues against Hume's absolute rejection of such testimony: '[Bentham's] main contention is that there is no absolute criterion for assuming the impossibility of any given fact . . . . The impossible is only the highest degree of the improbable. And the improbable is really only the measure of our ignorance.'[27] For example:

> Take a case of witchcraft. It must be recollected, that, what, in our own days, is never spoken of seriously, was a source of terror to our forefathers. The alleged fact is, that an old woman travelled through the air on a broomstick. Do you believe it? No. Why? Because it is impossible. Impossible! how do you prove that? Where is the necessity for proof? To reason about such a thing is mere madness.
>
> This is no doubt a most legitimate prejudice, and one which does honour to the knowledge of the age; but those whose opinions are founded only on this prejudice, would have condemned the very same witches, had they lived in the times when the prejudice was in favour of their existence.[28]

Thus, as Twining comments: 'the basis of my belief [against the existence of witches] is not the intrinsic impossibility of such a phenomenon; it is the circumstantial evidence of two physical laws'.[29] For Bentham the 'laws of nature' are relative to the contemporary state of knowledge and, furthermore, to the judge's personal knowledge of those laws.[30] Such is of course the case with the 'law' invoked by the newspapers in the question of the drowned body in 'The Mystery of Marie Rogêt'. Dupin argues from the newspaper's assertion that 'All experience shows . . . ' to his conclusion, 'All experience does *not* show', by examining the 'probability' of the laws invoked by the journalists in terms of their 'rationale' and of the limited knowledge of the laws of nature possessed by the authors and the reading public (the truth, in all probability, is that Dupin invents a new 'law of nature' to support his own interpretation! – III, pp. 740–43).

By introducing a relativity into the laws of nature and the judge's knowledge of those laws, Bentham radically transforms the question of the probability of 'facts': 'Improbability and impossibility are names not for any qualities of facts themselves, but for our *persuasion* of their non-existence' (my italics).[31] It follows that the probative force of evidence is dislocated from the objective nature of the evidence itself – whether what is alleged is itself probable – to its subjective effect on the mind of the judge – whether, in the circumstances in which it is alleged, it is credible to the listener: 'The task of the judge is to assess the probative force of the relevant evidence in terms of the degree of persuasion that it produces in his mind.'[32] Here, then, Bentham's contribution goes well beyond evidence theory, like John Mill and the associationists, shifting the empiricist model from the sphere of philosophy into that of psychology, from an attempt to describe the world towards what Victor Sage calls 'a grammar of human expectation'.[33]

This shift into psychology is clearly subjectivist, taking us back, as it were, to the more radically empiricist perspective of Hume's first *Treatise* . . . .[34] It might also remind us, as I suggested above, of the rival legal paradigm emerging in the courts of Equity, and hence of the novel. But even Equity had to establish itself as a form of 'ruled justice'. In any case, one could hardly expect the author of the 'Police Machine' to leave it at that. Reducing judgment to the personal beliefs and credulity of judges alone, would be as bad as establishing artificial *a priori* rules of exclusion, surrendering justice only to arbitrariness. In his attempt to develop some form of regulation, as we might expect, Bentham seeks to articulate the radically empiricist, subjectivist and individual with an equally radical rationalistic, systematic and objective position. So what was referred to above as 'the degree of persuasion' is to be taken fairly literally as a *measurable* mathematical formulation: it is 'a function of the probative force of all the positive evidence minus the probative force of all the infirmative evidence'.[35] In other words,

Bentham requires some systematic way of assessing evidence, some rational theory of persuasion applicable to any human individual which, like all utilitarian virtues, may be calculated in numerical terms – precisely what Dupin calls a 'calculus of probabilities' (III, p. 773)

Bentham's proposal for a 'moral thermometer' or a 'thermometer of persuasion', as, in consonance with the contemporary discursive intersection of Psychology, Medicine and Law, it came to be called, became the focus of the controversy which has surrounded his theory of evidence. It is not clear 'whether he was advancing a "subjectivist" or "objectivist" theory of proof or an incoherent mixture of the two . . . . [O]n one view, the proposal represents a plunge into pure subjectivism and on another it introduces precise mathematical calculations into an area that is not susceptible to this kind of (presumably objective) analysis.'[36] The contradiction reflects that of his social projects, on the one hand liberal in its focus on the individual, on the other tyrannically repressive in its articulation into a political order. Thus Twining's conclusion does not, to my mind, solve the paradox: 'Bentham's theory . . . gave a place to subjective judgements and objective standards, but . . . his views were not as fully worked out nor as coherent as [one of his defenders] suggests. Nevertheless . . . he attempted to accommodate both subjective psychological factors and objective standards of rationality within his theory – as, indeed, any rounded theory of evidence must do.' This is all well and good, but it rather begs the question: how to calculate the psychological force of influence? What is crucially lacking for Bentham – as it was for the moral managers – is precisely a science of the mind capable of articulating in the quantifiable terms which dominated contemporary science, the factors, hitherto philosophical, which he has shifted into the realm of psychology. How to articulate a science of subjectivity?

Let us return then to Dupin. As we have observed, the difference and superiority of his methodology to that of the police is that it is itself based on difference. Just as in Bentham's argument on miracles, Dupin counters one of the basic postulates of Humean empiricism (the inference from the past to the present): 'It is no longer philosophical to base, upon what has been, a vision of what is to be' (III, p. 752). This being so, 'it should not be so much asked "what has occurred," as, "what has occurred that has never occurred before"' (II, p. 548, III, p. 737) since 'it is by these deviations from the plane of the ordinary, that reason feels its way, if at all, in its search for the true.' This postulate becomes a defence of his character's theoretical idiosyncrasy and his own, different, writing. For Dupin, the truth of modern mysteries – the point of coincidence of their fictions and their realities – is found in what is normally marginalized, the 'outskirts' (III, p. 751) of phenomena – like the piece of cloth torn from Marie's dress, the 'clew' in the Rue Morgue, or the letter-rack in the Minister's apartment. Dupin links what is assumed to be marginal in significance precisely to the 'deviations from the plane of the ordinary' which disturb the probabilities of plot. His expertise lies in the mastery of the irrelevant and the unlikely:

> It is the malpractice of the courts to confine evidence and discussion to the bounds of apparent relevancy. Yet experience has shown, and a true philosophy will always show, that a vast, perhaps the larger, portion of truth arises from the seemingly irrelevant. It is through the spirit of this principle, if not precisely through its letter, that modern science has resolved to *calculate upon the unforeseen*. (III, p. 752)

But note: although Poe's hero claims the fantastic territory of the 'unforeseen' – in short, the improbable – he has already disavowed (his own) literary sensationalism. Further, 'In my own heart dwells no faith in praeter-nature' (III, p. 772). In dealing with the marginal and the improbable, the word 'calculate' is crucial here in distinguishing the Dupin experiment from Poe's gothic mode.

We should also note that in Dupin too, although questions related to forensics are the occasion for his intervention, the sphere in which calculation is applied is, as in Bentham, less that of Law than of Psychology. It seems to me far from incidental that neither Dupin nor the narrator ever talks about 'detecting'. What they do talk a great deal about is 'analysis'. From his initial and most dramatic demonstration of his peculiar talents, when he makes good his boast that 'most men, in respect of himself, wore windows in their bosoms' (II, p. 533), and explains 'the method – if method there is – by which you have been enabled to fathom my soul in this matter', through his assessment of the Minister's thought-processes, and his speculations on those of the characters (eloping girls, romantic busy-bodies, murderous lovers, and gangs) involved in Marie's 'discursive' walk (III, p. 749), Dupin demonstrates that, like Bentham, the object of his analytic calculations is precisely the human mind. Dupin is less the first 'detective' to apply scientific methods to crime, than an 'analyst' applying 'science' to the hitherto largely religious or metaphysical mysteries of the psyche.

However, if Dupin claims the territory of the fantastic for scientific analysis, by the same token, his 'science' is plainly not that of traditional positivism, as the footnote from Landor makes clear: 'when law becomes a science and a system, it ceases to be justice. The errors into which a blind devotion to *principles* of classification has led the common law, will be seen by observing how often the legislature has been obliged to come forward to restore the equity its scheme had lost' (III, p. 747). 'The Purloined Letter' is equally clear in its criticism of the 'purely' mathematical: 'If the Minister had been no more than a mathematician, the Prefect would have been under no necessity of giving me this check' (III, p. 988). Simple mathematics falls under the category of the ordinary. What defeats the legalistic, positivistic Prefect is precisely the Minister's difference – the fact that he is both a mathematician *and* a poet. In contrast, Dupin, analytic and Romantic, occupies symmetrically the extraordinary site of the synthesis of the scientific and the poetic – the very articulation Bentham himself requires to conciliate the objectivist and subjectivist components of his calculus of influence. As in Bentham this results in contradiction, in Dupin it generates the unnatural and double methodology – textually, an 'anomaly' in which 'the most rigidly exact in science [is] applied to the shadow and spirituality of the most intangible in speculation' (III, p. 724) – Dupin employs to master the very place from which emanates the political threat that the police and the Law cannot control.

By shifting probability from the 'laws of nature' to the degree of persuasion of the witness or hearer and thereby 'psychologizing' reality, Bentham is, in effect, dissolving the objective barrier between fact and fiction. Indeed, according to Twining, 'the main philosophical basis of his theory of evidence' is his 'theory of fictions'.[37] According to this theory, our only instrument for articulating our beliefs about the real world is language:

> yet language is not merely an imperfect instrument for such a purpose – rather it is systematically misleading. In particular, it commits us to think and talk in terms of non-existing entities as if they exist . . . The main link between Bentham's theory of fictions and his theory of evidence is that the latter is dependent on fictions of a special kind, viz. 'ontological fictions'

such as probability, possibility, and necessity. These are fictions concerned with existence. They are special because they are 'fictitious qualities', which are doubly fictitious because qualities are themselves fictitious entities and because these qualities are falsely ascribed, in ordinary parlance, to facts or events rather than to modifications of belief . . . . [38]

In the absence of a psychological mathematics, it is possible, then, to conceive that it is the writer of fiction, the specialist in these 'fictitious qualities' applied to fictitious entities, who best can 'calculate' the persuasiveness of narratives.

But for Poe the application of fiction to the truth would appear to be the province of not just any writer of fiction – or just any form of writing fiction. Herein lies the explanation for the particular articulation of theory and narrative in these stories and for their ultimate contradiction. His critique of the police paradigm demonstrates his unsuitability for the 'romance of the detective' in part by proposing, as the quote from Landor might suggest, a reform of writing in the direction of the equitable principles of realism. But, as I have also suggested, despite this, the reform of writing proposed by the Dupin stories differs from that of realism. If sympathetic identification serves in realism to conceal the ideological and sexual position of the creative subject, what is at issue is that very position. As we have already seen, the paradigm of the 'ordinary' employed by the police, the Law and journalism and its cognate fictions is adequate in that it holds a symmetrical relation to the 'mass' – very much a 'common' law. It would follow then that, in such discourses of 'common sense', their theoretical assumptions need not be explicit for the very reason that they are, purportedly, commonly shared by both writer and reader. Thus, the transformation of realist 'sympathy' in Dupin's application of it to what cannot be embraced by 'common' discourse – that which, actively or passively, denounces the communality of the 'mass' and its police discourses and is hence marginalized or excluded by 'ordinary' realism – has two decisive effects. First, it means that this writing, rather than 'natural' and 'universal', has to be 'idiosyncratic' – 'idio-' in the sense of both individually and ideologically specific (and we might note how Dupin's theory is almost always expressed as a contradiction of 'common sense'). Second, it makes the explicit presence of the master necessary as a site of difference, symmetrical to that of the object of mastery: in short, *his theoretical position has to be present as part of the narrative.* Though the realist author may indulge in occasional excursions into philosophical or personal comment, he or she tends to conceal the process of production of his or her simulacrum beneath the 'natural' surface; Dupin, on the other hand, is committed to subjecting the techniques of fiction to a discourse of method, including the theoretical explanation of how he reconstructs the plot and signifies its agent in his text. Here, in short, in contrast to Miller's account of the realist novel, the theoretical 'eye' is made visible to the reader (if not, as notoriously in the personal combat between the twin monsters in 'The Purloined Letter', to the opponent).[39]

Poe's attempt to include the theoretical difference of his science of the subject in his narrative can of course only occur within the historical limitations of the dominant scientific terms available to him at the time. For this reason both he and Bentham look to mathematics for an objective means of analysing subjective judgments of probability – in narrative terms, the ability to 'calculate upon the unforeseen' and to make 'chance a matter of absolute calculation' – in short, a mathematics of expectation. Within mathematics, Bentham, like Dupin, looks to contemporary probability theory, what was called at the time 'the doctrine of chances'. However, for his juridical purposes ('making a case'), this theory although 'perfectly correct . . . unfortunately . . . will be found not applicable to the present purpose.'[40] In this context, the closest Bentham can get is the theory of wagering and insurance – in the first case, at least, precisely that used by Dupin in his example of the guessing game ('The Purloined Letter') and the outrageous theory of the dice at the end of 'The Mystery of Marie Rogêt'. Although mathematics remains the measure of objectivity, and shows signs of developing in a suitable direction, it remains here a theoretical gesture, in the end a form of science fiction, not in this case, of technology but of theory and methodology. Both Dupin and Bentham phantasize a dialectic between theory and fiction, between the model of objective science – mathematics – and the subjective material of the mind.

In consequence, we hesitate before a Dupin who remains fantastic and, ultimately, monstrous. Although his 'acumen', like the ape's strength in the Rue Morgue, 'appears . . . praeternatural', the narrator tries to reassure us that he is not 'detailing any mystery, or penning any romance. What I have described in the Frenchman was merely the result of an excited, or perhaps of a diseased intelligence' (II, p. 533). None the less, 'I often dwelt meditatively upon the old philosophy of the Bi-Part Soul, and amused myself with the fancy of a double Dupin – the creative and the resolvent' (II, p. 533). Perhaps the most important monster of all is thus Dupin himself, impossible and double.

Of course, in this way the experiment in a 'novel' form of writing in 'The Mystery of Marie Rogêt' cannot help but fail, denouncing the contradictions of Poe's new experiment, the ideological limitations of science and the fictionality of fiction and, as we observed in chapter I, the necessarily retrospective nature of their epistemology. In the end, as we now know, Poe was reduced to revising the conclusion, retrospectively adjusting the fiction to events as they unfold beyond it.[41] But, even then, it is likely that he still got it wrong. Was the attempt to use his form of writing to solve the mysteries of the real serious? As opposed to the realist novel in which the theoretical position of the subject tends to be concealed in the self-evidence of its texture, the foregrounding of theory here does draw our attention to the location of the gap between realism and the historical world in the theoretical model which intervenes between the world and its simulacrum. I hope to have suggested how, in the context of Bentham's contribution to evidence theory and the limitations of contemporary science, Dupin's theorizing is not as absurd as it is sometimes taken to be, but an acceptable imaginative figure for a science of the subject generated from a dialectic of theory and narrative, whose inadequacy is the consequence of those historical limitations which ensure that a phantastic synthesis remains a contradiction. But at least it enables a theoretical discussion, if not of its own theory, then at least of the undeclared theory of its contiguous discourses, both literary and scientific.

It is here we find the major problem: in locating the question as the persuasive impact of testimony under a theory of fictions, Bentham – and Dupin – make it a question of psychology, rather than of rhetoric – of mind rather than language. This has indeed been the major tradition of evidence theory since Bentham until recently, when questions of the rhetorical role of language in persuading judges of testimony have come to the fore. This has meant shifting the very Poe-like issue of the referential relation between testimony and the 'facts' (the 'correspondence theory of evidence') to that of its rhetorical form (the 'coherence theory of evidence') and, eventually, to that of the narrative pragmatics of the courtroom.[42] This of course presupposes a very different model of language from that available to Poe in the nineteenth century. But, clearly, a theory of fictions and a theory of mind without a theory of language is doomed to the idealism that guarantees the failure of this text.

We shall return to the question of theories of fiction, mind, and language in Chapter 8, to which one more element will have to be added. For it is not, however, only a theory of language that is missing here. The figure that appears to lie 'in fact' at the end of Marie's story, filling the space between its signifiers and the historical reality, is another form of monstrosity: an 'abortion'. The gap lay within the woman, and the text responds symmetrically with its own gap: its theory of the subject also lacks a theory of gender. Indeed, we were all wrong again; we were searching for a man responsible for murdering a beautiful young woman, but, as it 'probably' turns out, she died in the criminal act of interrupting her pregnancy: in the end, the 'murderer' was the girl herself, responsible for a crime committed on her own body. The mind of the young woman is one that Dupin cannot master. The guilt of the female, suggested by Mary Shelley's preface to her own 'abortion', will be one of the main themes of our study of sensation fiction in Chapter 7.

7

Sensation

THE NERVOUS STATE

Before he was made into a writer of 'detective fiction', Poe was known, as we have seen, as a writer of 'enigma' stories, one of the terms used in the early 1860s to describe the sort of fiction which was based on the unravelling of plots and secrets. The term 'detective fiction' employed from the 1880s inherited and intensified the critical stigmatization and devaluation to which this sort of fiction was subjected. A classic example of the decay of the literature of mystery supposedly represented by 'detective' fiction is seen in the changing attitude of Henry James to the narrative of the servant, Mrs. Beard, in *The American*: as she pauses in her telling of her 'lurid tale of family murder', James comments in 1877: 'the most artistic of romancers could not have been more effective. Newman made a movement as if he were turning over the page of a novel'; but in the 1907 revised edition, James writes: 'the most *expert story-teller* couldn't have been more *thrilling*. Newman made *almost* the motion of turning the page of a *"detective story"'* (my italics).[1] The appellation 'detective' serves to denigrate the artistry and belittle the effect of what of course remains the same tale.

It is above all the effect on the reader that is in question. That novels had become influential was clearly perceived in the second half of the nineteenth century – as Trollope testified in 1870: 'We have become a novel-reading people. Novels are in the hands of us all: from the Prime Minister down to the last-appointed scullery-maid. We have them in our library, our drawing-rooms, our bed-rooms, our kitchens, – and in our nurseries. Our memories are laden with the stories which we read, with the plots which are unravelled for us, and with the characters which are drawn for us.'[2] This does not however warrant calling the mid-Victorian period 'the Age of the Novel'; rather, as Alfred Austin declared in 1874: 'It may be the age of anything else people like; but assuredly it is the age of Novels'.[3] The plural is important, for the former title would immediately have at least one rival: as *Punch* observed nervously in 1861, 'Some would have it an age of sensation'.[4] *Punch* is not yet speaking of the 'sensation novel', for that term would only be coined the following year, in Mrs. Oliphant's famous review of 'Sensation Novels' in *Blackwood's Magazine*,[5] yet this was what very soon challenged the 'serious' novel at the height of its respectability. Trollope again testifies, somewhat ironically, to the former's popularity and the competition between them: 'Among English novels of the present day, and among English novelists, a great division is made. There are sensational novels and anti-sensational, sensational novelists and anti-sensational, sensational readers and anti-sensational. The novelists who are considered to be anti-sensational are generally called realistic.'[6] To a large extent the 'realistic' novel did take its definition by disavowing its popular competitor: by accusing the sensation novel of, amongst other things, mixing genres (romance and realism, domesticity and melodrama), breaking literary decorum and probability, demolishing class barriers in the reading public, and threatening the morals of young ladies, realist fiction clearly disclaims earlier accusations directed against it for doing much the same things.

But sensation probably denounced something more fundamental in the Novel, the very thing whose disavowal was essential to the institution of 'Literature': the fact that it was the product of an industry. Thanks to increasing literacy and an organized market – dominated by Mudie's Circulating Library – fiction was becoming important not only in 'the mind of the nation', but in its pocket too. Indeed, the very coining of the expression 'sensation novel' occurs in a literary review – a development which accompanied the proliferation and resultant competition in the novel industry, as an indirect means of advertising and as a space in which the criteria for judging fiction were debated and gradually worked out. One of the major novelties of the label would appear to be that of a literary category defined by commercial terms. As one reviewer put it in 1864, 'two or three years ago nobody would have known what was meant by a sensation novel; yet now the term has already passed through the stage of jocular use . . . and has been adopted as the regular commercial name for a particular product of industry for which there is just now a brisk demand':[7] 'sensation', like the later 'best-seller', represents trade-mark as genre.

It is the manufactured aspect of writing that most seems to irritate the respectable novel, which was to turn on sensation as 'mechanical' – in other words, 'hack' writing. *Punch* views the prospect of 'an age of sensation' and 'the vulgar excitement it brings' as an exotic importation to 'this common sense nation' from America: 'that land of fast life and fast laws/ Laws not faster made than they're broken'. And it concludes its satiric warning with the following advice:

> If you've got something good, never doubt it
> By deeds will avouch its vocation;
> And be sure that not talking about it
> Is the true way to *make* a 'Sensation'.

According to Richard Altick, the direct source for the modern use of sensation is the term 'sensation scenes', introduced from America into the London theatrical vocabulary in 1860 to describe the spectacular effects achieved in contemporary popular melodramas by the elaborate mechanical paraphernalia which had been developed in the Shakespearian drama.[8] *Punch* is thus already aware that sensation is not only crime, action, and secrets, but more to the point, it is essentially something *made*, a manufactured effect, as opposed to the common sense experiences which come about naturally.

Wilkie Collins was particularly and significantly annoying in this respect. He makes the legal paradigm of realism explicit; he foregrounds the unreliable idiosyncrasies of his narrators; he delights in making his readers aware that we are being manipulated, teasingly denying us omniscience and parading before us the gaps which inform narrative. Furthermore, against Dickens' advice,[9] he writes prefaces answering the reviewers and explaining his literary and/or political positions and intentions to the public, in which he also frequently specifies the scientific, legal and medical authorities which serve as explicit guarantees for the authenticity of his fictions. The display of the mechanics of narrative construction and, more particularly, of their grounding in external knowledges and prejudices particularly irritated the *Westminster Review*: 'It is not artistic to tell this to the reader. The process of watching our dinner being cooked takes away our appetite.'[10]

In a crime story, it is clearly someone's goose that is being cooked. In pursuing suspects, these tales cannot help but foreground the means by which the narrative and its protagonists read events and character, detect secrets, and characterize the guilty and the innocent; but, contrary to the opinion of much generalized formal criticism of detective fiction, they do not have to endorse them. More frequently, they oblige us to experience their effects at the same time as, at another level, they draw a critical attention to the mechanisms by which that effect is produced. A key example is identified by D. A. Miller in *The Woman in White* when, coming to the end of Marian's diary, we find that Fosco has been there before us. Our shocked sense of this violation of privacy rebounds on us: 'For the Count's postscript only puts him in a position we already occupy. Having just finished reading Marian's diary ourselves, we are thus implicated in the sadism of his act, which even as it violates our readerly intimacy with Marian reveals that "intimacy" to be itself a violation.'[11] Sensation fiction exhibits a particular awareness of the positions of the narrators/'detectives', how the paradigms they employ to represent the mystery and to rewrite the plot into order are necessarily, as Barickman *et al.* put it, 'obtrusive' (or, in Fosco's case, 'intrusive').[12] As a result, we cannot help but recognize that what we are reading are the readings conducted by the story's 'detectives'. Indeed, much of the suspense and mystery results from the gaps which are a consequence of the frames imposed by the narrators' or detectives' ideological, theoretical or personal positions on the elements in the narrative and the characters, including the narrators/detectives themselves, which escape his or her – and most usually 'his' – control. As we read, these elements begin to constitute what Barickman *et al.* refer to as a 'symbolic counter-plot' (and/or, I would add, what may be called a 'discursive' counter-plot). This most especially affects the pre-judged stereotypical roles into which characters, and particularly women, are forced by the narrator's or detective's position in relation to them.

As we will remember from the fictional and factual source for two of the Dupin stories, another fund for 'sensation' and an obvious realm in which stereotypes constructed their universe were the dramatic press reports of contemporary crimes.[13] Such crimes became 'sensational' by analogy with the popular melodramas – and not, as one might expect, vice versa. Witness Thackeray's treatment of the 'Northumberland Street affair' in *The Cornhill Magazine* in September 1861: 'Have any novelists of our days a scene and catastrophe more strange and terrible that this which occurs at noonday within a few yards of the greatest thoroughfare in Europe? At the theatres they have a new name for their melodramatic pieces, and call them "Sensation Dramas." What a sensation drama this is!'[14] Thackeray is referring to what was known as the 'Major Case', but he might equally well have been referring to the contemporary cases involving Vidil, Lafarge (1839), the Mannings (1849), William Palmer (1856), Madelaine Smith (1857), Thomas Smethurst (1859), or Constance Kent (1860) – to mention only the more dramatic criminal scandals which occupied so much of the press up to that date. These cases 'created a sensation' as much as any in the contemporary theatre, and part of the sensation they created was the manufacture of an 'obtrusive' discourse about many things, from the moral and psychological state of civilization to the novel, passing, far from incidentally, through the role, nature and particularly the criminality and pathology of women.

Such sensational crime played a central part in the recognition of the failure of Reform and in the generation of public anxieties and new responses. In reacting to the Northumberland and Vidil cases analysed by Altick, for example, *Fraser's Magazine* made the following observation: 'That the fierce passions of men are not tamed by the progress of civilization is evidenced by the prevalence of deadly outbursts, such as a few months ago wrung from the *Times* an appeal to the rulers of the people, to "diminish crime by terror, if they could not do so by discipline"', whilst the *News of the World* appeared to sum up the result of over a half-century of attempted melioration and the reversion, soon to be implemented by a reactionary reading of Darwin, to biological determinism: 'Our agencies of detection are generally successful; we may not hope that detection will always lead to prevention. Human nature is just as bad in some people as it always was'.[15] But it also challenged, with a measure of irony, the prevailing model of fiction immediately prior to the sensation novel. Referring to the Vidil case, the *Daily Telegraph* commented: 'What novelist of the present day, even though as fond of the morbid as Poe, or of the marvellous as Dumas, would take for this theme the attempt of a father on his son's life . . . ?' As for the motives alleged in the case, the *Morning Post* commented: 'If this story be true, let no novelist despair'; whilst, as for the 'plot', Thackeray observed: 'After this, what is the use of being squeamish about the probabilities and possibilities in the writing of fiction?' Life had become more extraordinary than fiction. Not only then was this a reality which would justify the most extravagant fiction, but, we have seen, no one had yet picked up Poe's mantle – the *Daily Telegraph* again: 'We have no Poe amongst us now to penetrate this mystery, and arrive through a dark labyrinth of evidence and deduction at that mental standpoint where all becomes open and clear.'[16]

Little of course did the *Telegraph* know that a 'new Poe' had in fact arrived, if not yet on the stage, at least on the page, with the first 'sensation scene' in *The Woman in White* (1860). Here, according to Mrs. Oliphant, when Anne Catherick lays her hand on Walter's arm in the Finchley Road, the reader experiences not a phantastic delusion of the imagination but a perfectly Humean sense of authentic experience: 'Few readers will be able to resist the mysterious thrill of this sudden touch. The sensation is distinct and indisputable. The reader's nerves are affected like the hero's . . . the silent woman lays her hand upon our shoulder as well as upon that of Mr. Walter Hartright.'[17] The principal effect manufactured by the sensation novel was 'sensation' itself, in the sense of a physiological reaction.

The nature of the sensation aroused is distinctly one of 'nervousness'. As Miller puts it: 'The genre offers us one of the first instances of modern literature to address itself primarily to the sympathetic nervous system, where it grounds its characteristic adrenalin effects . . . . The fiction elaborates a fantasmatics of sensation in which our reading bodies take their place from the start, and of which our physiological responses thus become the hysterical acting out.'[18] In order to obtain this effect, the actual tale and its characters have already to represent a prevailing environment of nervousness, what Miller again describes, ambiguously, as 'the nervous state',[19] a world populated by characters in which, as the *Christian Remembrancer* complained (of Mrs. Braddon) in 1863, 'nerves, feeling, excitement, will, and inclination are the sole motive powers'.[20] For this reason, the taste for sensation in the press, the popular theatre and the commercial novel was seen to be itself a form of nervous disease infecting the middle-classes from the poor:

Just as in the Middle Ages people were afflicted with the Dancing Mania and Lycanthropy . . . so now we have Sensation Mania. Just, too, as those diseases always occurred in seasons of dearth and poverty, and attacked only the poor, so does the Sensation Mania burst out only in times of mental poverty, and afflict only the most poverty-stricken minds. From an epidemic, however, it has lately changed into an endemic. Its virus is spreading in all directions . . . '[21]

The sensation virus attacks 'the nerves'. This was a central topic in the mixing of moral and medical language and the battle between psychological and physiological theories of mental disorder during the nineteenth century: 'in 1800 the "nervous doctor" had treated functional diseases of the nervous system, whereas psychiatrists had confidence in the underlying organic nature of the diseases which concerned them. By the century's end, the roles were reversed: nervous doctors – neurologists – were concerned primarily with organic diseases, whereas the psychiatrists had accepted the reality of primary mental disease.'[22] In short, 'the nerves' focus the rivalry between the post-Reform recapture of the moral terrain by medicine, in which neurophysiology was a principal instrument, and the development of an alternative psychological theory of the 'neuroses' out of which, of course, psychoanalysis was to develop.

The theory of nervous disease was descended from the earlier catch-alls, 'melancholy' and 'hypochondria'. The French called this 'spléen', and held that it was a 'maladie hypochondriaque propre aux Anglais'.[23] In *The English Malady* (1733), Edward Cheyne accepted the insult, maintaining that it was not a genuine madness but merely a state of nervous sensibility which had earlier been kept within the bounds of health by the old organic, paternal order, but had now been exacerbated by progress. In other words, in a similar way to the figure of crime, the 'malady' of the English was the price they had to pay in their nerves for their superior level of civilization and development, their very modernity.[24] But, as a descendent of hypochondria, the nervous disease of modernity is necessarily intimately connected with the disorder cognate with the former: hysteria, the disease that, through its etymological inheritance, could not help but invoke the woman. This association did not diminish when hysteria began to pass from an organic disorder to a disease of the 'sensitive principle' (Robert Whytt, 1764) since, due to their peculiar sexual nature and the weakness of their 'nerves', women were held to be more inclined to such disorders than men. The characteristic symptomology of hysteria, a physical sensation or reaction (pains, spasms) with no apparent organic cause, had led Thomas Sydenham (1681) to identify the disease in terms of its mimetic quality, the way in which hysterical or hypochondriacal symptoms mystify medicine by 'the multiformity of the shapes it puts on. Few of the maladies of miserable mortality are not imitated by it.'[25]

Hypochondria and hysteria were an ironically pathological comment on the eighteenth-century Reform notion of the power of mind to affect the body. The extreme case of ideological influence over physical sensation and behaviour represented by the fashionable success of Mesmer in the 1760s to 1780s was particularly worrying in relation to the women patients he mainly treated and the political implications of his practice, which were only laid to rest by Louis XVI's Royal Commission of 1784. Although the Commission tried to discredit Mesmer by attributing the trance or 'crises' provoked not to the power ('animal magnetism') of the mesmerist but to the 'imagination' of the patient, the implications of such a psychological theory were not to be drawn until James Braid's work in the 1840s. Braid's major contribution was 'to recognize more clearly the importance of the factor of suggestion in inducing the phenomena'.[26] He elaborated a theory of dislocated attention which he variously termed 'neuropnology', 'nervous sleep', or 'hypnotism' (1843). As a committed physiologist, Braid sought to explain the nature of the phenomenon in terms of its effect on the optical nerve; but when he discovered that even the blind could be hypnotized, he shifted his explanation to 'the sentient, or motor, and sympathetic nerves, and the mind'.[27] His perception that the trance was achieved 'entirely through the imagination' led him, in 1847, to coin the term 'monoideism' to describe the state of suspended will in which the patient became open to suggestions from the hypnotizer.

Artificially induced 'monoideism' in its turn mimics the pathological notion of 'monomania', one of what came to be known in the nineteenth century as the 'obsessional disorders', another category of central importance to the development of a distinct science of psychology and, of course, to Freud's theory of the neuroses. The term 'monomania', was first used in 1838 by Esquirol in characterizing an 'intelligent madwoman' whose form of 'moral insanity' he attributed to the overpowering and unresistable influence of a single idea or passion (Tuke called them 'imperative ideas') which resulted in a 'délire partiel'.[28] This remained a highly controversial concept in that, in the light of the traditional view that madness was the simple contrary to reason, it represented a contradiction in terms, as the alternative expressions used to define it, such as 'folie lucide', 'folie avec conscience' or 'folie raisonnante', make even clearer. It was therefore a sensational category in both senses of the word: not only in the somatic realization of hysterical notions but also in denying that insanity was an absolute state. The moral implications of the dissolving of the absolute line between sanity and insanity provoked by the notion of partial insanity, as figured in monomania, hypochondria, hysteria and hypnotism, can be seen in its repercussions on the distinction between insane and criminal.

The standard legal doctrine on insanity defences as handed down by Bracton and Hale made an absolute distinction between the mental states of 'idiocy' and 'absolute madness' – which were acceptable pleas of insanity, since the subject in these conditions was deprived of moral sense and a sense of the meaning of his or her acts by being reduced to the state of an animal (either dumb or as a 'wild beast') -, and partial insanity – that is to say, an insanity restricted to particular topics or periods – which, since everyone, under the influence of 'fears or griefs', may be subject to such crises, was not acceptable as a defence.[29] But when Hadfield tried to shoot George III in 1800, his counsel, Erskine, successfully argued that there are cases of madness in which reason is not totally destroyed, but in which it is subdued by 'distraction'. The subject reasons, sanely, from false premises 'because a delusive image, the inseparable companion of real insanity, is thrust upon the subjugated understanding'.[30] As Hale had indicated, this was a dangerous doctrine, made all the more so by a psychological reflection bred from the reform of the Asylum. The Bracton 'wild beast' test (as it was known) was held to be related to the animalistic treatment of the insane, whereas moral treatment had shown that the line between sanity and insanity was much harder to determine: as the Reformer Isaac Ray argued in his *Treatise on the Medical Jurisprudence of Insanity* (1838), 'Could Lord Hale have contemplated the scenes presented by the lunatic asylums of our own times, we should undoubtedly have received from him a very different doctrine.'[31]

The problem of this blurring of the distinction between criminality and insanity came to a crisis in the trial of Daniel M'Naghten. M'Naghten had an undisputed history of eccentric behaviour, and complained of persecution by, in turn, the Church of Rome, the New Police, and the Tory Party. In 1843 he shot Peel's secretary, mistaking him for the Prime Minister. With the help of the testimony of various medical witnesses, including Alexander Morison (one of only two teaching physicians currently lecturing on mental disease), Alexander Cockburn managed to obtain what is known as a 'special verdict': 'not guilty on grounds of insanity'. Another sensation. The *Times* commented: 'we would . . . ask those learned and philosophic gentlemen [the judges in the case] to define, for the edification of common-place people like ourselves, where sanity ends and madness begins . . . '.[32] The scandal led to the extraordinary decision of the House of Lords to call the judges to answer a set of specific questions. The answers they gave became known as the 'M'Naghten Rules' and remained the basic doctrine on insanity defences until 1959. The judges admitted the Erskine defence of partial insanity with an all-important rider: 'If the insanity of the accused is limited to a delusion, then only a delusion which, if true, would have justified the act in law will excuse him from the penalty.'[33] And so the issue was decided: partial insanity did exist as an argument which took one out of the realm of legal accountability, but the delusions which determined it would have to be, as it were, 'respectable'. It was only in 1959 that the idea of 'irresistible impulse' became a potential defence. The only thing left to decide was the moral status of the insanity defence, and this was settled when Roderick Maclean distinguished himself as the seventh would-be assassin of Queen Victoria, the latter being so enraged by the special verdict of 'not guilty on the grounds of insanity' that she demanded and in 1883 obtained a change in the law which transformed such verdicts into 'guilty but insane'. In harmony with the moralization of medicine in the post-Reform period, being 'mad' was in no way an alternative to being 'bad'.

Part of the reason for this may lie in the political overtones of the notion that, through pathological and, more particularly, hypnotic influence, a single 'delusive image' can take control of the rational being's will. This anxiety becomes clear as soon as it is asked where these ideas or passions come from and why they are not resisted – particularly, whether the responsibility derived from the hypnotizer or the hypnotized. When the Nancy School, led by Bernheim, returned to the question of hypnotism in the 1880–90s, it challenged Charcot's powerful contemporary theory which presented hypnotic suggestibility not as an analogy but as a symptom of the hysterical personality, by exploring the question of the generalized suggestibility of the imagination raised by Braid. The two theories clashed in France in the murder trial of Gabrielle Bompard in 1891. The debate surrounding the trial linked the dangers of suggestibility, on the Charcot side, to female moral and sexual vulnerability and perversity, and, on the Nancy side, to the power of the doctor over his patient and to the dangers of popular oratory in the manipulation of crowd psychology and mass demonstrations. The latter amounts to an ironic and pathological inversion of moral treatment: the idea that one person, be he a doctor or a rabble-rouser, could implant a delusive or compulsive idea in the mind of others and provoke them to transgress the law and morality.[34] A second central question was thus whether anyone was vulnerable to suggestibility or principally the undisciplined and weak-willed hysterical woman, and the contemporary tendency was to recognize the fundamental susceptibility of the latter – as in the neuroses of the eighteenth century, if not for organic, then for emotional reasons.

Thus, given the pathological model of the psycho-somatic offered by hysteria, precisely because of the sensation novel's concentration on nervous sensitivity and its technology of suggestion, although the 'nervous state' it depicted, exploited and produced affected everyone in the novel and everyone who read them, from the Prime Minister to the scullery-maid, it necessarily focused primarily on the young heroine. As we saw in Miller, the 'sensation mania' is itself a form of hysteria, which the middle-class characters 'catch', in *The Woman in White*, from the hysterical fugitive from the asylum. This was something which clearly most shocked the reviewers. Against the backdrop of the notorious Contagious Diseases Acts of 1864–9 which sought to make the woman's body – rather, the body of the female poor – the source of physical and moral contamination, the fear was that the form's promiscuous mixing of popular and sensitive classes (in both its characters and its readers) would open the vulnerable middle-class reader to hysterical contamination from its lower-class sources. Indeed, the sensation novel seemed to embody that very contamination. Comparisons with French romances were again employed, noting not only that the latter centre their scandals on adultery, whilst the English centre them on murder, but, equally importantly, that, whereas in the French novel there is almost always 'one virtuous central figure [who] is modest and dignified, and that one is generally the girl of 17 or 19. In the English, the most unlimited manifestations of passion proceed from the girl herself, who is created expressly to charm the young people of good society.'[35] The class dimension of this view of the woman is sustained by the fact that, although the contaminating or contaminated heroine in these novels may be the wife of a member of the middle- or noble classes, it is almost always the case that she has risen to this place from a more lowly social origin, and her calamity is often linked to the return of that repressed origin.

CHERCHEZ LA FEMME!

'I do not ask for my rights, I have no rights; I have only wrongs.'

Caroline Sheridan Norton, 1853.[36]

The *locus classicus* of the corrupt lower-class female hiding hysterically behind an angelic middle-class exterior is obviously the second work, after *The Woman in White*, to establish itself as a 'sensation', Mary Braddon's *Lady Audley's Secret* (1862). Contemporary critics would have the public believe that a 'secret' is the sum total of the genre, the motive power of its plot in a fraud perpetrated on the reader by the exaggerated concealment of information. However, although secrets are indisputably an important ingredient in many sensation and detective stories, it is not true that they are the necessarily mechanical or specious centre.[37] *Lady Audley's Secret* is an obvious case in point. If a sensation novel starts with a concealed secret, explores its dramatic consequences, and ends with its transformation from a disturbing lacuna to a plenitude of clarity and order, what, one might ask, *is* Lady Audley's secret? Is it that Lady Audley murdered her first husband, that she did not, that she had been married before, that she was married still, that she is not 'Lady Audley' but Helen Talboys, or Helen Maldon, that the innocent-looking lady is evil, or that she is insane? Or, given that, in the end, the family makes Lady Audley herself the secret, a skeleton in the *maison de santé*, is it simply that, whatever the secret, it cannot cease to be secret? Rather than being dissipated by the plot, the secret simply proliferates, denying us a signified which will exhaustively fill the gap it opens. Lady Audley's secret is, like Poe's purloined letter and, as we shall see, Collins' moonstone, most basically a sensational signifier, an absence which generates nervous and discursive reaction in the characters and the reader.

By having and becoming a secret, Lady Audley becomes an object which must be mastered – like Dupin, 'the cynosure of policial eyes'. But her mystery, constantly escaping the capture of a single code, fragments the homogeneity of the dominant discipline. The victim is Robert Audley, the family lawyer who, acting in a private and personal capacity (much more family than lawyer), subjects her and her life to his scrutiny. Thanks to Lady Audley, Robert finds himself at the centre of a complex web of conflicting desires and obligations: in his running debate with himself as to what he should do, he is torn between his professional duty, his personal apathy, his obligations to Providence, his acknowledged attraction for his aunt, his love and duty to his uncle, and his affection for his friend, George (and for his sister, Clara). The secret that is Lady Audley makes itself felt by fracturing the different codes – personal and public, sexual and familial – which define Robert's modern social position.

Robert represents to himself that it is his commitment to a code of family duty that, despite his being an officer of the court, makes him fear the Law.[38] None the less, the family can no longer deal with its own secrets; professional and administrative help is needed. So, running from the Law, the family turns to the physician to bring Lady Audley under control. However, on the basis of what Robert tells him, Dr. Mosgrave (who has 'the face of a man who had spent the greater part of his life in listening to other people' – p. 316) does not believe that she is mad, either in medical or legal terms: there is 'no evidence of madness in anything that she has done' (indeed the crime would be evidence of her sanity) and 'I do not think any jury in England would accept the plea of insanity in such a case as this.' What is worse, the doctor, here taking on the professional expertise relinquished by Robert, reminds the lawyer that, barring her motive, there is in fact not even any evidence that a murder has been committed. Be that as it may, the family demands she be incarcerated.

Lady Audley, like the monsters we looked at in the previous chapter, threatens to escape in the gaps she opens between family, legal and medical codes. Having generated these conflicts, her secret can only be mastered by a conspiracy which brings them back into an alignment in defence of family respectability and the ultimate complementarity of asylums and prisons in the modern police system. But in order for psychiatric medicine to take the punitive place of the Law in defending the family, it too has to shift its paradigm. As in the reading of crime and insanity after the failure of Reform, the only way to sustain the mastery of this 'police' is by invoking the woman's physiology against her. The impasse which Mosgrave describes is only resolved by his invocation of the convenient post-Reform diagnosis that replaces the failure of moral treatment by a biological destiny: Lady Audley's secret is that she is intrinsically 'dangerous' because she suffers from hereditary latent (i.e., partial, intermittent) insanity (p. 321). If Robert is punishing her, without benefit of trial, for a crime she had not committed, Dr. Mosgrave agrees to commit her because he believes her innocent of any crime except her blood. Were it not for this, he would not assist in 'smuggling her away out of the reach of justice'. A special verdict indeed: insane on the grounds of being not guilty and, at the same time, in Victoria's revision, guilty because insane.

Lady Audley is hence incarcerated in the disciplinary codes which are invoked to deal with what disrupts their order. But, conscious that she is the victim of a conspiracy in which the family use the threat of Law and Medicine to keep its secret by locking up the woman, it is here that we become aware of the working of a discursive 'counter-plot'. The interweaving of criminal and medical codes appears throughout the novel, and in many other sensation novels of the period, not only as a conspiratorial complementarity but as alternative, conflicting readings. One of the curiosities of this tale is the apparent early resolution of its principal narrative mystery. Although Robert declares at the end of chapter XX that 'I can understand all now' (p. 135), yet his investigation continues, not, as might be expected, in order to find his missing friend (to which he only returns after he has dealt with his aunt because, as he had accused her, he too is 'haunted' by George) or to gather evidence admissible in a court of law, but as an exhaustive investigation which will make him master of every detail of Lady Audley's biography. In order to sustain the constant postponement of confrontation and resolution a dynamic of hesitation has to be introduced into the tale. One major theme responsible for postponing resolution is the debate on duty referred to above. However this is accompanied by another theme which uses the medical and legal codes not as a means of capturing the woman, but as weapons in the conflict between the woman and the man.

What is at issue here is the hesitation of the reliability of witness discussed in the previous chapter now clearly cast in a struggle for dominance between a legalistic position which codes its narrative as 'evidence' and a medical (psychiatric) coding which denies the former as a subjective delusion produced by the influence of a 'monomania'. Robert first attacks his aunt by donning a professional position: 'Lady Audley . . . I have never practiced as a barrister . . . but we are sometimes forced into the very position we have most avoided; and I have found myself lately compelled to think of these things. Lady Audley, did you ever study the theory of circumstantial evidence?' (pp. 103–4) The mere articulation of this theory has a 'sensational' effect on the woman; it is enough to make Lady Audley faint. However, when Robert next invokes the 'right of

circumstantial evidence' against his aunt, she counter-attacks with
the accusation that he is being 'hypochondriacal' (pp. 230–1). The
conflict escalates to the last confrontation. Robert imagines himself
at the ritualistic height of his profession ('I wonder if the judges
of the land feel as I do now, when they put on the black cap'
– p. 233); for which he receives the most categorical retort from
Lady Audley: 'You are mad, Mr. Audley!' She defies his 'chain of
evidence' with the same theory that Robert will use, in the absence
of legal evidence, to incarcerate her ('It is no fault of mine if my
husband's nephew goes mad, and chooses me for the victim of his
monomania' – p. 236), even using the same argument of hereditary
insanity in spreading the idea that Robert is insane: 'Do you know,
Alicia,' she says to her step-daughter, 'that madness is more often
transmitted from father to son than from father to daughter, and
from mother to daughter than from mother to son? . . . but he must
be watched, Alicia, for he is mad!' (p. 239). This is not a merely
desperate evasion; from the moment Robert first appears 'On the
Watch' (chapter XV), he is regarded by the Christmas visitors at
Audley Court as 'an inoffensive species of maniac' (p. 98). More
to the point, even Robert has suspected this (of) himself. When his
policeman-like attempt to follow his victim to London fails, he asks:
'Am I never to get any nearer to the truth, but am I to be tormented
all my life by vague doubts, and wretched suspicions, which may
grow upon me till I become a monomaniac?' (p. 125). This is soon
confirmed by the text – 'The one idea of his life had become his
master. He was the bond slave of one gloomy thought – one horrible
presentiment' (p. 180) – and becomes a general comment on the
melodramatic narrative he builds:

> Why did that unaccountable terror seize upon me? . . . Why was
> it that I saw some strange mystery in my friend's disappearance?
> Was it a monition or a monomania? What if I am wrong after
> all? What if this chain of evidence which I have constructed
> link by link is woven out of my own folly? What if this edifice
> of horror and suspicion is a mere collection of crotchets – the
> nervous fancies of a hypochondriacal bachelor? (pp. 217–18)

The dialectic between the evidence of circumstance and the delusive ideas of subjective obsessions is a constant in sensation fiction.
Walter Hartright, recognizing that he has no grounds for his suspicions, 'Judging by the ordinary rules of evidence', asks himself,

'Had the events of the morning so unnerved me already that I was at the mercy of any delusion which common chances and common coincidences might suggest to my imagination?'[39] The very hermeneutic enterprise of the mystery novel begins to appear like a hypochondriacal obsession: 'It seemed almost like a monomania to be tracing back everything strange that happened, everything unexpected that was said, always to the same hidden source and the same sinister influence.'[40] The same dialectic also frames, even more self-consciously, Anna Katherine Green's 'Lawyer's Story' of 1878, *The Leavenworth Case* (a story which bears out Poe's intuition on the value of fiction in being used at Yale in the late nineteenth century to teach lawyers the dangers of circumstantial evidence). The focus is again the woman's secret – or the relation between two women and their secrets – generated by their reticence and by a collection of material clues, including a handkerchief stained with gun-oil. Both investigators, Mr. Raymond, the family lawyer, and Mr. Gryce, the detective, interpret a chain of 'evidence', which leads, ambiguously, to each of the nieces in turn, and, through them, to the suspicion of a secret marriage and the guilt of the supposed husband. However, Raymond constantly resists the force of evidence in favour of his irresistible and obsessive attraction to the women. He represents this as masculine honour – 'Miss Leavenworth, I am but a man; I cannot see you so distressed. Say that you are innocent, and I will believe you, without regard to appearances'[41] – yet it is precisely her 'appearance' which convinces him against the apparent evidence: '"She must be innocent; she cannot be otherwise," I reiterated to myself, and then, pausing, asked what warranty I had of this? Only her beautiful face; only, only her beautiful face.'[42] On the other hand, as one would expect, Mr. Gryce the detective is the unconditional spokesman for circumstantial evidence: 'Now it is a principle which every detective recognizes, that if of a hundred leading circumstances connected with a crime, ninety-nine of these are acts pointing to the suspected party with unerring certainty, but the hundredth equally important act one which that person could not have performed, the whole fabric of suspicion is destroyed.'[43] But what is this one crucial 'circumstance'? It is that the culprit had cleaned the weapon after the murder, and Gryce could not reconcile this fact with 'what I know of womankind.' What the detective Gryce knows about women is, for him, not an ideological and gendered theory, in short a masculine *idée fixe*, but a piece of circumstantial evidence on a par with a stained handkerchief. For all the talk of evidence, the narratives that both the family lawyer and the lower-class detective construct are so determined by their models of women that they fail to discover the real culprit; the case is resolved, to their joint surprise, by the old-fashioned and somewhat fortuitous confession of the insane secretary, Hanwell.

Both Mr. Raymond and Robert Audley (not to mention Walter Hartright) demonstrate that the detective eye turned on women is a sexualized eye, the eye of a voyeur, whose sense of reality is obsessively dominated by its idea of women. Although Robert, like Mr. Richmond, falls in love with the suspect at the very start, in his case the attraction battles with a profound and explicit mysogny: 'I hate women' (p. 178); it is women who are responsible for the loss of his friend George. He feels that women are 'the stronger sex, the noisier, the more persevering, the more self-assertive sex', and resents the power they exercise over him and his friend. It is, after all, George's sister, Clara, who forces him to continue with his investigation, disturbing his own tendency to passivity and leading him to threaten the family with exposure: 'What am I in the hands of this woman . . . ?' (p. 221). In sum, it is all a conspiracy against men: 'What a world it is, and how these women take life out of our hands. Helen Maldon, Lady Audley, Clara Talboys, and now Miss Tonks – all womankind from beginning to end' (p. 203). Robert expresses his anger against women and their power over him with the violence (and the cowardice) of the rapist. He wants to go 'straight to the arch-conspirator, and . . . tear away the beautiful veil under which she hides her wickedness' (p. 217), but, again like the rapist, he can only do so when he sees her 'no longer [as] a woman; a guilty woman with a heart which in its worst wickedness has yet some latent power to suffer and feel; I now look upon you as the demoniac incarnation of some evil principle' (p. 292). The chain of evidence he builds out of Lady Audley's life represents an obsessional delusion as violent and murderous as that of which she herself is accused.

None the less, it would appear that the plot endorses Robert's 'chain of evidence' in binding Lady Audley's biography. No one disputes the 'facts', and Lady Audley confesses both her criminality and her madness. Yet, although it makes little moral difference, the fact that the reader is deliberately surprised by the revelation that George is not, after all, dead, creates a major epistemological reserve about the inferences and beliefs constructed from circumstantial evidence. The whole narrative is premised on a delusion suggested to Robert (and, through him, to us) by circumstances, fears and expectations. However, in marrying the Baronet, Lucy was guilty of no more than a similar inference (after her husband had abandoned her for three years she believed that she had 'a right to think that he is dead, or that he wishes me to believe him dead' – p. 300). In this context, the fact that Lady Audley herself endorses the charge against her becomes particularly important. But the confession she makes to Robert explicitly equates 'the secret of my life' with 'the story of my life' (pp. 293–4) – in short, the secret she is to reveal encloses an alternative reading of the circumstances out of which Robert constructed her biography. And this reading, if it draws the same *ultimate* inferences of guilt and insanity as Robert's, does so *precisely because it is constructed by the same obsessive idea of insanity, criminality and evil.*

The key is clearly the early suggestion planted in her mind, there to dominate her reading of her own life: the idea that she has inherited insanity from her mother, whose image of a golden, peaceful, childish woman concealing a ferocious beast will characterize her own stereotypical portrayal. She recounts a life of motherlessness, internalized stigma, and poverty, how she was abandoned by her husband, forced to leave her child and enter into service, her good fortune, George's return, and now her persecution by Robert. If the latter organizes his reading by a conspiracy of women to take men's lives, Lady Audley is governed by her terror of its obverse, her imprisonment in the life, circumstances and obsessions men have created for her: 'afraid of my mother's horrible inheritance; afraid of poverty; afraid of George Talboys; afraid of *you*' (p. 331). Like any genuine obsessive idea, Helen's fear of her own suggested insanity is, by its nature, a self-fulfilling prophecy. Even in terms of the more strictly legal question of her bigamy, here too we see the circumstantiality and homocentricity of the dominating idea which condemns the woman. Like the heroine of Braddon's *Aurora Floyd* (1863), Lady Audley is only guilty of bigamy in a contingent and strictly legalistic sense. Even apart from her claim to believe her husband, for all intents and purposes, dead, her idea that she has the moral right to re-marry is more reasonable than the circumstances which prevent it; she is forced into secrecy by both George's selfish and inconsistent behaviour and the irrationality of the law. Abandonment was an area which the Divorce Act of 1857 – the year, we should note, of Helen Talboys' 'death' (p. 36) –, favouring the male partner in all its considerations (except custody of the children), had left incomplete. Although it was finally recognized as grounds for the breakdown of marriage, it did not yet allow for remarriage, but, by making the husband liable for his ex-wife's upkeep, maintained the woman's dependence. It is, in this case, the Law which frames Helen Talboys in an illegal state by keeping her imprisoned in a non-marriage.

In short, the circumstantial story she tells of her inheritance and her marriage clearly demands a different reading from that which, by mimicking Robert and Mosgrave's conspiracy, testifies to the power of the male obsession about women's madness and criminality and its legal and medical supports. If Lady Audley is, in the end, 'mad', it is clearly *'circumstances' which have made her mad*. The key 'circumstance', as with Gryce, is her idea about herself, and that is a conspicuously gendered idea based on contemporary medico-moral theories (although she is condemned as her mother's daughter, no anxiety is of course felt about her son). This then is what Robert, and George (who 'treated me as you treated me' – p. 333) had not realized: that by '[using] your power basely and cruelly' (p. 330), they 'did not know it was possible to drive me mad' (p. 332).

There is one more level at which the text subverts its own diagnosis of evidence in the light of monomaniacal obsessions. As we have seen, partial insanity cannot help but invoke the question of its status as madness. Lady Audley describes its first manifestation (not, as the diagnosis of her mother led her to suspect, when she had her child, but when she was abandoned by her husband shortly afterwards) in the following terms: 'at this time I became subject to fits of violence and despair. At this time I think my mind first lost its balance, and for the first time I crossed that invisible line which separates reason from madness' (p. 299). Whilst her 'hereditary' susceptibility to crossing that line makes her dangerous, we find that, once she has been rendered harmless, the charge of hypochondria against Robert is accepted, not as a danger, but as an extenuating circumstance: 'Do not laugh at poor Robert because he grew hypochondriacal, after hearing the horrible story of his friend's death. There is nothing so delicate, so fragile, as that invisible balance upon which the mind is always trembling; mad to-day and sane to-morrow .... Who has not been, or is not to be, mad in some lonely hour of life?' (p. 341 – cf. the earlier and equally sympathetic consideration of the question on pp. 175–6). In short, the text itself endorses hypochondria, the male counterpart of hysteria, like Cheyne had, as a natural and universal modern state, but only after the same model of partial insanity has served to bury Lady Audley alive.

If Robert is hypochondriacal, nervous, obsessional, and prone to cross the line between sanity and madness, what price the 'evidence' he invokes against his aunt's accusation? Whilst the plot obliges us to read Lady Audley's story as what Robert, the Law and Medicine 'know of womankind', its 'counter-plot' makes us aware how women are incarcerated in the obsessional concerns of men in relation to them. If their obsessions find support in circumstances, those circumstances are always already interpreted by the obsession. Indeed, the obsession is not only part of the circumstances, it is the circumstance with the greatest probative force. As Mosgrave diagnoses from Robert's story, the question of material evidence is secondary to the principle 'fact': 'you suspect!' (p. 320).

In the press reports of murder trials, the texts and reviews of sensation fiction, the studies of poverty and the textbooks of criminality and psychopathology, not to mention the legislation of the period, the men are obsessed by the nature of women, hesitating nervously between a vision of the woman as an 'angel in the house' who may turn out to be a 'madwoman in the attic' or a 'maniac in the cellar' – to invoke the obviously related titles given to their studies of the subject by Gilbert and Gubar and Winifred Hughes. A major source for this obsession lies in the growing gap between the world of the home and the world of work. As *Dombey and Son* makes pathologically clear, whilst in the public sphere the code of capitalist production and exchange consolidated its hegemony, the code of the private middle-class domestic environment, which must sustain the former without being contaminated by it, comes under increasing pressure, a pressure which falls on the woman:

> More than ever before, the home was an area quite distinct from the public sphere, a private world upholding different values, in theory the woman's domain, a family sanctuary . . . The anxieties concentrated on the lady of the house . . . stemmed precisely from the fact that she was . . . the guardian of the inner sanctuary, the 'angel in the house' . . . . Moreover as she was exclusively identified with the private sphere, it was not clear what her relation with the public sphere should or could be. Novelists who centre their mysteries on female members of the household are often uncertain whether they should be seen as rebels against the home and its legitimate head, or as partisans

so committed to the defence of the home's interests as to be incapable of understanding the just claims of the public sphere.[44]

As the relation between the home and the public sphere became
subject to interrogation, it is the women who, given their special
place as the point of articulation of the two spheres, become *suspect*.
Although the word exists before the nineteenth century, according
to the *Oxford English Dictionary* it gained a new currency 'due to its
revived use in connexion with the events of the French revolution',
specifically the *loi des suspects* of 1793.

The difference between the 'suspected person' of the English
Vagrancy Laws (reinforced by the Thames Police Act of 1800) and
the French 'suspect' is that the former is suspected of plotting an
economic crime, whereas the latter represents an explicitly political
threat. Individuals became suspect when 'soit par leur conduite,
soit par leurs relations, soit par leurs propres écrits, se sont montrés
les partisans de la tyrannie e du fédéralisme, et ennemis de la
liberté; ceux qui ne peuvent justifier de l'acquit de leurs devoirs
civiques; ceux à qui il a été refusé des certificats de civisme; ceux
des ci-devant nobles . . . qui n'ont pas constamment manifesté leur
attachement la révolution'.[45] Being suspect was sufficient condition
to suspend the regulation barring the police from invading the home
during the night: it was, in short, the extreme complement of the
total French police model. Translating this into a non-revolutionary
context, a suspect is someone who does not *actively* manifest their
support for the regime. The woman is necessarily suspect, in this
sense, because she *cannot*, given her contradictory position in the
conflicts between public and private spheres, give *positive* proof of
her support for the regime – except by the possibility offered by the
courts of the Terror, by denouncing others as suspect.

SUSPICION

In her article on 'Sensation Novels' Mrs. Oliphant complained that
'The sensation novel is . . . a literary institutionalisation of the
habits of mind of the new police force.' Since it is rarely the
policeman who solves the crime, this cannot be meant in the
terms in which we saw the 'romance of the detective' claiming
the territory for policing. Rather, as Anthea Trodd argues, the actual
police officer is 'tamed' in the course of the narrative, taught to

restrict himself to his sphere – basically that of the servant class – and to leave the question of middle-class family crime to 'genteel amateur detectives'.[46] In this way, D. A. Miller appears, in the end, to see no difference between realism and the sensation novel; in both the police corporation is disavowed the better to enforce its function indirectly.[47] A key text for this argument is Wilkie Collins' *The Moonstone* (1868) – the novel usually invoked, after Poe, as the 'first English detective novel'.

According to a review in the *Spectator*, 'The Moonstone is not worthy of Mr. Wilkie Collins's reputation as a novelist . . . ', whilst *The Nation* argued that, in relation to Collins, 'The word "novel" . . . is an absurd misnomer, however that word is understood.'[48] *The Moonstone* appears to register Mrs. Beard's transition as the text in which the sensational effects of the popular novel initiated their decline by reducing the neurotic effect to the 'thrilling', a mechanical narrative of merely intellectual curiosity. But I do not feel that the notion of 'thrill' is really adequate. What *The Moonstone* does is to select one of the sensations experienced in the genre and build it into the universe of the text. It represents the habits of thought of the modern 'police' to the extent that it portrays the 'nervous state' specifically as a 'state of suspicion', and what it most suspects is, of course, the woman. Thus, if, as Miller argues, 'one of the major sites' of its 'ideology' lies 'in the perception of everyday life as fundamentally "outside" the network of policing power', this is only true in a strictly institutional sense.[49] Its reintroduction of an informal police 'discipline' within the family cannot necessarily be taken to imply a reassuring limitation of police when the text makes us equally aware, as Miller also says, that 'a policing power is inscribed in the ordinary practices and institutions of the world from the start'.[50] What critics refer to as the 'amateur genteel detectives' (in Franklin's case, more amatory than amateur, and more cruel than genteel, since, amongst other things, his behaviour drives Rosanna to her death) may be seen to represent not a reassurance against police but a recognition that the global project of policing in its multiplicity of forms had become the modern condition informing all human relations, even the private and middle-class – what Franklin Blake refers to as 'the atmosphere of mystery and suspicion in which we are all living now'.[51] In sum, in contrast to the realist novel, sensation fiction cannot disavow the 'police' universe for that, indeed, is its subject. Suspicion is not an ideological subterfuge but a deliberate narrative principle which draws attention to itself by the way it makes us aware that, obviously, we too are contaminated. Part of the effect *The Moonstone* manufactures is to deny us refuge from its universe, as suspicion comes to structure the reading experience itself. What we catch here is not hysteria but what the archetypically eighteenth-century figure, the head servant Betteredge, unconsciously ironizing the narrative's effect, significantly calls 'detective fever' (pp. 160 and *passim*).

The Moonstone, like many of Collins' other novels, is frequently castigated for adopting a legalistic frame. Some of the issues this involves have already been discussed in the previous chapter. Once again, the legalism is firstly epistemological and literary: 'I am to keep strictly within the limits of my own experience . . . In this matter of the Moonstone the plan is, not to present reports, but to produce witnesses' (Betteredge, p. 232); '(alas!) I am not permitted to improve – I am condemned to narrate' (Miss Clack, p. 241). It puts in explicit confrontation the police paradigm of knowledge inferred from 'circumstances' and 'experience' and the family paradigm of personal knowledge (see the debate between Cuff and Lady Verinder, pp. 205–7). More dramatically in this particular case, we are placed 'in all respects like a Judge on the bench' in order to hear a crime story which is at the same time a love story and a family story. In arguing that Collins' penchant for the 'judicial model' represents a desire to extend the Law and its discipline beyond what it ordinarily covers, Miller overlooks the fact that this discipline has already been reaching into these areas, with the full panoply of legal, hygienic and moral 'police' since the early days of Reform.[52] If, as Barickman *et al.* point out, 'The Victorian novel in general shifts attention from courtship as a relation between individuals to courtship as a ritual conditioned by family life',[53] Collins' novels present that family life not primarily as a natural phenomenon but as an institution increasingly inscribed in Law. At least it was so for the woman, who, when she married, literally lost her independent legal identity and her right to her own personal property, and found herself 'in the same category with criminals, lunatics, and minors as being legally incompetent and irresponsible'.[54] 1867 saw the failure of John Stuart Mill's attempt to have 'persons' substituted for 'men' in the Reform Bill, and the following year a massive decade-long campaign by women resulted in the unsuccessful presentation of a Bill to reform the married women's property law. To regard sexual relations in this light in the late 1860s puts in place the central preoccupation of women during the period: their legal status within marriage, particularly the identity of married women and their position as owners and transmitters of property.

If Collins' *No Name* takes off from the dependence of women for their very identity on the Law, *The Moonstone* is primarily a story of the woman as owner and transmitter of inheritance, an issue of clear importance in relation to the Social Darwinism which was to legitimize the collapse of Reform. The universe of this story – with the important exception of the Indians – is circumscribed by the family, almost all the characters being members, servants or employees. It is also a family in crisis. The patriarch, referred to only by the biblical form of 'the old lord' (p. 41), has been dead for some time, as have his two sons, Arthur (the inheritor of the title) and John (the original thief of the diamond). Neither son had married, but his three daughters, Adelaide, Julia and Caroline married Mr. Blake, Sir John Verinder, and Mr. Abelwhite respectively. The issues of these marriages are three cousins: Franklin Blake, Rachel Verinder, and Godfrey Abelwhite. However, the family is divided by a dispute between Julia Verinder and John Herncastle because of the diamond which Julia's brother posthumously leaves to his niece. It is this inheritance which lies at the heart of the story. Thus we find Rachel: about to celebrate her eighteenth birthday, she receives from her maternal uncle a diamond which, theoretically, should enhance her marriageability.[55] But the question the legacy poses is whether the gift represents a family reconciliation, or a mortal attack on the family's future: 'In bringing the Moonstone to my aunt's house,' Franklin asks, 'am I serving his vengeance blindfold, or am I vindicating him in the character of a penitent and Christian man?' (p. 75). In this deliberately closed universe, Rachel's marriage choice is restricted to her cousins, and the future of the family depends on her opting correctly between Godfrey, the modern, self-made liberal philanthropist and 'manager', 'the man whom the women couldn't do without' (pp. 89–90), and Franklin, 'one of those men the women all like' (p. 224). The Moonstone, responsible, in Cuff's words, for 'upsetting your sleeping arrangements' (p. 180), nearly brings Rachel to make a fatally wrong marriage choice – or does it ensure she makes the right choice?

What then is the Moonstone? Like the purloined letter, its principal value is symbolic and depends on the position of the subject – the two extremes being Godfrey, for whom it has merely commercial value, and the Hindus for whom it has only religious value. At the

same time, as the Prologue makes clear, it is first of all the source
of the family rupture (which explicitly cannot be resolved by the
courts), and, at the last, a threat to the family's future, passing, in
the meantime, as the occasion for the intervention of the police in the
family's affairs. It is the 'wicked Colonel' himself who establishes
the broad terms of the diamond's action:

> He never attempted to sell it . . . . He never gave it away; he
> never even showed it to any living soul. Some said he was afraid
> of its getting him into a difficulty with the military authorities;
> others (very ignorant indeed of the real nature of the man) said
> he was afraid, if he showed it, of its costing him his life.
>
> There was perhaps a grain of truth mixed up with this last
> report: It was false to say that he was afraid; but it was a
> fact that his life had been twice threatened in India; and it
> was firmly believed that the Moonstone was at the bottom of
> it. When he came back to England, and found himself avoided
> by everybody, the Moonstone was thought to be at the bottom
> of it again. The mystery of the Colonel's life got in the Colonel's
> way, and outlawed him, as you may say, among his own people.
> The men wouldn't let him into their clubs; the women – more
> than one – whom he wanted to marry, refused him; friends and
> relations got too near-sighted to see him in the street . . . .
>
> We heard different rumours about him from time to time.
> Sometimes they said he was given up to smoking opium and
> collecting old books; sometimes he was reported to be trying
> strange things in chemistry; sometimes he was seen carousing
> and amusing himself among the lowest people in the lowest
> slums of London. Anyhow, a solitary, vicious, underground life
> was the life the Colonel led. (p. 64)

The main characteristic of the stone is the need to keep it hidden,
since its revelation would bring its owner into conflict with the
Law ('the military authorities') and, eventually, cause his death.
However, although hidden, the stone continues to work its effect,
placing its owner outside the law and outside society: he is denied
masculine friendship, marriage and normal family relations. It com-
pels him to an 'underground' life, a life of transgressive knowledge
and vicious pleasures. This is how the diamond continues to work
in the text. From the moment it is hidden it reveals that the major
figures it touches all have a secret which, in one way or another,

isolates them from their community and brings them into potential conflict with the Law which should bind them.

Mainly of course the diamond affects Rachel's matrimonial value. For a brief moment it seems to enhance her as a potential bride, but very soon:

> 'this is a more important matter than you may suppose'.
> 'It's a matter of twenty thousand pounds, sir!', I said, thinking of the value of the diamond.
> 'It's a matter of quieting Rachel's mind', answered Mr. Franklin gravely. (p. 130)

As events develop and suspicion actually falls on Rachel, Betteredge rapidly realizes that 'It was no longer a question of quieting my young lady's nervous excitement; it was a question of proving her innocence' (p. 179). As the Moonstone attacks Rachel's 'innocence' via the 'nervous excitement' its loss provokes in her 'mind', once again, the woman falls under the alternative and successive scrutinies of medical and legal codes. Rachel is as respectable a young lady as one could wish to see in a nineteenth-century novel; yet she is as incarcerated by fixed ideas as Lady Audley. As Barickman *et al.* again point out, one of the means of manifesting and questioning dominant stereotypes is through the symbolic pairing of characters, often linking the genteel with the lower class.[56] In Rachel's case, she is clearly paired with the servant, Rosanna, the only figure who might 'save' her: 'Nothing but the tracing of the Moonstone to our second housemaid could now raise Miss Rachel above the infamous suspicion that rested on her in the mind of Sergeant Cuff' (p. 179). If Rachel's strength is her 'independence', going 'on a way of her own', her 'secrecy and self-will' (p. 87), and her 'self-control' (p. 172), Rosanna's vice is her 'silent tongue and her solitary ways' (p. 55). This bears out the class- as well as the gender-base of contemporary theories of suspiciousness which permitted the articulation of the Contagious Diseases Act with the vision of middle-class genteel sexual purity. Indeed, according to Betteredge's sympathetic appreciation of the servant, 'there was just a dash of something that wasn't like a housemaid, and that *was* like a lady, about her.'

Rosanna also suffers from an 'unquiet mind' (p. 58). This is visible even before the loss of the Diamond, being related to her obsession with her criminal past and her attraction to the 'melancholy'

Shivering Sands, a place which, like Rachel's Moonstone, obeys the cycles of the moon. Her 'unaccountable behaviour' defeats both Franklin's 'foreign training' and Betteredge's 'English' criteria, 'age, experience, and natural mother-wit' (p. 60). After the loss of the diamond the servant comes under closer scrutiny. Whilst Rosanna is, from the moment Franklin arrives, 'merry without reason, and sad without reason' (p. 79), her 'strange language and behaviour' (p. 129) finds a parallel in Rachel's 'extraordinary language and conduct' (p. 123): Rachel is 'In a rage, one moment; in tears, the next! What did it mean?' (p. 123) It means, as Rachel's London doctor diagnoses from these classic symptoms, that she is suffering from hysteria. So too, of course, is Rosanna, who has 'what they call an hysterical attack' (p. 130) immediately following Franklin's confession of 'uneasiness' about Rachel's mind, and who is led by her hysteria to suicide (this being seen at the time as a common danger with hysterics).[57]

As Rachel's behaviour places in danger first her mind and then her innocence, in Rosanna's case, according to Franklin, 'either . . . [her] head is not quite right, or I am afraid she knows more about the Moonstone than she ought to know' (p. 127). The only alternative to the confirmation of the incorrigible criminality of this deformed ex-Reformatory girl, is the suspicion of an insanity caused by an uncontrollable and illicit sexual passion for the gentleman – 'mad enough to set her heart on Mr. Franklin Blake' (p. 151). The difference between Rosanna and Rachel is that, whilst the former's strange language and behaviour gives rise to explanations which offer a choice between madness and badness, her sexual or her criminal guilt, in Rachel's case the sexual explanation cannot be contemplated. Cuff outrages everyone by suspecting her of stealing her own diamond; but in fact no other explanation for her hysteria is entertained. Not even the policeman is capable of suspecting that the young lady is as capable as the prostitute's daughter of harbouring illicit sexual passions.

Yet the irony is that the two alternative readings turn out to be equally true in both cases. Both Rosanna and Rachel conceal from the family and the police what they believe to be the criminal truth of the theft, and both are led to defy the Law because they are irresistibly in love with the thief. It is precisely this that makes Rachel hysterical. When Godfrey declares his love, Rachel offers to make her own 'confession'. For Rachel, love is something one 'confesses', like a guilty secret. But both Godfrey and Miss Clack suspiciously assume 'that she was about to divulge the mystery of the Moonstone'. The confession turns out, after all, to be both these things. The truly shocking is what no one could suspect; the confession of the mystery of the Moonstone is a confession of her own, literally unspeakable, sexuality:

> Oh, how can I find words to say it in! How can I make a *man* understand that a feeling which horrifies me at myself, can be a feeling that fascinates me at the same time? It's the breath of my life, Godfrey, and it's the poison that kills me – both in one! . . . Are you doctor enough, Godfrey, to tell me why I feel as if I was stifling for want of breath? Is there a form of hysterics that bursts into words instead of tears? I dare say! (p. 279) .

How could she 'dare say', some thirty years before Anna O. coined the felicitous phrase for the uncovering of the sexual origins of hysteria, the 'talking cure'? None the less, she is able to signal the area of the mystery: a morally ambivalent sexual feeling ('the breath of my life') which both horrifies and fascinates her, but which, in any case, a man cannot understand. Of course, Godfrey and Clack are no more capable of reading Rachel's hysterical discourse than anyone else had been.

In short then the Moonstone attacks Rachel's mind and her innocence by making her hysterical, like Rosanna. The discourse of this hysteria becomes the focus for a conflict between legal codes (criminal guilt) and medical codes (sexual guilt). In the context, Freud's lecture to law students on 'Psycho-Analysis and the Ascertaining of the Truth in Courts of Law' (1906) must strike us as particularly remarkable. But, given Bentham's 'moral thermometer' and Dupin's mathematical science of the spiritual for assessing evidence, perhaps not so. Especially as, under the modern state, sexuality becomes increasingly dominated by the codes of Law, then perhaps there is no reason not to invert the relationship and use the science of the (sexual) subject to read testimony in court. Indeed, Freud's intervention in this field is provoked by a peculiarly Benthamite – and realist – concern: 'There is a growing recognition of the untrustworthiness of statements made by witness, at present the basis of so many judgments in Courts of Law.'[58] In *The Moonstone* too, we find that the governing empiricist paradigm and its agents prove capable of presenting, but incapable of resolving, the mystery. The only way to achieve this is through the intervention of a

psychologist, Ezra Jennings, who, in a procedure which can be read
as an anticipation of psychoanalysis, introduces a novel strategy,
like Freud's proposal, which will by-pass the empiricist test and
render Bentham's 'moral thermometer' of persuasion redundant
by, in Freud's words, leading 'the accused person to establish his
own guilt or innocence objectively.' But even Freud recognizes the
outrageousness of his proposal to install the medical authority in the
place of the judge: 'To allay your surprise,' he writes, 'I must work
out an analogy between the criminal and the hysteric.'[59] The once
again potentially conflicting interpretations of a given behaviour by
Law and Medicine can be brought back into alignment because, in
fact, their two objects, the criminal and the hysteric, are analogous.

The point is that the analogy was always, in a sense, there, at
least since witches were burnt under criminal ordinance. Hysteria
was, as we have seen, a form of partial insanity in which the subject
surrenders control of her will, even of her body; at the same time
it was always seen as the locus of the moral pathology of female
sexuality. Although it freed hysteria from the organic association
with the female suggested by its etymology, the theory of moral
insanity retained the association with the sexual nature of the
woman, particularly her emotional instability and her sensuality.
For the spokesman of the mid-Victorian fashion for hysteria, Robert
Carter (1853), although sexual passion was not the only factor, it
was by far the most frequent and important, largely because women
were more sensitive and more obliged to repress their sexual needs;
those women who failed to do so successfully – the hysteric – were
probably suffering from an excess of sexuality.[60] At the same time,
its imitative tendency came to be seen as an aspect of women's
basic and essentially sexual duplicity – Jules Falret, psychiatrist
at the Salpêtrière, arguing a similar case to Carter in his 'Folie
raisonnante ou folie morale' (1866), characterized the emotionally
volatile, sensitive women suffering from exaggerated passions as
'veritable actresses; they do not know of a greater pleasure than
to deceive . . . . In one word, the life of the hysteric is nothing but
one perpetual falsehood; they affect the airs of piety and devotion
and let themselves be taken for saints while at the same time
secretly abandoning themselves to the most shameful actions'.[61]
If, from one point of view, women were trapped into hysteria by
their criminal sexual excess, they were kept there by the denial
of any sexuality at all. In post-Reform England, William Acton's
Prostitution considered in its moral, social and sanitary aspects (1857) and

his highly influential *The Functions and Disorders of the Reproductive Organs* (1865) distinguished two models. For lower-class women, the danger continued to be a consequence of a pathological sexuality. But 'the average, healthy woman does not experience sexual feelings and submits to sexual advances only in so far as these are subservient to the maternal instinct'.[62] Middle-class hysteria was a result of the contradictory forces of the biological need to reproduce and the natural repugnance that sensitive women felt for sexual activity. In either case, then, women were perceived as pathological and anti-social to the extent that they manifested sexual passion.

There are three constants in the story of hysteria: its connection to the sexual nature of women, its quasi-criminal association with immoral excess and loss of self-control, and its protean nature. As Ilza Veith says, 'the manifestations of the disease tended to change from era to era . . . The symptoms, it seems, were conditioned by social expectancy, tastes, mores, and religion, and were further shaped by the state of medicine in general and the knowledge of the public about medical matters . . . .'[63] But 'knowledge' would appear to be the wrong word. Already in the eighteenth century Willis had observed that

> when at any time a sickness happens in a Woman's Body, of an unusual manner, or more occult original, so that its causes lie hid, and a Curatory indication is altogether uncertain, presently we accuse the evil influence of the Womb (which for the most part is innocent) and in every unusual symptom, we declare it to be something hysterical, and so to this scope, which oftentimes is only the subterfuge of ignorance, the medical intentions and use of Remedies are directed.[64]

In other words, according to Foucault's gloss, 'the idea of hysteria is a catchall for the fantasies, not of the person who is or believes himself ill, but of the ignorant doctor who pretends to know why'.[65] As in *Lady Audley's Secret*, what informs that ignorance are masculine fears and disapprovals of female sexuality.

We have already seen that what the detective Gryce knows about women is a fact constitutive of truth. What men don't know about women is a challenge to their authoritative position as masters of the code which defines and narrates reality and has to be expelled into the non-existent or the unnatural. So, if they insist in behaving 'impossibly' or monstrously, what men do not know can only be what women are not telling. This is what makes them suspect: their reticence, their hysterical weeping rather than speaking, their tendency to imitate and to lie, their commitment to private secrecy is nothing less than a challenge to the mastery of masculine knowledge.

In this way, it is Rachel's idiosyncratic independence that becomes responsible for making her an object of suspicion. This begins in the sexual register, before the loss of the diamond. Whereas Franklin's desire for his cousin is transparent, 'The difficulty was to fathom Miss Rachel' (p. 86). As soon as the diamond disappears, it is her silence that perpetuates the mystery – as Cuff observes, 'But for her self-control, the mystery that puzzles you, Mr. Betteredge, would have been at an end to-night' (p. 172). The two moments are clearly related: just as she refuses to 'show her mind' after Franklin's proposal (p. 91), 'the whole of this case . . . will tumble into pieces, if we can only break through Rachel's inveterate reserve, and prevail upon her to speak out' (Bruff, p. 384) – speak out and 'show her whole mind in this matter, without reserve' (p. 387). This is, of course, specifically what characterizes the woman as, in the French sense, 'suspect': the refusal to denounce. It becomes essential to take her roof off. Bruff, the family lawyer, advises Franklin to exploit Rachel's 'certain perverse weakness for *you*' (not knowing that this is precisely what is causing her silence): 'Touch that – and . . . trust to the consequences for the fullest disclosures that can flow from a woman's lips!' (p. 387) For Rachel, this 'seems a cowardly experiment, to try an experiment on my weakness for you . . . . But that is only a woman's view. I ought to have known it couldn't be your view. I should have done better if I had controlled myself, and said nothing' (p. 391). Franklin insists, and is temporarily reassured to know that 'while her hand lay in mine I was her master still!' (p. 393) But even then her hysterical language remains opaque to him; it merely confirms 'that she was in a state of dangerous nervous excitement' and resuscitates his earlier suspicion 'whether the loss of the jewel was as much a mystery to her as to the rest of us' (p. 401) – leaving Rachel, in short, in the same position as Rosanna.

Rachel's refusal or inability to speak her '*whole*' mind is related to the very model of characterization in this book. As we know, the attack on plot in sensation novels is related to a critique of the superficiality of characterization, the lack of a developed discourse of individual consciousness. But, as Barickman *et al.* point out,

authors like Collins and Dickens 'implicitly challenge their culture's
growing reliance on a consciously directed moral will as the means
to correct the world's evils. None of them even locates the center
of fictional interest in consciousness . . . Consciousness is not the
source of primary conflict, nor the agent of resolution . . . . Consciousness in these novels is a partial, imperfect register of conflicts
whose psychological depth and social range can only be represented
through symbolic configurations of plot and character.'[66] The characters of the realist novel have a mind to speak, but here neither the
hero nor the heroine can be that sort of 'character', for, in a very
important sense, their problem is that they do not know their minds
– in the sense that it is not their 'minds' which are responsible for
their actions.

This then is another effect of the Moonstone, it takes life out of
the hands of consciousness. 'At the turn of the tide, something
goes on in the unknown depths below, which sets the whole
face of the quicksand shivering and trembling' (p. 55); or, as
Betteredge complains, 'The cursed Moonstone had turned us all
upside down' (p. 118). Franklin reasons in his absurd dialectical
way that 'Rachel . . . is not Rachel, but Somebody Else' (p. 215).
Yet, he will find this out about himself – in Rimbaud's words, 'Je
est un autre'. Although he too is a man who is 'in a state of perpetual
contradiction with himself' (p. 77), nothing could be more dramatic
than his discovery that he is himself the thief. He is 'innocent of
all knowledge of having taken the Diamond . . . But there is the
witness against me' – his stained nightgown, which is as likely to
raise our sexual suspicions as it did Rosanna's (pp. 361, 366). We
should note that the section in which Franklin discovers this truth is
the first one that he, the editor of this story, himself narrates, putting
into sharp contradiction the reliability of the subject as witness and
the subjectivity to which he bears witness. This contradiction, the
lack of knowledge of one's own (criminal) behaviour, is monstrous,
'the abominable impossibility which, nevertheless, confronts me as
an undeniable fact' (p. 360).

Who is to narrate this, and how? We might remember how 'the
mystery of the Colonel's life got in the Colonel's way' (p. 64). So
too, Betteredge asks as he begins his empiricist, legalistic narrative,
so clearly related back to the eighteenth-century model of realism
through his religious commitment to *Robinson Crusoe*, 'I am asked
to tell the story of the Diamond, and, instead of that, I have been
telling the story of my own self. Curious, and quite beyond me to

account for. I wonder whether the gentlemen who make a business and a living out of writing books, ever find their own selves getting in the way of their subjects, like me?' (p. 45) People's mysteries, their selves, get in their way, subverting their lives and their narratives and characterizations. Franklin can only be saved when he finds not himself but 'the irrepressible Ezra Jennings getting in my way again!' (p. 409).

The hysterical behaviour of Rachel and Rosanna is subject to interrogation by the various codes to be found within the family (servant, lover, mother), by caricatures of eighteenth-century empiricism, continental dialectics, and evangelism, by the public police (circumstance and experience), the private lawyer, and the doctors. A very lively and complete epistemological debate is established between 'characters' who, in place of an illusion of self-consciousness, become identified, in a Dupin-like fashion, by their theoretical or ideological positions. Winifred Hughes claims that here 'the professional viewpoint begins to take over' in what has become a 'tidy, complacent literary product'.[67] For Philip O'Neil, on the other hand, the text puts in question 'the validity of philosophical premise and the ability to provide interpretations of our world' in which 'what are at issue, are the difficulties involved in all interpretation rather than the relative merits of any particularised philosophy.' For him, 'it would be a mistake to read his success as a vindication of Jennings' scientific method'.[68] It seems to me however that the truth lies between these two positions: the foregrounding of the mechanisms for narrating this mystery do manifest a world of professional and ideological power, but it does so in a far from 'complacent' manner; rather, critical discriminations are introduced between the way the various discursive positions construct and interpret the mystery. How one views this question necessarily depends on how one reads Ezra Jennings.

One of O'Neil's points against Jennings' importance as any more than a providential device relates to his sources, W. B. Carpenter and John Elliotson. He dismisses any serious claims for Jennings on the grounds that 'while Carpenter was a respectable scholar and genuine scientist, Elliotson, on the other hand, was a suspect character and had something of the reputation of a quack'.[69] Elliotson, Professor of Physic at University College, London and Fellow of the Royal Society, was converted to mesmerism in 1837, when he began to use it as an anaesthetic during surgical operations. Because of this practice and his publicizing of mesmerism through his journal of social improvement, *The Zooist*, Elliotson was hounded out of his job. Yet, as L. S. Hearnshaw argues, his anaesthetic technique 'may have overcome professional opposition had not Sir James Simpson discovered the anaesthetic properties of chloroform in 1847'.[70] By the same token, the only alternative to his mesmeric and phreno-logical explanation of the phenomena was that elaborated by Braid which, despite being explicitly designed to free the phenomena from their mystical associations, was also 'greeted with incredulity in scientific circles'.[71] Given the continuing lack of interest in the subject, it is clear, as J. H. Conn suggests, that it was not Elliotson's reputation that brought his mesmeric practice into disrepute, but vice versa.[72]

Contemporary psychology remained fixed in its two models: a philosophical theory of consciousness (associationism) and a physio-logical theory of nervous organization (neurology); what it very simply could not cope with was any theory of 'automatism' that presupposed what was held to be a contradiction in terms, an intelligent psychological unconscious. Even Carpenter, with his physiological notion of 'unconscious cerebration' (1853), did not produce so much a theory as what his colleague, Sir Henry Holland, called a 'programme' – a programme of a very disreputable sort for the study of the structure of the human mind: 'Dreaming – insanity in its many forms – intoxication from wine or narcotics – and the phenomena arising from cerebral disease, are the four great mines of mental discovery open to us.'[73] We might of course note how these are also four great themes for sensation fiction. Despite Braid, work on hypnotic automatism remained as suspect to professional science as the Indian's 'hocus pocus', their 'trick' with 'some black stuff, like ink' (p. 50), is to Betteredge. Throughout the second half of the nineteenth century, the study of the unconscious was forced into association with disreputably 'mystical' areas, with the result that, by the end of the century, the only place in England where such matters as hypnotic phenomena were pursued with any scientific seriousness and where Freud's theory received any sympathetic attention was the Society for Psychical Research (whilst the Society welcomed his work on hysteria in 1893, a meeting of the British Medical Association walked out on a paper read by the Freudian M. D. Eder as late as 1911). Although they were accused of resurrecting mysticism in their use of hypnosis with hysterics, none the less it was initially hypnosis that offered the first approaches to a science of the unconscious for Charcot, Janet and Freud before the latter abandoned it for the not much more respectable materials of the hysterical discourse (the 'talking cure') and the dream.

This is the context in which Ezra Jennings' providential intervention to save the family should be viewed. It would represent a complacent recuperation of policing and a careful marking of its public limits, were Jennings, like Mosgrave, a representative of post-Reform medicine working as a *complement* to the detective police. But Jennings is not the nineteenth-century psychopathologist – that is Dr. Downward of *Armadale*, the abortionist and murderer whose transformation into a fashionable psychiatrist is greeted ironically at the end of the book: 'In this enlightened nineteenth century, I look upon the doctor as one of our rising men.'[74] Jennings is, like Elliotson, a 'médécin maudit', on the margins of his science, his profession, and his society (like the Colonel and like Collins, especially at the time of writing *The Moonstone*, he is addicted to opium). As a doctor, nobody trusts him (p. 187), 'Nobody likes him', more than that, 'Nobody knows who he is' (p. 372). By his own confession, he is a man 'whose character is gone' (p. 428) of whom all we know is that he has a secret which has resulted in 'a horrible accusation' and the loss of a past love, but what that secret is, we shall never know – 'My story will die with me' (p. 427) – and, indeed, before the story ends, Jennings is already dead: 'His story is a blank' (p. 515). Without a character or a story, but only a hidden secret, Jennings is entirely a mystery. A man who looks 'old and young both together', with hair that is half black, half white, an Englishman with exotic foreign blood (pp. 419, 371), Jennings is, in short, not a character but, like Dupin, a site of incompatibilities in search of a synthesis. The last, and, in the context of the gendered ideological positions of this universe, perhaps the most important, of his contradictions is his sexuality. He tells Franklin that, after saving Dr. Candy, he burst into tears: 'An hysterical relief, Mr. Blake – nothing more! Physiology says, and says truly, that some men are born with female constitutions – and I am one of them!' (p. 422) *Anima mulieris in corpore virili inclusa*, to use the German lawyer Karl Ulrichs' medical expression for homosexuality as a congenitally-determined form of moral insanity.[75] This confession is, in narrative terms, so redundant that it cannot help but subvert the dominant masculine narrative of power – what men know about women – of Medicine. If Jennings, as the figure who enables the mystery to solve itself, obeys the principle of symmetry we have hitherto observed, then he clearly reinforces the association of the

Moonstone with female sexuality (Rachel and Rosanna's 'hysteria', the Shivering Sands, and the diamond itself). And lastly it follows that, if the mystery he has to reveal is Franklin's unconscious, that unconscious becomes signalled as a site of similarly contradictory (or, as Freud was to have it, 'polymorphous') sexuality.

Jennings is a 'nerve doctor' whose manuscript on 'the brain and the nervous system' certainly articulates precisely what was rejected by the orthodox neurophysiology which had recaptured the asylum, most particularly, the existence of an intelligent unconscious (p. 423). In order to solve the mystery of the Moonstone, he has to invoke a reading of Dr. Candy's fragmented delirium and a theory of intelligent unconscious action on the basis of an obsessive anxiety under the influence of a narcotic-induced hypnotic trance. This theory is as unacceptable to the Law as it is to contemporary science because it is, given the potential fields of research on unconscious phenomena, inevitably based on 'circumstances entirely out of the experience of the mass of mankind.' The only epistemological guarantee that can be offered is Jennings himself, and he has already been disqualified as a witness because of his difference, his lack of 'character' (p. 438). It would equally well be unacceptable to realist narrative, inasmuch as it is postulated on the superiority of the fragmentary symptoms of obsessive unconscious thought to the novelistic sense of consciousness (p. 424). Jennings proposes material and a mode of reading which, bearing in mind the accusations made against *The Moonstone* itself, he compares provocatively to 'a child's "puzzle"' in which one has to fill in the blanks in the text.

Even more impossible than Dupin, Jennings breaks the empiricist paradigm of knowledge, witness, character and narrative in which the novel is so strictly cast both in theory and person. He cannot reassure, because for him to exist the epistemological structure of Science and Law and its cognate narrative structure of literary realism would have to change radically. He is the one blank that the narrative cannot fill. Thus, in order to make his theory acceptable and useful to the family it is to save, Jennings is obliged to re-enter the novel's explicit epistemology and undertake an experiment which, by artificially reproducing the original event before witnesses, overcomes the epistemological objections to his theory. He is successful; even Bruff, 'immersed in Law; impenetrable to Medicine' (p. 471) is persuaded to abandon his view that this was a case of 'mesmerism, clairvoyance and the like' (p. 452). But of course, the salvation of the family – and of the compatibility of Law and Medicine – is extremely fragile, nerve-wracking in the way it stretches our credibility. To imagine this science bringing its extraordinary truths of the unconscious subject into alignment with the empiricist paradigms which, historically, was always to deny its scientificity, particularly in terms of its inability to predict and reproduce its results in the laboratory,[76] is only likely as science phantasy, a gesture towards the resolution of a contradiction. The reader knows that such perversive behaviour is unreproducible – except perhaps in a text this which so perversely subtitles itself 'A Romance'.

Well, a happy ending; *The Moonstone* is, after all, more a comedy than a melodrama – but if it is a comedy, it is a somewhat nervous one. Although we might be tempted by the surface of the text, we should not forget that Rachel's double, Rosanna, has been sacrificed, and her friend's invocation against Franklin, 'the day is not far off when the poor will rise against the rich. I hope they will start with *him*' (p. 227) still lingers, as does the revenge extorted by the jewel of Victoria's crown. In the meantime, as it circulated, the mystery of the Moonstone has opened a number of new mysteries and turned the suspicious eye on two genteel young lovers. Apart from denouncing the hypocrisy of the philanthropic Godfrey, it has shown that the gentleman Franklin is not the self-sufficient, self-conscious and self-controlled subject he should be as a hero, and that he is governed by an unconscious in which, it is implied, the gender identities attributed to characters may not be so decisively clear. It has also shown that Rachel, capable of loving and protecting a man she believes to be a thief and incapable of mastering her sexuality, is considerably closer to Rosanna than one might 'suspect'. The fact that, providentially, it turns out that Franklin's unconscious is well-intentioned (all he did was, despite Rachel's not having accepted his proposal, to act as her husband, treating his desired wife's property as if it were already his!) and that Rachel's belief in his guilt was misplaced, does not alter the equally important fact that, believing otherwise, she protected her criminal lover like the worst villainness of a sensational novel. More radically still, in a story which claims 'to trace the influence of character on circumstance' (Preface, p. 28), it has shown that the notion of 'character' is incapable of narrating the truth of the 'underground' life and of female sexuality which is uncovered by the cursed diamond.

The Moonstone is, like Jennings and his experiment, quite anomalous. It clearly has extremely little to do with the 'romance of the detective'/'detective story'. Yet Miller claims that the novel 'begins by invoking and observing the norms of detective fiction' but 'with Cuff's failure and departure, [it] stages a conspicuous modification of what had seemed to be its program.'[77] But how can the 'first detective novel' violate the norms it is claimed to establish? Certainly, Cuff is a stock figure clearly recognizable from Dickens' 'real' policemen (and from the real policeman in the Constance Kent case on whom he too is modeled) who does serve as a model for the later Gryce and Holmes. But his failure here cannot be equated with Jennings' success in the way that Mosgrave fills the police/law gap in *Lady Audley's Secret*. He is the phantastic personification and the embryonic theorization of precisely what contradicts the police 'habits of thought' which Miller would have him uphold, in the same way as *The Moonstone* contradicts the genre it is held to found.

Collins recognizes more perhaps than any other writer that Law is the master code, which, having recruited Medicine to the same 'police' project, is responsible for the oppressive suspicion against women. But the text senses the possibility of another 'medical and metaphysical theory' (p. 438) which contradicts that 'police', contradicting at the same time the image of the individual and his coherent narrative of consciousness where reason disciplines all mysteries. If it is reason which wins here, it is a reason against that which underwrites the paradigm of empiricist witness on which modern law, science and fiction are based. Until a science emerges which can narrate Jennings' mysteries, the Moonstone returns to its place in the forehead of the Hindu Moon goddess, from whence, although temporarily invisible to English eyes, it still insists: 'What will be the next adventures of the Moonstone? Who can tell!' (p. 526).

Part IV
Writing Right?

8

The Master

In one of its senses, the Moonstone does keep coming back in the early Sherlock Holmes stories. Of the twenty-five stories published in four volumes up to Holmes' 'death' (*A Study in Scarlet*, 1887; *The Sign of Four*, 1890; *Adventures of Sherlock Holmes*, 1892; *Memoirs of Sherlock Holmes*, 1894), in no less than ten the crime is connected with events in or wealth from the former colonies. We have wicked colonels, hidden crimes, secret societies, and savage assassins; but, despite the insistence of the Indian Mutiny, transportation and the American Civil War, thanks to Holmes, in no case will the sins of the imperialist fathers be visited upon the children. Indeed, in one of his rare sallies into social comment, Holmes defends a new imperial federation: 'I am one of those who believe that the folly of a monarch and the blundering of a minister in far-gone years will not prevent our children from being some day citizens of the same world-wide country under a flag which shall be a quartering of the Union Jack with the Stars and Stripes' ('The Adventure of the Noble Bachelor').[1]

As this case might remind us, another common theme here is the sensational crime of bigamy. But this is now of the most innocent kind, and we are chastened, with Holmes, to find out how wrong such old suspicions can be ('The Yellow Face'). The question of sexuality is perfectly defused in these stories, as it is in its hero. In *The Leavenworth Case* one of the central debates between the family lawyer and the detective concerns the question of motive. Whilst Mr. Raymond argues that the suspect murdered Mr. Leavenworth because he 'stood in the way of Eleanore's acknowledging him as a husband', Gryce thinks that this argument based on love is 'weak': 'One should never deliberate upon the causes which have led to the destruction of a rich man without taking into account that most common passion of the human race', avarice.[2] In Holmes, this 'police habit of thought' becomes triumphant, particularly in the three stories in which stepfathers or fathers try, by various means (seduction ['A Case of Identity'], imprisonment ['The Adventure of the Copper Beeches'] and murder ['The Adventure of the Speckled Band']), to prevent their daughters from marrying so as to continue to enjoy their property (in 'The Greek Interpreter', the young lady is also abducted in order to obtain her property). Here, sexuality is entirely subordinate to financial motives. Holmes' celebration of an Anglo-American federation is in fact aimed at disarming the objections raised by the press to 'the present free-trade principle' in the 'marriage market' which was leading to the 'management of the noble houses of Great Britain . . . passing into the hands of our fair cousins from across the Atlantic' (p. 289).

It is not, in the end, surprising that Holmes is seen as the culmination of a tradition, for Conan Doyle is careful to sprinkle references to that tradition throughout his stories, be they explicit (and usually derogatory) comments on Dupin and LeCoq, or themes which refer with varying degrees of obviousness to Poe or Collins (the constant fascination with the closed room and its subjection to exhaustive measure and the hiding and discovery of the photograph in 'Scandal in Bohemia' ['The Purloined Letter'], the description of the savage in 'The Sign of Four' and the stoat in 'The Crooked Man' and the mind-reading episode in 'The Resident Patient' ['The Murders . . . '], or the cursed diamond in 'The Adventure of the Blue Carbuncle' [*The Moonstone*] and the substituted woman in 'The Adventure of the Copper Beeches' [*The Woman in White*], etc.). There are, furthermore, indirect references which clearly serve to mark and demark Holmes in relation to his antecessors. In 'A Study in Scarlet' Holmes is distinguished from Cuff in having no interest in gardening and from Dupin in having no interest in astronomy, whilst the stupid constable lives in 'Audley Court'; it is Mrs. Forrester – recalling the name of the author of 'The Female Detective' – who rejoices in the 'romance' of the story in 'The Sign of Four', and the 'crooked man' turns out to be no other than Henry Wood (Mrs. Henry Wood being the author of *East Lynne* and other successful sensation novels, and H. F. Wood the author of *The Passenger from Scotland Yard*, discussed below); in 'The Musgrave Ritual' (itself perhaps recalling Mosgrave of *Lady Audley's Secret*) Holmes paraphrases Dupin – 'you know my methods in such cases, Watson. I put myself in the man's place, and, having first gauged his intelligence, I try to imagine how I should myself have proceeded under the same circumstances' (p. 392). But throughout these references it is essential that we be aware of Conan Doyle's strategy: Holmes is accumulating a set of antecedents in a selective and entirely revisionary way.

That is not of course to say that Holmes himself does not embody characteristics of a series of fictional detectives, rather the contrary. His physiognomy and characteristics clearly direct our attention towards precisely those detectives in sensational fiction, like Cuff and Gryce, descended from Dickens' real-life portraits, but who, we should remember, had been signalled in the fiction as objects of criticism by being made to *fail* to solve the mysteries with which they were charged. So Holmes is right to disavow this paternity at the same time as he advertises it, for he takes the inheritance he creates and he revises its status from a critical signifier of the failure of a model of 'police' to an image of success. His revision goes further: his frequent involvement in cases on behalf of the crowned heads of Europe and the English royalist nobility, along-side his general demeanour, make it clear that the class limitations of the former detectives have been fully overcome.[3] In contrast with the government spy of X.Y.Z., Holmes makes middle-class interference in the privacy of the genteel home entirely respectable and the residual anxiety of the detective in relation to suspicions of spying and tyranny are totally absent. This is in fact perhaps one of Holmes' most significant innovations in relation to his competitors: even Gaboriau's LeCoq has something to prove, both to society and his superiors; but Holmes is the perfection of the detective function enthroned in the confidence of its right and its power. Rather than anxiously negotiating that power, here the detective condescends. Lastly, he can do so because, like Cesare Lombroso in his new science of 'criminology', Holmes has definitively homogenized the potential crisis of conflicting codes. We first see him in the hospital laboratory, conducting a medical experiment. The doctor, Watson, cannot see the 'practical' significance, but Holmes enlightens him: 'it is the most practical *medico-legal* discovery for years' (p. 18 – my italics). Its significance is simply that 'Had this test been invented, there are hundreds of men now walking the earth who would long ago have paid the penalty of their crimes.' As sexuality is subordinated to economics, medicine is unequivocally subordinated to the punitive law.

The absence of class, political or methodological problematization and anxiety also hints at the equally important fact that, by directing us towards the specious and discreet intelligences of the eccentric detectives of sensation fiction, Holmes is most of all diverting us from his other ancestors, the policemen of the 'romance of the detective', whom he appears to supply with the discourse of method and intelligence they had lacked. Holmes is of course celebrated as, finally, the first detective really to bring, as he constantly claims, scientific method to bear on social mysteries. Ousby, for example, sees in Holmes the celebration of that 'spirit of scientific rationalism which had come to dominate the intellectual climate of the late Victorian period'.[4] But that is to take a certain amount for granted about both the contemporary 'intellectual climate' and Holmes' methodology. In fact, the intellectual and scientific bases of his practice have nothing to do with the ferment of epistemological ideas generated by the revolutions in physics from the 1880s (and which were only resolved in the first two decades of the twentieth century by the paradigmatic rupture initiated by Henri Poincaré and Einstein), and everything to do with an older, more stable science. As Stephen Knight observes, at bottom lies 'Doyle's wish to protect old values, ideas and their social setting as innate to his hero's methodology: the weakness of his own reasoning is clear in misnaming his hero's methodology'.[5] Holmes may well seem to provide the methodological content lacking in the earlier 'romances', and to ensure its contact with Dupin through a similar vocabulary, but he does so with a bad conscience and a fraudulent and patronizing attitude towards his readers.

The 'misnaming' of his scientific methodology is related to his disavowal of his literary origins. Poor old Watson is the butt of his insistence. Whilst Mrs. Forrester declares of 'The Sign of Four' that 'It is a romance!' (p. 129), Watson has already been warned:

> 'Detection is, or ought to be, an exact science and should be treated in the same cold and unemotional manner. You have attempted to tinge it with romanticism . . . '
>
> 'But the romance was there,' I remonstrated. 'I could not tamper with the facts.'
>
> 'Some facts should be repressed, or, at least, a just sense of proportion should be observed in treating them. The only point in the case ['A Study in Scarlet'] which deserved mention was the curious analytical reasoning *from effects to causes* . . . .' (p. 90 – my italics)

We shall be returning to the question of repressing facts, but for now it is important to note how, strangely, in 'The Adventure of the Copper Beeches', when Watson returns to the question of romance and facts, confessing that 'I cannot quite hold myself absolved from the charge of sensationalism which has been urged against my records' (p. 317), Holmes admonishes him: 'you have erred perhaps in attempting to put colour and life into each of your statements instead of confining yourself to the task of placing upon record that severe reasoning *from cause to effect* which is really the only notable feature about the thing' (my italics). In stark contrast to the attention given to methodological positions in Dupin and Collins, here the exact nature of the epistemology does not seem to matter, so long as it drives out the 'romance' and 'sensationalism'.

It is very possible that the fraudulent nature of Holmes' scientificity was apparent to Doyle's competitors. At least H. F. Wood appears to see through it in *The Passenger from Scotland Yard* (1888). This amusing tale plays with a number of conventions. The first mystery is the identity of the 'passenger from Scotland Yard': the need for invisibility leads everyone to suspect each other of being a detective and a criminal. In Paris itself, much is ironically made of French police methods in contrast to the English – for example, when obliged to fill in the hotel register form, Inspector Byde exclaims: 'What a help . . . if we had all these papers to work from in England!', to which his assistant replies: 'Yes . . . and people sometimes do fill them up honestly by mistake.'[6] Indeed, this 'sleeper' returns later, when Byde's assistant goes to the Prefecture to check up on the presence of suspicious foreigners in Paris: only one irregularity is noted – 'A gentleman who came from London by the night-mail, described himself as an English detective officer when the train reached Paris . . . and gave a different description of himself entirely when he filled up the police-sheet at his hotel' (p. 138).

Now, the problem with Byde is that he has an obsessive prejudice against the evangelical temperance movement, which has already got him into trouble, and here his prime suspect is a temperance preacher. He tries to protect himself against his obsession by defending 'a process of pure logical induction' against his colleagues' subjective 'impressionism' (p. 183); in fact he is known and ridiculed at Scotland Yard because of his proposal for 'a scientifically-trained detective force applying mathematics to their regular work, reasoning on infallible processes, with symbols and by formulas' (p. 211). Byde celebrates this triumph of method as 'climbing to an irrefragable conclusion through irrefutable steps', and the author comments: 'The foregoing is the inspector's language, and the reader will anticipate us in a smile . . . These were elegances of diction and proprieties of metaphor due in great part to the evening class in rhetoric at the institute in Camberwell' (p. 183). Byde, it turns out, has taken various courses, on 'the art of rhetoric, the palaeozoic period, the Aryan race, elementary physics'. But, most of all, his belief in and use of mathematical reasoning is explained as follows:

> He had not soared to lofty mathematical eminences, as the reader will no doubt have observed. Indeed, he had never been able to push his researches into the eternal truths of Euclid's elements farther than proposition 12, the scholastic advantages which he had almost religiously procured for Master Edgar Byde, the sole scion of his house, and possibly a future ornament of the Yard, having been as a rule beyond his own reach, notwithstanding the popular institute at the corner of the terrace. But the inspector could do eight out of those twelve, he flattered himself, as lucidly as anyone, and five of them he knew by heart. Was this bad, when you were a busy man, and self-instructed? He could not bring himself to seek assistance from his erudite son; but he borrowed Master Byde's old school-books, and retained them – having paid for them himself – and frequently consulted those portable volumes, in secret. (p. 50)

For all the talk, then, what does Holmes actually do in these stories? To a very large extent he still displays the qualities and employs the techniques of the pseudo-factual detectives: he suspects with uncanny accuracy; he follows suspects or their trails; he adopts disguises in order to infiltrate establishments where his visibility would inhibit his action, and he gains the confidence of potential informers, supplementing these time-honoured 'detective' strategies with his own private spy force (the 'Baker Street Irregulars' – 'they can go everywhere, see everything, overhear everyone' – p. 127) and the use of advertisements, and other forms, to entrap suspects. Brilliant of course is his innovation of reading footprints. Except that, already in the 1840s, prior to 'the developments of fingerprinting and forensic science, detection still often involved matching a suspect's shoes to footprints at the scene of the crime, perhaps with the occasional refinement of digging such footsteps up, preserving them between boards and presenting them in court as evidence.'[7] Furthermore, the innovation in fiction – like so much in Holmes – had already been claimed by the young LeCoq.[8] Neither the real detective nor LeCoq of course had Holmes' good fortune so often to find culprits with wooden or 'gamey' legs. From feet to hands: another astounding 'fresh weapon among the many with which he waged his lifelong battle against crime' is his ability to 'deduce' character from handwriting – not only character, but also age – 'You may not be aware that the deduction of a man's age from his writing is one which has been brought to considerable accuracy by experts' ('The Reigate Puzzle', pp. 398, 408).

We may well not be aware of this remarkably spurious biologism, but it is the sort of esoteric knowledge that Holmes most relies on, for all his talk of method. As Michael Shepherd observes, Holmes' 'method' is 'a counterfeit, a simulacrum of the real thing', in short, less method than 'mythod'.[9] The 'mythod' rapidly made itself felt in a revitalization of the tradition of female detectives: like Paschal and Holmes, Catherine Pirkis' Loveday Brooke (1893) constantly demonstrates her superior intelligence in contrast to ordinary citizens, the police and even her own employer who, on the basis of the evident, all immediately suspect the wrong person. Like Mrs. Paschal, she disguises herself as a servant, a secretary, a nursery governess and an interior decorator. But whilst her invocation of superior intelligence contrasts with her predecessors by appearing to have a more genuine specialized content, it is Holmes, not Dupin, who provides the model. As in Holmes a mystique is created around her superior perceptivity, methodology and knowledge, but her appearance of superhuman intelligence is achieved mainly by concealing key information from the reader. Miss Brooke solves her cases not through a methodology but by the recondite knowledge which she alone possesses and only shares with us in the explanation of her solution – her expertise in such esoterica as popular recitation books, cabman's slang, Genoese guild rings, heraldry, Wesleyianism and ghost psychology. Given this, her processes of investigation are an ironic commentary on her employer's recommendation:

I only know she is the most sensible and practical woman I ever met. In the first place, she has the faculty – so rare among women – of carrying out orders to the very letter; in the second place, she has a clear, shrewd brain, unhampered by any hard-and-fast theories; thirdly, and most important item of all, she has so much common sense that it amounts to genius.[10]

In this way, Dupin's impossible 'genius' of theorized difference is domesticated to the triumph of the mastery of 'common sense'.

We know that Doyle tried to enlist his professor, Joseph Bell, as his model for Holmes. He wrote to Bell that 'Round the centre of deduction and inference and observation which I have heard you inculcate I have tried to build up a man who pushed the thing as far as it would go.'[11] But, interestingly, Bell was the first to recognize that this was quite unexceptional: 'The precise and intelligent recognition and appreciation of minor differences is the real essential factor in all successful medical diagnosis. Carried into ordinary life, granted the presence of an insatiable curiosity and fairly acute sense, you have Sherlock Holmes as he astonishes his somewhat dense friend Dr. Watson; carried out in a specialized training, you have Sherlock Holmes the skilled detective.'[12] What Doyle left out in his praise of Bell was the third quality whose absence explains the difference between Holmes and the fictional French detective (and translator of Holmes), François le Villard. When Watson points out that 'He speaks as a pupil to his master', Holmes replies that: 'He has considerable gifts himself. He possesses two out of the three qualities necessary for the ideal detective. He has the power of observation and that of deduction. He is only wanting in knowledge' (p. 91). The triumph of method is then a false democratic promise; what is at issue is the power of accumulated knowledge of individual criminals and of criminal London, his filing system of newspaper reports, and, most of all, his records and memory of parallel cases, supplemented by his encyclopaediae – in other words, the fruits of his (and others') 'specialized training' not in skills but in information.

Holmes is aware of the power this knowledge grants him if he knows how to manage it. In a not so rare moment of disavowal, he comments to Watson:

It is one of those instances where the reasoner can produce an effect which seems remarkable to his neighbour, because the latter has missed the one little point which is the basis of the deduction. The same may be said, my dear fellow, for the effect of some of these little sketches of yours, which is entirely meretricious, depending as it does upon your retaining in your

own hands some factors in the problem which are never imparted
to the reader. (p. 412)

In response to Mr. Jabez Wilson's remark, 'I thought at first that you
had done something clever, but I see that there was nothing in it,
after all', Holmes complains to Watson, 'I begin to think . . . that
I made a mistake in explaining. *"Omne ignotum pro magnifico"*, you
know' (p. 177) – likewise, in 'The Stock-Broker's Clerk', 'I am afraid
that I rather give myself away when I explain . . . Results without
causes are much more impressive' (p. 363). Yet the concealment
and timely revelation of clues and pieces of knowledge unknown
to the reader is the fundamental dynamic of these tales, with Watson
collaborating in distracting our attention. Our role is not to compete
or to suffer neurotically the suspense of ignorance. It is to trust and
to admire.

The point is, then, as Haycraft was the first to point out, 'Subjected
to purely technical analysis, in fact, [the Holmes stories] will be
found all too frequently loose, obvious, imitative, trite, and repetitious in device and theme.'[13] For him, as for Julian Symons, Doyle's
'real originality or inventiveness' resides almost exclusively in 'his
masterly creation of character'. Not so much, however, a masterly
character as the character of mastery. Like Dupin, Holmes is not
exactly a 'character' in the traditional sense; but, in contrast to
Dupin, Holmes is not the site for theory but for mastery itself,
mastery in a very particular sense.

The structure of the stories signifies an important displacement,
in which the mystery itself is shifted from the crime, its sequel, and
even its solution, to the detective's explanation of how he solved
it, in which much depends on the timely revelation of the master's
earlier acts of concealment ('I'll tell you what I did first, and how I
came to do it afterwards' – p. 466). In this sense, *A Study in Scarlet*,
borrowing its structure from M. LeCoq, is paradigmatic: the first
narrative takes us from the crime to the capture of the culprit;
the second provides the story behind the crime; but it is the third
narrative, the explanation of the solution, which bears the brunt of
our attention. Holmes' power is exercised in a clear division of
narrative labour in which the two senses of narration have become
split: the telling of events and the telling of their significance. There
are two typical structures here: the cases where a witness (normally
victim) recounts the events, to which Holmes returns their meaning;
or those in which Holmes hypothesises a meaning, requiring only

the confession to fill in the detailed events (to 'confirm our own deductions' – p. 445). In both, Holmes has an absolute and exclusive monopoly on the meaning of events.

Holmes' character is of major importance to his success, especially as Doyle inflects the Gaboriau model into the short story. In the first place, it offers a defence of novelistic respectability against the attack on the emphasis on plot; and in the second place, it provides a mechanism for binding the new literary form Doyle is here exploiting. Whereas a cliff-hanging plot was essential to the serial publication of sensation fiction and for the coherence of the three-decker, the cheap edition designed to be bought at the railway stall and read on the train journey needs to be complete in itself and to be identifiable as a trade-mark in order to sell subsequent, equally self-contained, numbers. The 'series', as opposed to the serial, implies then the repetition of a 'formula', which is most productively centred on a strong, unifying 'character'. One reads almost as much to find out about Holmes, as to find out 'who done it'. As Watson observes, 'During my long and intimate acquaintance with Mr. Sherlock Holmes I had never heard him refer to his relations, and hardly ever to his own early life. This reticence upon his part had increased the somewhat inhuman effect which he produced upon me, until sometimes I found myself regarding him as an isolated phenomenon, a brain without a heart, as deficient in human sympathy as he was preeminent in intelligence' (p. 435). Doyle is of course himself masterful in managing Holmes' 'reticence' about himself as about the material of his cases, dosing his stories with just enough timely family detail and signs of affection to prevent Holmes from turning into a monster. His eccentricities, in contrast to Dupin's, are anything but significant (with the possible exception of the drug-taking – which, however, contrasts with his temperance). If Holmes is (another) one who takes trivia seriously, he also trivializes the serious (e.g. music). This makes the stunningly banal Watson his (and our) ideal reader, the perfect means for knowing him.

Watson and Holmes are brought together by a new modern mystery, how to live in the modern city as professional people on a small income: 'Trying to solve the problem as to whether it is possible to get comfortable rooms at a reasonable price', as Watson says to Stamford. The latter replies: 'That's a strange thing . . . . You are the second man today that has used that expression to me' (p. 16). Who is this 'second man' who so rhymes with Watson? He is 'a little queer in his ideas – an enthusiast in some branches of science';

although he is working in the hospital laboratory, he is not a medical
student – 'His studies are very desultory and eccentric', resulting in
'a lot of out-of-the-way knowledge'. Indeed, mystifyingly, he is not
studying for a 'degree in science or any other portal which would
give him an entrance to the learned world' (p. 20). We should note
that the very first thing Watson had told us about himself was his
degree in medicine (1878) and his further education as a surgeon
in the Army. We are clearly in the modern universe – of the rise
of higher education and the professions – in which a man *is* the
professional position he occupies, and his profession is a function
of his accredited knowledge. In these stories, not only sexuality, but
knowledge itself is subordinate to economics, a means of gaining
a livelihood. Watson simply cannot conceive of the pursuit of
knowledge for its own ends: 'Surely no man would work so hard
or attain such precise information unless he had some definite end
in view.'

Whilst Watson unsuccessfully analyses his curriculum in order
to solve the mystery of Sherlock Holmes, Holmes, in contrast,
discovers Watson's – or anyone else's – profession at a glance.
That, in fact, is the subject of his article on 'The Book of Life' –
'Let him, on meeting a fellow-mortal, learn at a glance to distinguish
the history of the man, and the trade or profession to which he
belongs . . . . By a man's finger-nails, by his coat-sleeve, by his
boots, by his trouser-knees, by the callosities of his forefinger
and thumb, by his expression, by his shirt-cuffs – by each of
these things a man's calling is plainly revealed' (p. 23) – and his
first stunning act as a detective is to prove this, his first thesis,
by identifying the 'retired sergeant of Marines' in the street below
(and he will continue to do this with almost everyone who comes
within his purview). On the other hand, his own profession is, of
course, impenetrable to the ordinary man (Watson). This, then, is
Holmes' mystery and his power:

'That's just his little peculiarity . . . A good many people have
wanted to know how he finds things out.'
'Oh! a mystery is it?' I cried, rubbing my hands. 'This is very
piquant. I am much obliged to you for bringing us together. "The
proper study of mankind is man," you know.'
'You must study him, then,' Stamford said, as he bade me
good-bye. 'You'll find him a knotty problem, though. I'll wager
he learns more about you than you about him.' (p. 19)

Holmes' mysterious profession of professional mastery is what makes him unique: 'That is why I have chosen my own particular profession, or rather created it, for I am the only one in the world' (p. 90). It is not surprising that Watson (and we) cannot 'deduce' Holmes' profession – it is entirely new. In the end, Holmes has to explain: 'I'm a consulting detective, if you can understand what that is' (p. 24). The 'consulting detective' is to be distinguished from the 'government detective', the 'private detective' (loc. cit.) and the 'unofficial detective' (p. 90) but, in accumulating, revising and developing their various traditions, it is clearly closest to the space previously occupied by Mrs. Paschal, particularly in not being limited by the law. Indeed, Watson reminds us in 'The Adventure of the Blue Carbuncle' that 'of the last six cases which I have added to my notes, three have been entirely free of any legal crime' (p. 245). Further, in two of the remaining three, punishment has been left to a providential Nature. Of the seven (if we include the present case), only one, 'The Red-Headed League', involves a recognized crime and a legal process.[14] Of course, the notion of 'legal crime' implies that of another sort of crime not circumscribed by law, and, in these cases as in so many others, it is this, above all, that Holmes investigates, like Paschal, taking a police discipline, on his own initiative, into the territories that the Law does not reach. Mrs. Paschal had stretched the official detective to the very margin of private enterprise. In the case of Loveday Brooke, we find that the problem of placing the daughter of Paschal independent of the police in 1893 is solved by the existence of a commercial investigative agency. Holmes turns the unofficial activities of interested parties and the extra-mural activities of police detectives into a profession capable of earning a living but, unlike Loveday and her ilk, Holmes is not part of a commercial market; he works entirely for himself and is professionally above both state ('government') and commerce ('private'). At the same time, then, he celebrates the power of the independent professional, answerable only to his own, self-invented, deontology: 'I follow my own methods and tell as much or as little as I choose. That is the advantage of being unofficial' (p. 345). Fortunately, and despite his personal misanthropy, his role is philanthropic, he is 'unofficial adviser and helper to everybody who is absolutely puzzled' (p. 191), but he is most of all *the* professional – the one whose livelihood and power derives from his knowledge. Not only, as he tells Mary Sutherland in 'A Case of Identity', 'it is my business to know things' (p. 192), but more specifically, as he tells the goose salesman in 'The Adventure of the Blue Carbuncle': 'My name is Sherlock Holmes. It is my business to know what other people don't know' (p. 254). And although not part of the police or market system, this archetypal professional, who, we should remember, has a monopoly on his profession and on narrative knowledge, is, like the Bank of England to the commercial banking system and the state accounts, the 'last resort' which underpins the modern capitalist 'police' system:

> I am the last and highest court of appeal in detection. When Gregson, or Lestrade, or Athelney Jones are out of their depths – which, by the way, is their normal state – the matter is laid before me. I examine the data, as an expert, and pronounce a specialist's opinion. I claim no credit in such cases. My name figures in no newspaper. The work itself . . . is my highest reward. (p. 90)

With this handy spin-off: like the pseudo-factual detectives, his anonymous disinterested work where the official police fail enhances precisely *their* reputation: 'That's the result of all our Study in Scarlet: to get them a testimonial!' (p. 86)

However, more than anything else, Holmes revives the police 'romance' tradition precisely by his own pretence of factuality. The measure of his success is of course the fact that Holmes is the only fictional detective to have always been treated by the public *as if he were real*. This is not only a popular and literary pathology; Michael Shepherd refers to a series of articles in the *Journal of the American Medical Association* which discuss, with all due medical seriousness, the nature of Holmes' cocaine addiction.[15] This pretence is clearly a central strategy in the tales, and is cognate with its use of narrative mastery. In sum, the air of factuality is achieved precisely by repressing the fictionality of fiction. We have already observed this in the way in which he refers to Dupin and LeCoq as if they were real. This is underwritten by a spurious metonymy which plays, like Holmes, on the reader's ignorance and his or her faith in the reliability of 'authoritative' discourses. The cases we are privileged to witness are constantly implanted in a continuum of 'actual' events, signified by references to imaginary newspaper reports of 'real' cases we are 'supposed' to have read. In other words, the fiction signifies the facts which disavow its fictionality by concealing them. Reticence, secrecy, exclusion of the reader become the guarantees of authenticity, obliging us to believe only in the text's testimony of what we are not allowed to know – that is to say, of course, precisely what Holmes alone does know. So it is really no surprise that the two most important and illustrative cases are the two we cannot read. The first was undertaken, we are told, immediately after 'The Sign of Four', but it

> deals with interests of such importance and implicates so many of the first families in the kingdom that for many years it will be impossible to make it public. No case, however, in which Holmes was engaged has ever illustrated the value of his analytic methods so clearly or has impressed those who were associated with him so deeply . . . . The new century will have come, however, before the story can be safely told. (p. 447)

The other is the 'last' case, Holmes' struggle with his only equal, the master of crime, Moriarty: 'if a detailed account of that silent contest could be written, it would take its place as the most brilliant bit of thrust-and-parry work in the history of detection' (p. 471). In Holmes, Conan Doyle, the man who could believe in the most obviously fraudulent photographs of fairies,[16] proves himself the master of a sleight of hand which does not so much conflate as reverse fact and fiction: like a *trompe l'oeil* – or Sherlock Holmes' 'clues' – fact becomes a mere trick of metonymic surface which imbues fiction with factuality just so long as we are denied access to the 'facts'.

Holmes represents then not only the triumph of professionalism, of the police discipline, and of the monopolistic mastery of the specialist; in making his fiction more real than actuality, he also celebrates the triumph of realism. Whereas Dupin's investigation into the relation between fact and fiction reinforces the fictionality of fiction, Holmes represents the deliberate repression of the very category. This is quite clear from the curriculum listed by Watson. Of 'Literature', Holmes knows nothing (although, with a typical disregard for consistency, Doyle later has him reading Plutarch), but his knowledge of 'Sensational Literature' is 'Immense': 'He appears to know every detail of every horror perpetrated in the century' (p. 22). In other words, the expression 'Sensational Literature' deliberately inverts the relationship between the literary and the factual: it is the name for the authentic record of crime, not melodramatic fiction.

It is in this sense that we should read the literary justification of his profession:

life is infinitely stranger than anything which the mind of man could invent. We would not dare to conceive the things which are really mere commonplaces of existence. If we could fly out of that window hand in hand, hover over this great city, gently remove the roofs, and peep in at the queer things which are going on . . . it would make all fiction with its conventionalities and foreseen conclusions most stale and unprofitable. (pp. 190–1)

Whilst Holmes here clearly denies his own role in creating ('inventing') his narratives, it might appear that he is in fact taking the sensationalists' part against Mrs. Oliphant, when she complained against the police-court justification for sensation fiction (particularly Collins' defence of 'the Actual'):

Facts are of all things in the world the most false to nature, the most opposed to experience, the most contradictory of all grand laws of existence. The oft-repeated words 'Fact is stranger than fiction', express the very apparent truth that the things which *do* happen are in many cases exactly the things which could not have been expected to happen, and, indeed, ought not to have happened had there been any consistency in life . . . for us truth and fact are two different things.[17]

As Watson says, in disagreement with Holmes: 'We have in our police reports realism pushed to its extreme limits, and yet the result is, it must be confessed, neither fascinating nor artistic'. But this would be to misread Holmes' 'case'. The point is that he is no more defending the 'police report' as a true reflection of life than Oliphant: in response to Watson he argues that 'A certain selection and discretion must be used in producing a realistic effect . . . . This is wanting in the police report'. Both Holmes and Oliphant in fact share Sam Johnson's notion of realism in his famous *Rambler* article: 'If the world be promiscuously described, I cannot see of what use it can be to read the account'. For both, it is the discreet selection which represents the 'truth'. The difference is that whilst Oliphant uses 'fiction' to represent a reflection of 'nature' and 'experience', Holmes, in his total need to disavow his fictionality, employs the term very much in Defoe's derogatory, 'romance' sense. He equates his 'de-tecting' ('gently remov[ing] the roofs') not with 'fiction', but with a realistic reflection of 'life'. In short, real life is that which is selectively and discreetly grasped within his mastery (the only truth he allows us to glimpse) – not the material 'fact' it purports to imitate, but the fiction he monopolizes and presents to us as fact in accordance with the 'natural' laws he invokes to justify his narrative.

Clive Bloom has pointed to the contradiction of how an escapist literature creates a 'social milieu . . . so powerful that later generations would comprehend the era in which these tales were written *through* the medium of the tales themselves . . . . As such, these tales would have replaced the 'real' world with themselves.'[18] In this way, the world of this fiction 'is a substitute for and not a mirror to social forces'. From all that has been said before, I clearly do not share Bloom's distinction between detective fiction and the novel, nor indeed do I feel that his remarks are applicable to the mystery/detective story before Holmes (this being one of the retrospective effects produced by Holmes as the fraudulent maker of 'true' histories). None the less, it remains indisputable that what he says is most of all true of the Holmes stories, which take the realist disavowal to its most extreme conclusion: 'An escapist and totally fictional landscape denies the 'facts' of its origin.' For it is something that Holmes inherits from his detective 'romance' predecessors – rather than from those tales which so clearly problematize the nature of the 'fact' – that, 'Strangely, perhaps, that very perspective is a result of the detective tale's being the only fiction that *insists* it is dealing with facts.'

And this, in the end, is Holmes' greatest reassurance: that the exceptional, the 'stranger' fact, which had earlier served as a justification for a 'sensational' fiction, is, in the end, *in his hands*, not exceptional or strange at all. For all the talk of the *'outré'*, 'I never make exceptions. An exception disproves the rule' (p. 96). The ambiguity of evidence is only apparent, and only to the likes of us and Watson (the police being as certain as Holmes, only wrong); to the master, clues are univocal, they always 'only point to one conclusion' (p. 363) and the stranger they are, the simpler the explanation: 'It is a mistake to confound strangeness with mystery' (p. 59). On the one hand, it is his fund of professional knowledge which guarantees this reassurance: 'There is nothing new under the sun. It has all been done before' (p. 29), 'I am able to guide myself by the thousands of other similar cases which occur to my memory' (p. 176). All that is required is to possess the knowledge, which, of course, only Holmes can.

But there is an equally outrageous reassurance from this 'eccentric'. No one of course has missed the relation between his 'method' and Huxley's 'Lecture on a Piece of Chalk' (1868). However, whereas Huxley's methodology scrupulously supports an agnostic model of knowledge, perhaps Holmes' most revisionist act is to recuperate it to a reassuring and anti-materialist theology:

> 'There is nothing in which deduction is so necessary as in religion . . . It can be built up as an exact science by the reasoner. Our highest assurance of the goodness of Providence seems to me to rest in flowers. All other things . . . are all really necessary for our existence in the first instance. But this rose is an extra . . . . It is only goodness which gives extras, and so I say again that we have much to hope from flowers.' (pp. 455–6)

Curiously, the organization dedicated to proving the existence of God through the rigorously scientific study of parapsychological phenomena, the Society for Psychical Research, proved too scientific and insufficiently credulous and religious for Conan Doyle.[19]

'WHAT WILL BE THE NEXT ADVENTURES . . . ?'

'In Fascism the nightmare of childhood has come true.'
Theodor Adorno, *Minima Moralia* (1935)

And just as you thought that the killer was dead, he lunges again . . . . No sooner had Doyle killed Holmes off, than, in 1897, Bram Stoker reinvoked the themes of the hysterical woman, hypnotism, insanity, criminality and sexuality, secrets and surveillance, the conflict of professional codes, the constructive role of ideology, sexuality and discourse, and the gaping holes of narrative. This time the threat comes from geographically closer to home, not a million miles from Sarajevo, from the historical and cultural 'whirlpool' where the Western world meets the Eastern, and its effect is even more devastating than that of the Moonstone. Stoker takes multiple narration to the extreme to show that it is the limitations of the narrator's point of view over reality and the silences between subjects that creates a space within which a monster of both sexuality and language can operate. Only an argument, curiously very like that of the Society for Psychical Research, allying the most heterogeneous and up-to-date science with the most comprehensive view of ancient mythological and religious superstition can, apparently, overcome this monster; and even here, once again, the success is highly fragile: what does the look of triumph in Dracula's eyes mean? does he crumble into dust as a result of, or to escape the knife? In any case, 'It was like a miracle.'[20]

The book redoubles the intervention of point of view and ideology in determining the action by also foregrounding the very *material* nature of discourse – recording, manuscript, newspaper report, telegramme, shorthand, typewriting, etc. The marked fascination with the various forms of documenting reality, along with its attention to 'real time', contemporary thought and technology and the paraphernalia of the modern world, impart a sense of actuality to the book. This feel of the real raised a central question for contemporary reviewers which reproduces the fantastic hesitation generated by this monster: 'How far the author is himself a believer in the phenomena described.'[21] The solicitor Jonathan Harker and the asylum psychiatrist Seward insist on the supremacy of literal and material 'fact'; Van Helsing makes the plea for 'belief' and 'faith'. But this is defined in an entirely heretical way; what Van Helsing requires of Seward for him to accept the existence of vampires is the sort of credence indispensable not to religion but to *fiction*: for him, faith is 'that which enables us to believe things which we know to be untrue' (p. 232). Now, although, as we have just observed, the text is insistent on the materiality of documentation as a guarantee of its factuality, it ends with an unsettling postscript: in consequence of a fire which destroyed all the originals, 'We were struck by the fact that, in all the mass of material of which the record is composed, there is hardly one authentic document!' (p. 449). Hence, in the end, who should believe it? What is the status of this writing?

The problem is put even more radically early in the novel by the ancient mariner Swales. Quite redundant in narrative terms, his lengthy speeches are written in a dialogue whose difficulty draws our attention to the materiality of his language, but they serve only to give the lie to both the sort of marvellous myths Van Helsing would have us believe in and the most 'concrete' and definitive of biographical testimonies, what is engraved on tombstones:

> It be all fool-talk, lock, stock, and barrel; that's what it be, an' nowt else. These bans an' wafts an' boh-ghosts an' barguests and bogles an' all anent them is only fit to set bairns an' dizzy women a-belderin'. They be nowt but air-blebs! They, an' all grims an' signs an' warnin's, be all invented by parsons an'

illsome beuk-bodies an' railway touters to skeer an' scunner
hafflin's, an' to get folks to do somethin' that they don't other
incline to. It makes me ireful to think o' them. Why, it's them that,
not content with printin' lies on paper an' preachin' them out of
pulpits, does want to be cuttin' them on tombstones'. (p. 83)

If we cannot trust traditional legend and what is written religiously
on stone, what narrative, what writing can we trust? The earthly
grave of the man lost at sea, like the vampire, puts the old question
of Common Law and Equity: wherein lies the truth of language, in
the material literality or the figurative 'spirit' of the word?

We return to the 'fantastic' question: how should we read *Dracula*,
as literal horror or as metaphor? In the light of the Catholic Mass,
the goddess Kali, the child who suckles at the mother's breast,
the bat and the mosquito, the sadist and the necrophiliac cited
by Krafft-Ebing in *Psychopathia Sexualis* (1886) and Ernest Jones'
discussion in 'On the Nightmare' (1920), the 'blood-sucking' capitalist (*Das Kapital*, ch. X [English translation, 1887]), the emotionally parasitic lover, mediaeval legends, the reported and studied
cases of vampirism in the seventeenth- and eighteenth-centuries and
twentieth-century crime reports (like the 'Vampire of Dusseldorf' of
the 1920s), Vlad Tepes himself and Elizabeth Báthory, the question
is not so much, do vampires exist as, *in what sense* do they exist? If
the vampire is not literally real, what does it 'stand for'?

In *Dracula*, at the moment of explanation Arthur Lord Godalming
exclaims: 'Un-Dead! Not alive! What do you mean? Is this all a
nightmare, or what is it?' (p. 247) That is rather the point of the
linguistic monstrosity of the vampire: not either/or, but both/and.
Throughout the novel the experience of the vampire, the creature
which breaks down the barrier between life and death, consistently
literalizes the figurative, turning dream into reality, metaphor into
metonymy. Jonathan already experiences this on his journey to the
castle: 'I think I must have fallen asleep and kept dreaming of the
incident, for it seemed to be repeated endlessly, and now, looking
back, it is like a sort of awful nightmare' (p. 22). So too Lucy and
Mina ('My dream was very peculiar, and was almost typical of
the way that waking thoughts become merged in, or continued
in, dreams' – p. 308) – only the lunatic Renfield is capable of
distinguishing reality from dream ('I must not deceive myself; it
was no dream, but all a grim reality' – p. 331). This is of course, as
we saw in effect in Hogg, the nature of horror: phantasy turns into

reality by the transformation of a figurative metaphor into a literal metonymy. Dracula himself is the personification of this, with his 'very bright eyes, which seemed red in the lamplight' (p. 19) and his hand, 'more like the hand of a dead than a living man' (p. 26), his talk of past battles 'as if' he had been present; his appearance in his coffin 'as if his youth had been renewed' (p. 67). The translation of metaphor into metonymy is put with particular force in the vampire precisely because it is not a ghost, the survival of the immortal human spirit, but the material body of the 'walking dead' sustained by the very material of life. If, in an orthodox Christian semiotics, the body is merely the 'vehicle' of the 'soul', to become a vampire is to be condemned to literality, a body devoid of its spirit: 'Lucy Westerna, but yet how changed'; we can only 'call the thing that was before us Lucy because it bore her shape' (p. 253).

The horrific effect of literalization is centred on our reading of the metaphor of blood. The term is used as a metaphoric commonplace by everyone: Dracula tells us that 'the blood of many brave races' flows in his veins (p. 42); Van Helsing says that 'A brave man's blood is the best thing on this earth when a woman is in trouble' (p. 180) and Seward remarks 'His very heart was bleeding, and it took all the manhood out of him' (p. 183). Of course, contemporary medical theory of hereditary transmission pushes the figure in a metonymic direction, and this is born out in the central episode in which an attempt is made to save Lucy by giving her blood transfusions from her three declared lovers. At the normal level of literality, the transfusion fails, but it succeeds at the 'spiritual' level of metaphor, only to 'succeed' in quite another literal sense. Arthur declares sentimentally at Lucy's funeral 'that he felt since [the transfusion] as if they two had been really married, and that she was his wife in the sight of God' (p. 209). In case the reader (like the literalist Seward) misses the irony, Van Helsing, the systematic misuser of language, explains in a burst of hysterics: 'If so that, then what about the others? Ho, ho! Then this so sweet maid is a polyandrist' (p. 212). However, this is not a 'meaning' arbitrarily imposed by the master on a linguistic association; it is the literal echo of Lucy's own desire: 'Why can't they let a girl marry three men, or as many as want her, and save all this trouble? But this is heresy, and I must not say it' (p. 76). Lucy's transformation into a vampire realizes the affectionate girl's heretical phantasy and turns the hysteric into a sexual wanton. In this text, all phantasy, all metaphor, has its revenge in the return of what is literally repressed in it. Likewise, Jonathan's first encounter with vampires is the perverse literalization of his half-spoken desire in something between a dream and a reality ('I suppose I must have fallen asleep; I hope so, but I fear, for all that followed was startlingly real'). Far from his fiancée, as he is dozing off in the room where, he imagines, 'of old ladies had sat and sung and lived sweet lives whilst their gentle breasts were sad for their menfolk away in the midst of remorseless wars', he sees three 'young women, ladies by their dress and manner' and 'felt in my heart a wicked, burning desire that they would kiss me with those red lips'; and so they do, with what one might call a vengeance! (pp. 50–52).

As it makes dreams and desires real, the vampire's destabilizing of the metaphor/metonymy of blood re-literalizes the idealized language of sexual affection. What its unstable trope shows then is that the literality of the (masculine) 'vital fluid' lies elsewhere than in its apparently 'literal' sense. In *Dracula* the semiotic mystery which the text opens (what does it mean?) indicates that metaphor is literalized in a double metonymy: it is both materialized and displaced. Hence again Jonathan and the vampires:

> Lower and lower went her head as the lips went below the range of my mouth and chin and seemed to fasten on my throat. Then she paused . . . Then the skin of my throat began to tickle as one's flesh does when the hand that is to tickle it approaches nearer – nearer. I could feel the soft, shivering touch of the lips on the supersensitive skin of my throat, and the hard dents of two sharp teeth, just touching and pausing there. I closed my eyes in a languorous ecstasy and waited – waited with beating heart. (p. 52)

This becomes uncontrollable in the text, all metaphorical expression becomes sexualized, carrying a latent meaning of literal carnality. When Dracula attacks Jonathan's wife, what is Mina being forced to drink? 'When the blood began to spurt out, he took my hands in one of his, holding them tight, and with the other seized my neck and pressed my mouth to the wound, so that I must either suffocate or swallow some of the – Oh, my God, my God! what have I done?' (p. 343). This destabilization and displacement survives the defeat (?) of Dracula, infecting even the happy end represented by Mina and Jonathan's marriage and the birth of their son, whom they name for Quincy. After what has happened to the 'spirit' of the characters and of language, how are we to read this: 'His mother holds, I know, the secret belief that some of our brave friend's spirit has passed into him' (p. 449)?

As Renfield makes quite clear, the vampire sense of 'The Blood is the Life' is not a metaphor, any more than is the Catholic sense which the story inverts and exploits. It is trans-figurative. And this is most strange, coming from the Anglo-Irish Protestant, Stoker. But it is in that sense that he has created a 'myth'. The question of whether the vampire exists in reality or only as a metaphor becomes the question of the source of the myth's power: does it derive from the thing itself or is it an effect of language? Harker too, 'as an English Churchman' (p. 13), is perplexed by the reassurance he finds in the crucifix offered him by a peasant woman. He wonders whether its power derives from the literal object in itself or from its figurative significance to a particular subject: 'Is it that there is something in the essence of the thing itself, or that it is a medium, a tangible help, in conveying memories of sympathy and comfort?' (p. 46). But it is the efficacy of the symbolic – the Host and the crucifix – in alliance with the technologies of modern science (a much more actualized science than Holmes') that will in fact, apparently, defeat Dracula.

'WHO CAN TELL?'

'Psychoanalysis challenges the various philosophies of the human subject on a number of different levels – at the level of theory, through its theories of action, its models of the mind and its insistence on the textuality of experience; and, in its practice, whilst mediating between the man of care and the subject of knowledge, it challenges both – the philanthropic motives of the former and the absolute mastery of the latter.'[22]

I began this book with a reference to the analogy between the detective and others for whom explanation requires reconstructing what lies buried in the past, and must hence end it with a discussion of the figure who is so often facilely presented as not only contemporary, but also analogous to Holmes. But I could not, in any case, avoid discussing Freud in that what I have been presenting as the non-Holmesian tradition of mystery fiction has been pointing us in the same direction: re-reading meaning and the mythical master-plot; the privilege of the confession; sympathy and authority; sexuality, ideology, the mystery of the subject and his or her mastery; the uncovering of secrets, particularly those that the women are not telling; hysteria and hypnosis and the sexuality of the unconscious; the pursuit of a science of the mind through an articulation of theory and fiction, and of idea and language, and hence finally the question of the symbol, all place Freud very much (as he would have it in 'Psychoanalysis and the Ascertaining of the Truth in Courts of Law') 'on the stand'.

It is Freud's professor, Martin Charcot, who links the articulation of myth, magic and science in *Dracula* with the development of Psychoanalysis:

> 'I suppose now you do not believe in corporeal transference. No? Nor in materialization? No? Nor in astral bodies. No? Nor in the reading of thought. No? Nor in hypnotism -'
> 'Yes,' I said. 'Charcot has proved that pretty well.'[23]

But in proving a measure of scientific respectability for Jennings' 'metaphysical theory' through his account of hysteria and hypnosis, Charcot also raised the central question of the relation between therapeutic efficacy and authority. Charcot was himself unequivocal in dealing with the hysteric – as one anorexic patient says to him: 'When I saw that you were the master, I was afraid, and, despite my loathing, I tried to eat'; and Charcot comments: 'I thanked the child for her confession, which, as you see, contains a complete education.'[24] For Freud, on the other hand, what effected the cure was not the (male) doctor's authority over the (female, hysterical) patient but precisely that element missing in Poe and Bentham' theory of influence – for Freud, it is *language* that is efficacious in influencing the psyche:

> Words are the essential tools of mental treatment. A layman will no doubt find it hard to understand how pathological disorders of the body and the mind can be eliminated by 'mere' words. He will feel that he is being asked to believe in magic. And he will not be so very wrong, for the words which we use in everyday speech are nothing other than watered-down magic. But we shall have to follow a roundabout path in order to explain how science sets about restoring to words a part at least of their former magical power.[25]

The 'magic of words' operates perversely in hysteria through a symbolization involving, like *Dracula*, 'the enactment of the literal meaning of a verbally figurative expression' which can be healed by bringing the hysteric to 'restore her literal expression to its rightful place as a metaphor'.[26] However, rather than saving Freud from Charcot's mastery, the emphasis on language merely displaces the problem onto the question Psychoanalysis is quite properly constantly being called to answer: what is the authority for its 'interpretations' of our signifiers?

For Carl Jung and Ernest Jones the 'magic of words' resided in their signifieds, and mastery therefore belonged to the psychological authority who possesses the code – a sort of 'polyglot dictionary' (*Dracula*, p. 14) or set of master-plots in which the variety of symbolic expression may be reduced to a fixed system of transcendental meanings. But Freud sought to grant space to the individual's difference, using the play of signifiers in 'free association' to generate the lost history of the subject and hence arrive at an interpretation of their present – a theory that answers Harker's question by locating meaning and hence 'magic' in the 'medium' rather than in the spiritual significance of the symbol itself. Hence, as John Forrester shows, Freud looked to the etymological method and evolutionary theory of contemporary Philology – 'the one discourse that could provide an alternative to the organic evolutionism of the later nineteenth century' – for a means of accounting for the 'watered-down magic' of words by attributing the universality of the symbol to a history embodied in the material medium of language. But, crucially, if Psychoanalysis – or, for that matter, Philology – was to establish itself as a *science*, the sliding of the signifier initiated by free association or by the etymological method had to stop somewhere. Committed to its diachronic and ultimately idealist view of language, Philology could do little more than spiritualize the race-oriented Biology it sought to replace, underpinning its potentially infinite regression with a mythical, primal 'Ur-text', expressive of a collective *Volksgeist*.[27]

Hence Freud too, in an early stage, insisted on the historical reality behind the explanatory 'primal scene'. In 1889, on discovering evidence of the primal scene in one of his patients, Freud wrote to his 'mythodical' master, Wilhelm Fliess:

Buried deep beneath all his phantasies we found a scene from his primal period . . . which meets all requirements and into which

all the surviving puzzles flow. It is everything at the same time –
sexual, innocent, natural, etc. I can hardly bring myself to believe
it yet. It is as if Schliemann had dug up another Troy which had
hitherto been believed to be mythical.[28]

As Freud seeks scientific support for his developing method, we
find him resorting to Archaeology, as a theory of history, to provide
Philology, as a theory of language, with a more substantial base:
whilst the former could uncover the magic in language, the latter
had shown itself capable of proving the historical reality of the
mythical. What is more, by invoking Schliemann, Freud in effect
reminds us that Archaeology was precisely the type of 'historical
or palaetiological' science – i.e., a narrative dedicated to 'the recon-
struction in human imagination of events which have vanished or
ceased to be' – that T. H. Huxley was talking about when he invoked
Voltaire's 'detective' as his model in 'On the Method of Zadig:
Retrospective Prophecy as a Function of Science' (1881).[29] Ah ha!
So the masterful detective does, after all, offer a model for Freud's
narrative strategy? But there is a major difference to be noted here.
As Malcolm Bowie has shown, for Freud, Archaeology is no more
than a *metaphor* of method: 'The straight causal road opened up
by archaeology provides not so much a logical foundation for
Freudian historical and hermeneutic procedure as an escape from
that procedure at its moments of crisis or overspill . . . . Archaeology . . . was the dream of an alternative logic to the threatening and
insidious logic of dreams.'[30] Notwithstanding the attractions of a
unitary retrospective 'science' like that phantasized in Holmes, this
represented a 'religious' logic that he could not, in the end, accept.
In sum, 'For Freud mental science, the history of which was a tissue
of competing fictions, could never be expected to outgrow the need
for fiction and it was a point of agnostic honour not to pretend
otherwise.'[31]

So, as I suggested at the start, it depends on the detective, and
Freud's is very much a fictional, metaphorical one. In fact, Freud has
himself anticipated us, as he writes to Jung in 1909: 'My reply was
ever so wise and penetrating; I made it appear as though the most
tenuous of clues had enabled me Sherlock Holmes-like to guess
the situation (which of course was none too difficult after your
communications) . . . '.[32] What Freud is referring to here is precisely the discovery which accompanied the shift in his work with
hysterics from hypnosis to the talking cure and lay the grounds for

resolving the problem of the 'primal scene' by making the truth of the analyst's discourse dependent on a dialectic with the discourse of the patient. This is the transference, 'that is, a moment in the treatment of a patient when sexuality erupted into the open in the form of a direct implication of the doctor'[33] and which, rather than any extraneous or mystical mastery, founded the latter's authority over the analysand. But, put that way, the concept of the transference might remind us of the 'cowardly experiment' Bruff incites Franklin to practice on Rachel. The reference to Holmes is oddly appropriate for, by revealing medical 'sympathy' as a relationship of sexual power generated through the linguistic exchange of the analysis, the transference, even more perhaps than hypnosis or the interpretation of symbols, obviously raises the spectre of Charcot's model of mastery.

Such a view is quite borne out by the context. In fact, Freud here is bailing Jung out of a frightful mess with Sabine Spielrein – at the time his patient, later Piaget's analyst, and the probable originator of the idea of the death instinct. As Jung himself writes: 'She was, so to speak, my test case . . . She was, of course, systematically planning my seduction, which I considered inopportune. Now she is seeking revenge.'[34] Later, sounding even more like Robert Audley: 'The way these women manage to charm us with every conceivable psychic perfection until they have attained their purpose is one of nature's greatest spectacles.'[35] In short, in an act of male professional solidarity, Freud assumes *ironically* the role of Holmes, conspicuously *playing the master* to silence an importunate patient who is terrorizing her analyst with her transference. Equating Freud with Holmes is, as in a horror story, to collapse a metaphor, or, as in Holmes, to masquerade a fiction as a factual reality. Holmes is a metaphor to be invoked at a moment when Psychoanalysis becomes a caricature of itself, a male conspiracy to keep the woman's sexuality in its place and to conceal its own, whilst at the same time blaming the woman for what the doctor fails to know.

Freud's reply to Jung contains a hint that it may not in truth be the patient's fault; analysts are still learning 'what part of the danger lies in the matter and what part in our way of handling it'. This did not of course prevent Freud from initially blaming Dora's transference for his failure in treating her:

> If cruel impulses and revengeful motives . . . become transferred on to the physician during treatment, before he has had time to

detach them from himself by tracing them back to their sources, then it is not to be wondered at if the patient's condition is unaffected by his therapeutic efforts. For how could the patient take a more effective revenge than by demonstrating upon her own person the helplessness and incapacity of the physician?[36]

Had Psychoanalysis stopped with there, Freud's irony would turn on him and the analogy with Holmes would indeed hold. But it can be argued that this science of the subject broke free of that model of mastery precisely through its capacity for a critique of its own postulates, and most particularly, through its reinstatement of the 'obtrusive', constructive sexual and ideological position of the analyst of the other's history and discourse. For Freud later acknowledged that what was responsible for the failure of the Dora case not so much her transference, but the influence of *his* sexual projections onto the analysand. If Forrester is right to identify Psychoanalysis with seduction on the grounds that in both the first 'manoeuvre' is a gesture which says 'I know what you're thinking', then he is equally correct in raising the question in the psychoanalytic encounter, who is seducing whom?[37] Freud's discovery of the countertransference occurred when he recognized that, whilst he had pushed Dora to recognize the hidden object of her desire in Herr K, it was really directed at Frau K; what Freud was thinking Dora was thinking was clearly 'what he knew of womankind'.[38]

According to Forrester, there is something even more important than Freud's own sexual psyche involved here: what Freud could not accept, as much as the 'father of psychoanalysis' as as a man, was that the position of *knowledge* in which he was placed by the transference should be that of a woman:

[T]he psychoanalytic situation would have to receive a new meaning once Frau K.'s significance had become the centre of attention. For the relation that Dora had with Frau K. . . . was one of intimate talk about sexual secrets between two women. The most hidden of all Dora's secrets that Freud's techniques failed to uncover was that the psychoanalytic conversation itself, in which Freud thought he held all the keys, had become the scene in which two 'women' talked about sex . . . The opposition between logos (Freud's technique, explicitly analogous to gynaecology) and philia (Dora's secret) . . . is what Freud wishes to maintain, so that psychoanalysis retains its scientificity, and is prevented from degenerating into natter, into old wives' tales. Not only had Freud's work been called a 'scientific fairy tale' by a respected senior colleague, Freud had himself, in 1895, pointed out that his case-histories read more like short stories, lacking 'the serious stamp of science'.[39]

Such is the seduction of the inherited model of mastery. The resurgence of tyrannical masculine mastery in analysis, as in other narratives, can only be avoided by the recognition that the scientific or epistemological authority of the subject passes through the authorship of 'science', and that this passes through the role of gender in determining the models of scientific mastery.

So the question is not, to paraphrase Humpty-Dumpty, who is to be 'master', but how *not* to be. I am, I think, arguing (in a way which necessarily puts potentially devastating questions to my own professional enterprise) that the very desire to master is, as it were, part of the problem, not the solution. Again, that is – I hope obviously – not to say that there is no meaning, that the play of the signifier is infinite, or that one should disown narrative, knowledge, reason and politics for fear of becoming a 'policeman'. The chance would be a fine thing; for most of us are rather more mastered than masters. Ideologically, we may not like detectives and their stories, but, largely invisible as they so often insist on being, we do not lack for them. What has been at issue here is the question: by what fiction is mastery installed, and by what fiction may it be challenged? My fiction is that what we are mastered by, what mystery structures our plots, is probably better approached by the sort of critical narrative of social and personal authority, of discourse, ideology, sexuality, and of science and fiction which has been the monstrous sub-text of the popular literature we have been studying, and which Holmes, very clearly, aims finally to silence. His greatest success, then, has been to blind readers to the questions opened by the predecessors he also seeks to master in bringing them within his revisionary narrative.

Notes

CHAPTER 1 MYSTERY

1. Peter Humm, Paul Stigant and Peter Widdowson, *Popular Fictions* (London: Methuen, 1986), p. 2.
2. Peter Brooks, *Reading for the Plot* (Oxford: Clarendon Press, 1984), p. 29.
3. Julian Symons, *Bloody Murder* (Harmondsworth: Penguin, 1985 [1972]), p. 29.
4. See Ian Ousby, *Bloodhounds of Heaven* (Cambridge, Mass.: Harvard University Press, 1976) and R. F. Stewart, *. . . And Always a Detective* (Newton Abbot: David & Charles, 1980).
5. Franco Moretti, *Signs Taken for Wonders* (London: Verso, 1983), p. 9.
6. Mystery/detective fiction has been analysed, formally and/or functionally, in relation to all these genres, as well as to comedy and realism. W. H. Auden ('The Guilty Vicarage' [1944], like Jan R. Van Meter ('Sophocles and the Rest of the Boys in the Pulps', in Larry N. Landrum *et al.*, *Dimensions of Detective Fiction* [Bowling Green, Ohio: Popular Press, 1976], pp. 12–21), Geraldine Pederson-Krag ('Detective Stories and the Primal Scene', op. cit., pp. 58–63) and, in a negative sense, Geoffrey Hartman ('Literature High or Low: The Case of the Mystery Story', in *The Fate of Reading and Other Essays* [Chicago: University of Chicago Press, 1975], pp. 203–222), see it as a survival of the tragic myth. But Hanna Charney (*The Detective Novel of Manners* [Toronto: Associated University Press, 1981]) follows George Grella ('Murder and Manners: The Formal Detective Novel' in Larry N. Landrum *et al.*, *Dimensions of Detective Fiction*, pp. 37–57) in placing it, as their titles indicate, in the tradition of the comedy of manners. Tzvetan Todorov (see note 12 below), and John G. Cawelti (*Adventure, Mystery, and Romance* [Chicago: University of Chicago Press, 1976]) relate it to the Romance, whilst Raymond Chandler and others clearly see it as a form of social realism.
7. Brooks, p. 4.
8. See Terry Lovell, *Consuming Fiction* (London: New Left Books/Verso, 1987).
9. Quoted in Stewart, p. 73. A classic modern site for this, and other objections registered here, is Geoffrey Hartman, 'Literature High or Low: The Case of the Mystery Story', see, for example, p. 218.
10. David I. Grossvogel, *Mystery and its Fictions* (Baltimore: Johns Hopkins University Press, 1979), p. 15.
11. Jean-Pierre Faye, *La Critique du Langage et son Economie* (Paris: Editions Galilée, 1973), p. 16.
12. See Tzvetan Todorov, *The Poetics of Prose* (Oxford: Basil Blackwell, 1977).

13. Brooks, *Reading for the Plot*, p. 94; pp. 22–3.
14. Op. cit., pp. 103–4.
15. Op. cit., p. 107.
16. Op. cit., p. 25.
17. Op. cit., p. 27.
18. Todorov, pp. 122–3.
19. Op. cit., p. 125. See Joel Fineman, 'The Structure of Allegorical Desire' in Stephen Greenblatt (ed.), *Allegory and Representation* (Baltimore: Johns Hopkins University Press, 1981) and Ronald Schleifer, 'The Space and Dialogue of Desire: Lacan, Greimas, and Narrative Temporality', in Robert Con Davis (ed.), *Lacan and Narration* (Baltimore: Johns Hopkins University Press, 1983) – particularly p. 872.
20. Frederic Jameson, *The Political Unconscious* (London: Methuen, 1983 [1981]), p. 22.
21. See op. cit., p. 115.
22. Op. cit., p. 105.
23. Op. cit., p. 131.
24. Op. cit., p. 141.
25. Op. cit., p. 144.
26. Brooks, *Reading for the Plot*, p. 6.
27. Grossvogel, *Mystery and its Fictions*, p. 38.
28. Op. cit., p. 3.
29. '*Enromancier, romanar, romaniz* meant to translate or compose books in the vernacular.' Gillian Beer, *The Romance* (London: Methuen, 1970), p. 4.
30. The term 'Miracle' is no more religious in origin than 'Mystery'; it refers to the tricks of mountebanks and magicians which were a popular form of secular entertainment in the Middle Ages. See Rosemary Woolf, *The English Mystery Plays* (London: Routledge and Kegan Paul, 1972), p. 36.
31. See op. cit., pp. 83–4.
32. W. Lewis Jones, 'The Arthurian Legend' in A. C. Ward and A. Waller, *The Cambridge History of English Literature*, Vol. I (Cambridge: Cambridge University Press, 1949), p. 243–71.
33. See Dieter Mehl, *The Middle English Romances of the Thirteenth and Fourteenth Centuries* (London: Routledge and Kegan Paul, 1968), p. 4.
34. Todorov, *The Poetics of Prose*, p. 129.
35. Marc Shell, *Money, Language, and Thought* (Berkeley: University of California Press, 1982), pp. 24–6, 41.
36. Op. cit., pp. 41–3.
37. Op. cit., pp. 37–8.
38. See Marc Shell, *The Economy of Literature* (Baltimore: Johns Hopkins University Press, 1978), pp. 12–13.
39. The 'trial of the pyx' continues to the present day, the authority under trial being the Chancellor of the Exchequer. I am grateful to my father for this information.
40. Shell, *Money, Language, and Thought*, pp. 37–8; Moretti, *Signs Taken*

for Wonders, p. 46.

CHAPTER 2 CRIME

1. Lennard Davis, *Factual Fictions* (New York: Columbia University Press, 1983), p. 125.
2. See Victor Neuburg, *Popular Literature: A Guide* (Harmondsworth: Penguin, 1977), p. 62. For the tracing of the term 'novels', see Davis, p. 45.
3. Davis, p. 47.
4. Op. cit., p. 97.
5. According to Davis, 'Of all the ballads in general in Rollins' *Analytic Index to the Ballad Entries in the Stationers' Register,* the most popular single subject, according to my count, was criminal behavior' – Davis, p. 56. As David Nokes puts it: 'rarely if ever have [criminal biographies] figured as pre-eminently in publishers' lists as in the first three decades of the eighteenth century' – David Nokes (ed.), *Henry Fielding: Jonathan Wild* (Harmondsworth: Penguin, 1982), p. 8. *The Tyburn Calendar* was published regularly from 1700, to be replaced by *The Newgate Calendar* in 1773 (which, according to Leon Radzinowicz, sold ten times more copies than *The Spectator, The Rambler* or *The Guardian* – Leon Radzinowicz, *A History of English Criminal Law from 1750,* I [London: Stevens & Sons, 1948], p. 181). See also the extensive bibliography in Lincoln B. Faller, *Turned to Account* (Cambridge: Cambridge University Press, 1987).
6. See J. A. Sharpe, *Crime in Early Modern England, 1550–1750* (London: Longman, 1984), pp. 100, 164–5.
7. Thomas Hobbes, *Leviathan,* I. 13.
8. Quoted in John Miller, *The Glorious Revolution* (London: Longman, 1983), p. 27.
9. See C. K. Allen, *Law in the Making* (Oxford: Clarendon Press, 1964), p. 10.
10. John Brewer and John Styles, 'Popular attitudes to the law in the eighteenth century', in Mike Fitzgerald *et al., Crime and Society* (London: Routledge and Kegan Paul, 1981), p. 30.
11. J. H. Baker, *An Introduction to English Legal History,* 2nd edn (London: Butterworths, 1979), p. 166. Baker is referring to Bracton, *De Legibus et Consuetudinibus Angliae,* c.1250; the other contemporary compendia were Coke's *Institutes of the Laws of England* (1628–40s), Hale's posthumous *History of the Common Law* (1713) and *History of the Pleas of the Crown* (1736).
12. See David Sugarman and G. R. Rubin, 'Towards a New History of Law and Material Society in England, 1750–1914', in G. R. Rubin and David Sugarman (eds), *Law, Economy and Society* (Abingdon, Oxon: Professional Books, 1984), pp. 25–8.
13. Radzinowicz, *A History of English Criminal Law,* I, pp. 77, 51; see also Michael Ignatieff, *A Just Measure of Pain* (New York: Columbia University Press, 1980 [1978]), p. 16.

14.   As 'Rudé and Hobsbawm have both shown . . . riotous protest was an accepted and mutually understood means by which the politically unrepresented masses communicated grievances to the ruling élite – "bargaining by riot"' – Robert Reiner, *The Politics of the Police* (Brighton: Harvester Press, 1985), p. 21.

15.   For an account of the Marriage Act, see Allen Horstman, *Victorian Divorce* (London: Croom Helm, 1985), p. 12.

16.   Henry Fielding, *Inquiry into the Causes of the late Increase in Robberies*, 1750, quoted in Radzinowicz, I, p. 416.

17.   Jonas Hanway, *The Defects of Police: The Causes of Immorality . . .* , 1775, quoted in Radzinowicz, *A History of the English Criminal Law*, III, p. 17.

18.   Radzinowicz, III, p. 409.

19.   Douglas Hay, 'Property, Authority and the Criminal Law' in Douglas Hay *et al.*, *Albion's Fatal Tree* (Harmondsworth: Penguin, 1977 [1975]), p. 29.

20.   See Radzinowicz, I, pp. 25–35, 83–118, 139–88.

21.   Hay, *Albion's Fatal Tree*, p. 23.

22.   Ignatieff, *A Just Measure of Pain*, p. 21.

23.   Michel Foucault, *Discipline and Punish* (London: Allen Lane, 1977 [1975]), p. 44.

24.   Sharpe, *Crime in Early Modern England*, pp. 161–2.

25.   Brooks, *Reading for the Plot*, pp. 33, 268.

26.   Davis, *Factual Fictions*, pp. 126, 128. See Lincoln B. Faller, *Turned to Account*, Chs 1 and 2.

27.   Davis, p. 131.

28.   James Beattie, 'On Fable and Romance', in *Dissertations Moral and Critical*, 1783, in Geoffrey Day, *From Fiction to the Novel* (London: Routledge and Kegan Paul, 1987), pp. 48–9.

29.   John Locke, *Some Thoughts Concerning Education*, 1693, quoted in Geoffrey Summerfield, *Fantasy and Reason* (London: Methuen, 1984), p. 6.

30.   Summerfield, pp. 9–10.

31.   Op. cit., pp. 79, 33.

32.   From a review of Fanny Burney's *Carmilla* in *The British Critic* (November, 1796), quoted in Day, *From Fiction to the Novel*, p. 6.

33.   Daniel Defoe, *The True and Genuine Account of the Life and Actions of the Late Jonathan Wild*, 1725, in David Nokes (ed.), *Henry Fielding: Jonathan Wild*, p. 223.

34.   Daniel Defoe, preface to *Roxana, The Fortunate Mistress*, 1724, ed. David Blewett (Harmondsworth: Penguin, 1982), p. 35.

35.   Terry Lovell, *Consuming Fiction*, p. 7.

36.   Daniel Defoe, *The Fortunes and Misfortune of the Famous Moll Flanders*, 1722, ed. Juliet Mitchell (Harmondsworth: Penguin, 1978), pp. 29 (preface), p. 273.

37.   Davis, *Factual Fictions*, p. 137.

38.   Defoe, *Moll Flanders*, p. 28.

39.   See Carol Houlihan Flynn, 'Defoe's idea of conduct: ideological fictions and fictional reality', in Nancy Armstrong and Leonard

Tennenhouse (eds), *The Ideology of Conduct* (New York: Methuen, 1987), pp. 75–6.

40. Defoe, *Moll Flanders*, pp. 35, 38.
41. It is perhaps Defoe's *Colonel Jack* (1722), that text which does most to exploit and explain the new financial capitalism, which is most clearly textured by these running metaphors. The other side of this inverted underworld of 'trade' is that of bills, discount and interest, and of colonial exploitation under modern management methods on which Jack builds his respectability.
42. Faller, *Turned to Account*, p. 123.
43. See the bibliography to Gerald Howson, *It Takes a Thief: The Life and Times of Jonathan Wild* (London: Cresset Library, 1987 [1970]).
44. Henry Fielding, *The Life of Mr. Jonathan Wild*, 1743, in David Nokes (ed.), *Henry Fielding: Jonathan Wild*, pp. 61, 78, 102.
45. Defoe, *The True and Genuine Account . . .* , in op. cit., p. 240. Future references to this edition are given in the text.
46. According to the 1911 edition of the *Encyclopedia Britannica* one of the designers of the South Sea scheme – obtaining monopoly trade privileges in exchange for taking on the National Debt – was the ubiquitous Defoe. Similar, albeit less ambitious, deals had existed before; the novelty in this case was the secondary market generated in the company's stock. When the ferocious boom collapsed in 1720, it was discovered that there was no legal framework for dealing with the situation created by the company's failure. For the 1733 Stock-jobbing Act, see Sugarman and Rubin, *Law, Economy and Society*, pp. 194–5.
47. Baker, *An Introduction to English Legal History*, p. 166.
48. L. B. Curzon, *English Legal History*, 2nd edn (London: Macdonald & Evans, 1979), p. 95.
49. Baker, p. 176.
50. Op. cit., p. 93.
51. Curzon, p. 113. Cf. the dispute between James I and Coke in 1616. James' decision that Equity should prevail in the case of conflict was overruled by the Commonwealth, which in fact proposed the abolition of the courts of Equity. See also James II's use of his rights in Equity in the matter of the Test Acts.
52. K. J. Eddey, *The English Legal System* (London: Sweet & Maxwell, 1971), p. 171.
53. Peter Stein, *Legal Institutions* (London: Butterworths, 1984), p. 168.
54. Op. cit., p. 161.
55. Allen, *Law in the Making*, p. 411, 415–16.
56. Curzon, *English Legal History*, p. 107.
57. Moretti, *Signs Taken for Wonders*, p. 137.

CHAPTER 3   POLICE

1. Daniel Defoe, *Moll Flanders*, p. 271.

2. Stephen Knight, *Form and Ideology in Crime Fiction* (London: Macmillan, 1980), pp. 11–12.

3. See Lincoln B. Faller, *Turned to Account*, p. 75.

4. Phillip Thurmond Smith, *Policing Victorian London: Political Policing, Public Order, and the London Metropolitan Police* (Westport, Conn.: Greenwood Press, 1985), p. 18.

5. Frank Mort, *Dangerous Sexualities: Medico-Moral Politics in England since 1830* (London: Routledge and Kegan Paul, 1987), p. 25.

6. Phillip P. Smith, p. 11.

7. See E. C. Midwinter, *Victorian Social Reform* (Harlow, Essex: Longmans, 1968), p. 21.

8. Clive Emsley, *Policing and its Context 1750–1870* (London: Macmillan, 1983), p. 2; Emsley, *Crime and Society in England, 1750–1900* (London: Longman, 1987), p. 171.

9. See Radzinowicz, III, p. 417.

10. [Adam Smith], *Lectures on Justice, Police, Revenue and Arms . . . Reported by a Student in 1763*, quoted in Radzinowicz, III, p. 421.

11. Sir Nathaniel Conant, quoted in Radzinowicz, II, p. 311.

12. In 1735 the citizens of St. George's, Hanover Square had obtained a Bill permitting the vestry to raise a rate to pay the watch. By 1740 most of London had adopted this system. None the less, by the early nineteenth century, 'Charlies' (the nickname for the watch) was still a by-word for uselessness. A mounted patrol around the London turnpikes instituted by John Fielding in 1763 proved too expensive, but a 'Foot Patrol' of some 100 men continued at night in and around the Metropolis. In 1805, a 60-strong Horse Patrol was reinstated; in 1821 the Foot Patrol was restricted to paved areas and a 'Dismounted Horse Patrol' of a further 100 men was created; finally, a smaller Day Patrol (27 men) was added in 1822.

13. See Radzinowicz, II, pp. 190–1.

14. J. P. Smith, *Account of a Successful Experiment for an Effectual Nightly Watch . . .* [1812], quoted in Radzinowicz, III, p. 344.

15. 1818 Select Committee, quoted in Op. cit., p. 357.

16. Charles Dickens, 'New York', in *American Notes* [1842] (London: Oxford University Press, 1957), p. 88; *Dombey and Son* [1848] (Harmondsworth: Penguin, 1970), chap. XLVII, p. 738.

17. Quoted in Radzinowicz, III, pp. 555–6.

18. Quoted in Michael Donnelly, *Managing the Mind: A Study of Medical Psychology in Early Nineteenth Century Britain* (London: Tavistock, 1983), p. 22.

19. Ignatieff, *A Just Measure of Pain*, p. 213.

20. Op. cit., p. 62.

21. It does not seem to me necessary to opt absolutely between the traditional account of Reform as progressive humanitarianism and the revisionist history of repressive tolerance. As in more recent works which steer a middle course after the polemical production which followed Foucault's pioneering work, it makes more sense to see the various aspects of the 'police' of Reform not so much as

the fulfilment of a single benign or sinister class project, but as the dialectical consequence of various endeavours and of resistance to them, including *ad hoc* responses to specific foci at specific times. A useful summary and bibliography of the competing schools in relation to the police force itself may be found in Reiner, *The Politics of the Police*, chapter 1.

22.   As Sir Peter Parker observed in 1987: 'Those of us who have been in management all our bloody lives know that this is our moment.' Management is still struggling towards autonomous and specific professional status. Proposals were published in 1987 for the institution of a professional qualification of 'Chartered Manager', distinct from the accounting charters or business administration degrees presently awarded, but this is far from obtaining the unanimous support of the managers. See the *Financial Times*, 25 March 1988, pp. 14–15, for the 'Charter Group Code for Management Development'.

23.   Colquhon's estimate is found in Radzinowicz, III, p. 239, Chadwick's in Midwinter, *Victorian Social Reform*, p. 8.

24.   Henry VIII's 1544 statute refounding St. Bartholomew's, in F. F. Cartwright, *A Social History of Medicine* (London: Longman, 1977), p. 34.

25.   Op. cit., p. 23.

26.   The first important legislation was the 1774 Private Madhouses Act which introduced inspection and legal certification for private inmates on the advice of a doctor. The 1808 County Asylums Act, authorizing but not compelling magistrates to erect asylums at public expense, was the result of a Parliamentary Inquiry provoked by the legal question of custodial provision for those acquitted of felonies on the grounds of insanity (provoked by the Hadfield case, discussed in its legal aspect in chapter 6). A subsequent inquiry into scandals at York and Bethlem led to the publication of a survey in 1816, but the series of Bills proposing a centralized inspectorate introduced annually up to 1819 were all defeated. The County Asylums Act of 1828 obliged inspecting magistrates to supply annual returns to the Home Office, whilst the Madhouse Act of the same year enlarged the Metropolitan Commissioners and made medical certification obligatory for all inmates, including the pauper insane who had not been included in the 1774 Act. It was this body, constituted by five physicians and five lay members under the Lords Shaftesbury and Somerset, whose national tour of inspection and comprehensive report led to the major legislation of the period, the 1845 Lunacy Act and County Asylums Act, the first establishing a centralized national full-time inspectorate and asylum registers and medical records, and the second finally making the provision of pauper asylums compulsory. This did not however resolve the problem of wrongful detention: the 'Alleged Lunatics' Friends Society' was also founded in 1845.

27.   See Ignatieff, pp. 81–7.

28.   Statement of principle from Thomas Bernard's 1798 *Report of the*

Society for the Betterment of the Conditions of the Poor, quoted in op. cit., p. 76.
29. Mort, *Dangerous Sexualities*, p. 21.
30. For example, John Howard's detailed survey of every prison in England and Wales (*The State of the Prisons*, 1777), Patrick Colquhon's surveys of poverty and crime between 1796 and 1814, the first national census (1801), G. O. Paul's evidence to the 1807 Select Committee on asylums, and Chadwick's report on the poor (1833). The first statutory obligation of institutions demanded by the Reformers was the provision of the sort of statistical returns they had been gathering privately, turning the police of information into a regular state instrument, as we see in the more important official inquiries of the mid-century: the Select Committee on the Health of Towns (1840), the Report on the Sanitary Conditions of the Labouring Poor (1842), the Parliamentary Commission on the State of Large Towns (1844), and the Report of the Metropolitan Commissioners in Lunacy (1844). These were still supplemented by private philanthropic and increasingly professional social surveys in various areas, such as the reports of *The Philanthropist* from 1810 on, of the *Statistical Society* and the *National Association for the Promotion of Social Science* (founded in 1857) and the *Lancet's* inquiry into sick wards in workhouses (1865). The failure of the Reform movement is registered in a new round of even more extensive reports, of which the most famous are obviously Henry Mayhew's *London Labour and the London Poor* (1861–62) and Charles Booth's *Life and Labour of the People in London* (1889–91).
31. Mort, *Dangerous Sexualities*, p. 23.
32. Op. cit., p. 29.
33. Op. cit., p. 26.

CHAPTER 4   DETECTIVES

1. Jeremy Bentham, *Panopticon; or, the Inspection House* (1791), in *Works* (Edinburgh, 1843), IV, pp. 39, 40 'c 44.
2. See Marc Shell, *The Economy of Literature*, pp. 17–18.
3. Bentham, 'The Rationale of Reward', *Works*, II, p. 222; quoted in Radzinowicz, *A History of English Criminal Law and Its Administration*, I, p. 369.
4. The change is not, as Bentham seems to have wished, only verbal, but concerns the public visibility of the inspector. Despite the adoption of his architectural technology and the placing of an invisible invigilator in the penitentiary tower, Bentham's proposal for an invisible institutional regime of private sub-contracting and self-financing was rejected by a Commons Committee in 1810 in favour of G. O. Paul's proposal of externally scrutinized provision and supervision. See Ignatieff, *A Just Measure of Pain*, pp. 112–13.
5. Donnelly, *Managing the Mind*, p. 34. Citizen Pinel's unchaining of

the inmates at Bicêtre in 1792 is regarded, especially in the wake of Foucault, again in Donnelly's words, as 'the founding gesture of the model asylum movement.' The Quaker William Tuke founded his model institution, The Retreat, in York in the same year; his work was publicized by William Start in 1806 and by Tuke's grandson, Samuel, in his *Description of the Retreat*, 1813. Benjamin Rush, a defender of the theory that criminality and insanity were both medical pathologies, was responsible for the reform of both the Penitentiary and the Asylum at Walnut Street in Philadelphia.

6. James Prichard, *A Treatise on Lunacy*, 1835. See Donnelly, p. 137.
7. Donnelly, loc. cit.
8. Andrew Scull, *Museums of Madness: The Social Organization of Insanity in Nineteenth-Century England* (London: Allen Lane, 1979), p. 69.
9. Robert Gardiner Hill, *Total Abolition of Personal Restraint in the Treatment of the Insane*, 1839; quoted in Vieda Skultans, *English Madness: Ideas on Insanity, 1580–1890* (London: Routledge and Kegan Paul, 1979), p. 59.
10. Joan Bursfield, *Managing Madness: Changing Ideas and Practice* (London: Hutchinson, 1986), p. 212.
11. Donnelly, *Managing the Mind*, p. 42.
12. Op. cit., p. 41.
13. Op. cit., p. 42.
14. Quoted in op. cit., p. 44.
15. Patrick Colquhon, *A Treatise on the Commerce and Police of the River Thames*, 1800, quoted in Radzinowicz, *History of English Criminal Law and Its Administration*, III, p. 143.
16. Colquhon, *A Treatise on the Police of the Metropolis*, 1796, quoted in Radzinowicz, III, p. 235.
17. The opening paragraph of the Colquhon's Preface to the sixth edition of *A Treatise on the Police . . .* , quoted in Radzinowicz, III, p. 247.
18. Radzinowicz, op. cit., p. 265.
19. Op. cit., p. 294.
20. Radzinowicz, II, p. 369.
21. Midwinter, *Victorian Social Reform*, p. 24.
22. Edwin Chadwick, 'Life Assurances', 1828; Radzinowicz, III, p. 450.
23. Here Rowan and Mayne anticipated a recent management strategy whose best illustrations continues to be derived from the myth of police: 'Early every morning at the TGI Friday's American-style bistro in Reading, south-east England, there is a scene redolent of the roll call in *Hill Street Blues*, the American television series. Waiters, waitresses and kitchen staff at the restaurant, just like the police in the fictitious US police station, attend a regular "pep talk" conducted by a member of the management team . . . .', Lisa Wood, 'Teaching the staff to spread a little happiness', *Financial Times*, 18 January 1990, p. 8.
24. Rowan and Mayne, *General Instructions*, quoted in Radzinowicz, IV, p. 163.
25. Rowan maintained that in the early years of the force four out of every five dismissals were for drunkenness (See P. T. Smith,

Policing Victorian London, pp. 49–50). The importance of sobriety is known to us as the literary folklore of not taking a drink on duty.

26. Radzinowicz, IV, p. 167.

27. Quoted in Rainer, *The Politics of the Police*, p. 53.

28. Quoted in P. T. Smith, *Policing Victorian London*, p. 39.

29. Junius Junior [Johnson], *Life in the Low Parts of Manchester* (Manchester, n.d.), quoted in David Jones, *Crime, Protest, Community and Police in Nineteenth Century Britain* (London: Routledge and Kegan Paul, 1982), p. 176.

30. Quoted in Emsley, *Policing and Its Context*, p. 149.

31. Robert D. Storch, 'The plague of blue locusts: police reform and popular resistance in Northern England, 1840–57' [1975], in Mike Fitzgerald *et al.*, *Crime and Society: Readings in History and Theory* (London: Routledge and Kegan Paul, 1981), p. 93.

32. Quoted in P. T. Smith, *Policing Victorian London*, pp. 122.

33. Emsley, *Policing and Its Context*, p. 131.

34. George Rudé, *Criminal and Victim: Crime and Society in Early Nineteenth Century England* (Oxford: Clarendon Press, 1985), p. 100. Jones' conclusion were published in the *Transactions of the Royal Historical Society*, XXXIII (1983), pp. 151–68.

35. See David Jones, *Crime, Protest, Community and Police . . .*, pp. 18–32.

36. Quoted in Emsley, *Policing and Its Context*, p. 129.

37. Charles Reith, *The British Police and the Democratic Ideal* (London, 1943), pp. 152–8. See Radzinowicz, IV, p. 188.

38. Quoted in P. T. Smith, *Policing Victorian London*, p. 86.

39. Belton Cobb goes further and suggests that Mayne always intended to create such a department and was building a dossier of officers from the earliest days – see Belton Cobb, *The First Detectives and the Early Career of Richard Mayne, Commissioner of Police* (London: Faber & Faber, 1957), pp. 11, 50–8.

40. Ignatieff, *A Just Measure of Pain*, p. 200.

41. A campaigning journal, the *Lancet*, had been founded by physicians in 1823. Medical degrees were instituted in London in 1828 and 1831. In 1855 the British Medical Association was formed and the profession was finally regulated by a General Council for Medical Education and Registration set up under the 1858 Medical Act. The major professional bodies formed to stake the claim of the medical profession over the asylums were the Association of Medical Officers of Asylums and Hospitals (1841) and its *Asylum Journal of Mental Science* (1853) under John Charles Bucknill (later joint-author of the standard work from 1858–80), and the group formed by Forbes Winslow, physician, asylum owner and expert witness in legal defences of insanity, around his *Journal of Psychological Medicine and Mental Pathology* (1848).

42. Morel, *Treatise on Mental Diseases*, 1860, quoted in Ian Dowbiggin, 'Degeneration and hereditarianism in French Mental Medicine, 1840–90', in W. F. Bynum, Roy Porter and Michael Shepherd

(eds), *The Anatomy of Madness: Essays in the History of Psychiatry*, Vol. I (London: Tavistock, 1985), p. 206.

43.   Rudolf Virchow, *Cellular-Pathologie*, 1858, quoted in Cartwright, *A Social History of Medicine*, p. 136.

44.   Thomas Plint, *Crime in England: its Relation, Character and Extent*, 1851, quoted in William James Forsythe, *The Reform of Prisoners, 1830–1900* (London: Croom Helm, 1987), p. 169.

45.   Quoted in Skultans, *English Madness*, p. 136. See also Forsythe's chapter on 'The Scientific Approach to Criminal Man 1860–1890' in *The Reform of Prisoners*, pp. 167–192 and Mort's chapters on 'Medical hegemony and social policy 1850–1870' and 'Female sexuality' in the same period, in *Dangerous Sexualities*.

CHAPTER 5   THE ROMANCE OF THE DETECTIVE

1.   D. H. Lawrence, 'Morality and the Novel' (1925), in A. A. H. Inglis (ed.), *D. H. Lawrence: A Selection from Phoenix* (Harmondsworth: Penguin, 1971), p. 177.

2.   Lennard Davis, *Resisting Novels* (London: Methuen, 1987), pp. 24–5.

3.   D. A. Miller, 'The Novel and the Police', *Glyph*, VIII (1981), p. 141.

4.   Op. cit., p. 17.

5.   Terry Lovell, *Consuming Fiction*, p. 11.

6.   Op. cit., p. 93.

7.   Op. cit., p. 29.

8.   See Katherine MacDermott, 'Literature and the Grub Street myth', in Peter Humm *et al.*, *Popular Fictions. Essays in Literature and History* (London: Methuen, 1986), pp. 18–21.

9.   Ian Ousby, *Bloodhounds of Heaven*, p. ix.

10.   Julian Symons, *Bloody Murder*, pp. 13, 15.

11.   Edmund Wilson, 'Why Do People Read Detective Stories?' in *Classics and Commercials: a Literary Chronicle of the Forties* (New York: Farrar, Strauss, 1950), p. 236. As this text will make clear, I do not share Wilson's 'enchantment' with Sherlock Holmes (nor, I might add, his distaste for Dashiel Hammett), and would myself locate the beginning of this decline in Holmes himself.

12.   Arthur Conan Doyle, 'A Study in Scarlet' [1887], in *The Complete Sherlock Holmes* (Harmondsworth: Penguin, 1981), p. 24.

13.   Dickens, 'The Detective Police' ('A Detective Police Party', 1850), in *The Uncommercial Traveller and Reprinted Pieces* (1858), (London: Oxford University Press, 1958), p. 485.

14.   Philip Collins, *Dickens and Crime* (London: Macmillan, 1965), p. 205.

15.   W. H. Wills, 'The Modern Science of Thief-Taking' [*Household Words*, 13 July 1850], reprinted in Thomas Waters, *The Recollections of a Policeman* (New York: Cornish, Lamport, 1853), p. 191. It is clear that Wills' opinions were shared by Dickens. See Philip Collins, Chapter IX.

16.   Dickens, 'The Detective Police', in *The Uncommercial Traveller and Reprinted Pieces*, p. 485.

17.   Dickens, op. cit., p. 502.
18.   Wills, 'The Modern Science of Thief-Taking' in Waters, p. 196.
19.   Dickens, 'On Duty with Inspector Field' [1851], in *The Uncommercial Traveller and Reprinted Pieces*, pp. 522–3.
20.   Dickens, 'Down with the Tide', in op. cit., p. 534.
21.   Dickens, op. cit., p. 516.
22.   Wills, op. cit., p. 194.
23.   Dickens, 'The Detective Police', p. 486.
24.   Dickens, 'On Duty with Inspector Field' p. 524.
25.   Dickens, op. cit., p. 520.
26.   Wills, op. cit., p. 196.
27.   Op. cit., p. 201.
28.   Dickens, 'Three "Detective" Anecdotes' [1850], in op. cit., pp. 504–12.
29.   Dickens, op. cit., p. 502. Dornton's skill is illustrated by his patient pursuit of a bill-stealing Jew with a very conspicuous carpet bag, by hiding in wait for thieves in 'The Sofa', and by tracing a pair of gloves; Mith's by his disguising himself and infiltrating the market for stolen goods; and Witchem is shown to be a notable pickpocket and confidence trickster.
30.   Wills, op. cit., p. 189.
31.   See Stewart, ... *And Always a Detective*, p. 29. Nowadays we find not only the highly popular sensational newspaper report and magazines devoted exclusively to such cases, but also the detective's memoirs, and more recently a new sort of 'police procedural' in which a writer/journalist claims to recount the 'authentic' activity of real detectives, changing names 'wherever it was necessary to protect the identity of my sources' – Carsten Stroud, *Close Pursuit. A Week in the Life of an NYPD Homicide Cop* (Harmondsworth: Penguin, 1988), p. 5. See also the recent work of Joseph Wambaugh and William J. Caunitz.
32.   [Thomas Gaspey?], *Richmond: Scenes in the Life of a Bow Street Runner, drawn up from his private memoranda* [1827], ed. E. F. Bleiler (New York: Dover, 1976). Page references to this edition are given in the text. I have selected this work not only because it antedates Vidocq's *Memoirs* by a year but because, as a rule, given the difference between the French and English policing models, I have sought not to confuse the issue by analysing what is necessarily a different ideological tradition.
33.   'Thomas Waters', *The Recollections of a Policeman* (New York: Cornish, Lamport, 1853). These memoirs, like those of 'Inspector F.', are believed to have been written by the journalist, William Russell. Serial publication was in *Chambers's Edinburgh Review*, 1849; an English edition was published in 1856. Page references to the earlier, American edition are given in the text.
34.   To give a flavour of these tales, let us take the case of 'Mary Kingsford', the provincial girl working in a London shop, preyed on by 'swells'. The story is set in 1836 when Waters is returning from Liverpool after having failed to catch a man who had absconded

with some funds which he held in trust. As often happens, he starts observing the other passengers on the train, noticing particular some finely dressed gentlemen who seem out of place in the cheap carriage: 'To an eye less experienced than mine in the artifices and expedients familiar to a certain class of "swells", they might perhaps have passed muster'. His eye is also caught, in another sense, by a young woman 'of a remarkably graceful figure'. He feels 'an instantaneous conviction that she was known to me'. The young lady, dressed in mourning, is distressed by the attentions of the 'swells'. Waters intervenes and clashes with the ruffians. She turns out to be Mary Kingsford, an old friend of his eldest daughter. On the death of her father, with her mother reduced to poverty, and her engagement broken off, Mary is going to London to work as a shop girl with a cousin. When they arrive in London, Mary is met by a friend, but Waters, apprehensive for the young girl in the city, notices that her cab is followed by another.

The next Sunday, he calls for tea and discovers that two characters, Hartley and Simpson, are often at the shop, encouraged by the cousin. He obtains information about these characters from a 'brother-detective'. Then, one night, as he is going to Scotland Yard, Waters passes a young lady sobbing. He decides to follow her, but he bumps into a man and loses the trail. As he lays in hiding, the young lady, who turns out to be Mary, returns and throws herself into the river. Waters tries to save her, but when he calls for assistance, the police arrest Mary for robbery. Waters offers to stand bail for her; the officers find this highly irregular, 'but I stood too well at head-quarters for them to do more than hesitate'. The next day, he goes to the Superintendent and obtains charge of the case. Mary tells him that she and Sophie had gone to the theatre with Hartley and Simpson. When a brooch is stolen and the men arrested, they and a man called Saville accuse her of the theft.

Waters discusses the case with his wife, who asks him how much the brooch is worth. Waters warns her that there is to be no 'compounding'; however, since his wife is 'a pretty good judge of the value of jewels', he shows her the brooch. She immediately discerns that it is a fake: 'my wife's words gave color and consistency to a dim and faint suspicion which had crossed my mind.' Waters puts an advertisement in the *Times* for the owner of a missing brooch. The man who comes to claim the brooch turns out to be the person who had first identified Hartley as the thief at the theatre. Waters forces him to confess that he had not told the whole truth because he had lost the original brooch, a gift from a relative, at gambling. Now he tells all and Waters confronts Saville and makes him send for Hartley and Simpson. The detective hides and overhears the conversation between the three in the course of which the latter confess their crime and their attempt to put the blame on Mary. They are arrested, the father of Mary's former fiancé lifts his ban on her engagement, and Mary is happily married.

35. Andrew Forrester, 'The Unknown Weapon' (1864), in E. F. Bleiler (ed.), *Three Victorian Novels* (New York: Dover, 1978), p. 25.

36. Michèle Slung, introduction to Catherine Louisa Pirkis, *The Experiences of Loveday Brooke, Lady Detective* [1893] (New York: Dover, 1986), p. ix.

37. W. S. Hayward [Mrs. Paschal], *The Experiences of a Lady Detective* (London: Charles Henry Clarke, n.d. [1861]). Page references to this edition are given in the text.

38. 'The Mysterious Countess' poisons herself, the political murderer Zini is struck by lightning ('The Secret Band'), the Duke hushes up his wife's theft ('The Lost Diamonds'), John Eskell forgives his wife and her temptress is punished by public shame ('Fifty Pounds Reward'), John Halliday forgives his wayward brother ('Mistaken Identity'), a deal is struck with the cruel Abbess ('The Nun, the Will, and the Abbess'), and 'Incognita' is left to find a new victim.

39. Andrew Forrester, 'The Unknown Weapon', in E. F. Bleiler (ed.), *Three Victorian Novels*, p. 59.

40. Op. cit., p. 24.

41. Op. cit., p. 50.

42. Op. cit., p. 25.

43. Op. cit., p. 57.

44. Op. cit., p. 54.

45. See Stewart, *. . . And Always a Detective*, pp. 73, 179.

46. See R. C. Terry, *Victorian Popular Fiction, 1860–80* (London: Macmillan, 1983), p. 56. The expression 'Enigma novel' is taken from *The Spectator*, XXXIV (28 Dec. 1861) 1428, and the review of *Uncle Silas* was published in *The Saturday Review* on 4 February 1865.

47. Stewart, pp. 71–2.

48. *The Quarterly Review*, CXIII (April 1863) 486, quoted in Terry, loc. cit..

49. See Stewart, pp. 61–5.

50. Op. cit., p. 30. The preference for 'the modern Gaboriau novel' also helps explain why Holmes is as scathing about LeCoq as he is about Dupin (*A Study in Scarlet*, p. 25). Note that the *Morning Post*'s review of H. F. Wood's *The Passenger from Scotland Yard* (as late as 1888) still maintains the inverted commas (Stewart, p. 27).

51. Anna Katherine Green, *X.Y.Z.* (London: Ward, Lock, 1883). Page references are given in the text.

52. Whilst Pinkerton was publishing his cases, Kenward Philip launched the earliest recorded dime novel detective story, *The Bowery Detective* (1870), whilst the first weekly to dedicate itself to detective stories began publication, like *X.Y.Z.*, in 1883 (*Old Cap. Collier Library*) – the same year which also saw the first publication of the *New York Detective Library*. See Chris Steinbrunner and Otto Penzler, *Encyclopedia of Mystery and Detection* (London: Routledge and Kegan Paul, 1976), pp. 125–6. For Allan Pinkerton, see the somewhat hagiographic James D. Horan and Howard Swigget, *The Pinkerton Story* (London: Heinemann, 1952).

53. Conan Doyle, 'A Study in Scarlet', p. 90.

CHAPTER 6   MONSTERS

1. Edgar Allan Poe, 'The Murders in the Rue Morgue' (1841), in T. Mabbott (ed.), *Collected Works of Edgar Allan Poe*, II (Cambridge, Mass.: Harvard University Press, 1978), p. 558. Future references given in the text.
2. In 'The Purloined Letter' there is a first question of who, if anyone, has committed what crime, if any: whether the Queen is guilty of treason, or the Minister of theft (blackmail not yet having been attempted). If the former, is the Minister committing a crime in defending the King? And, of course, is Dupin himself compounding the offence by stealing the letter from the Minister, and committing the offence of compounding by selling it back to the Queen, via the Prefect? Secondly, does the Minister have the intention 'permanently to deprive', necessary for the crime of theft? Lastly, to whom does a letter 'belong', so that it can be 'stolen'? This last, of course, is a question to which Lacan directs our attention in 'Le séminaire sur "La Lettre volée' [1956], *Ecrits*, I (Paris: Seuil, 1966), p. 37.
3. Mabbott, introduction to 'The Murders in the Rue Morgue', p. 521.
4. Robert A. W. Lowndes, 'The Contributions of Edgar Allan Poe', in Francis M. Nevis, Jr. (ed.), *The Mystery Writer's Art* (Bowling Green, Ohio: Popular Press, 1970), pp. 2–3.
5. Poe, letter to Philip Pendleton Cooke, Aug. 8, 1846, quoted in Mabbott, II, p. 521.
6. Chris Baldick, *In Frankenstein's Shadow: Myth, Monstrosity, and Nineteenth Century Writing* (Oxford: Clarendon Press, 1987), pp. 16 et seq.
7. Cf. Sheridan LeFanu's 'Green Tea' (1838), an account of a priest who is 'haunted' by a devilish monkey and driven to suicide. Dr. Hesselius, professor of 'metaphysical medicine', diagnoses the apparition of the monkey as an emanation of a diseased nervous state, brought on by excessive consumption of green tea. His medicalization of the Rev. Jennings' visions continues with his diagnosis of his suicide as caused by hysteria and hereditary suicidal mania. See E. Bleiler (ed.), *The Best Ghost Stories of J. Sheridan LeFanu* (New York: Dover, 1964). The suggestion of the possible influence of this story on 'The Murders in the Rue Morgue' was raised by Patrick Diskin in *Notes and Queries* (Sept., 1966).
8. That is not to say that it does not 'stand for' anything, rather that it stands, in a sense, for too much. For a particularly interesting discussion of some of the meanings it may invoke, see Richard Godden, 'Edgar Allan Poe and the Detection of Riot', *Literature and History*, VIII. 2 (Autumn 1982), 206–73.
9. See Todorov, *The Poetics of Prose*, pp. 155–6.
10. David Hume, 'An Inquiry concerning Human Understanding', in

Essays and Treatises on Several Subjects, II (Edinburgh, 1793), p. 126. Future references given in the text.

11. Victor Sage, *Horror Fiction in the Protestant Tradition* (New York: St. Martin's Press, 1988), p. 167.

12. Mary Shelley, *Frankenstein, Or, The Modern Prometheus* [1817/1831] (New York: New American Library, 1965), p. vii. Future references to this edition are given in the text.

13. Ian Michael, *The Teaching of English from the sixteenth century to 1870* (Cambridge: Cambridge University Press, 1987), p. 221.

14. James Hogg, *The Private Memoirs and Confessions of a Justified Sinner* [1824], ed. John Wain (Harmondsworth: Penguin, 1983), pp. 106. Future references to this edition are given in the text.

15. David Hume, *A Treatise of Human Nature* [1739–40] (London: Dent, 1911), p. 114. So radically sceptical was this text that Hume was forced to more or less retract it in the Advertisement to the *Inquiry* . . . on the grounds of his youth at the time or writing and the unfairness of the critics. Future references to this edition are given in the text.

16. I am aware that the Laird's sexual claims on his Lady are also ideological – indeed, George is the issue of a marital rape. But, especially in a story which plays for its horror on crimes against the blood, I think that such an interpretation would be anachronistic here.

17. Karl Miller, *Doubles: Studies in Literary History* (Oxford: Oxford University Press, 1985), p. 39. Cf. 'The word "familiar" has meant an attendant spirit or demon, and therefore a double, and there was once a synonym for it in 'fly' – which could also mean spy, can still mean mischievous, and is a word for what the literary orphan does' (p. 24).

18. Hogg of course mercilessly doubles himself: as author, Editor, and as a character in the Editor's narrative. But even his status as the material author of this book has been challenged 'by those who thought it too good for him to have written' – hoist by the petard of his professional self-parody as a highland peasant. See Miller, pp. 16–17. Other 'authors' should include Nicol Muschet, whose *Confessions of Nicol Muschet of Boghall* (1818), attributed the authorship of the murder for which he was to be hanged to a double called 'Burnbank'; and, at the ideological level, James Hog and Thomas Boston of Carnock who had revived Antinomianism in the eighteenth century with their dialogue, *The Marrow of Modern Divinity*, parodied in the novel. See Sage, p. 98.

19. Lennard J. Davis, *Resisting Novels*, p. 3.

20. See Sage, *Horror Fiction* . . . , pp. 132–3, 195.

21. Poe, letter to George Roberts, editor of the Boston *Nation*, June 4, 1842, quoted in Mabbott, III, p. 718.

22. 'The Mystery of Marie Rogêt' might at first sight be thought to contradict this, especially as Dupin draws attention to the fact that, in contrast with the earlier case, 'There is nothing *outré* about it' (III, p. 736). But, however sociologically banal it may appear, the case is still theoretically extraordinary. Having introduced the notion of the

simplicity of the difficult in 'The Murders . . . ', here Poe presents the complexity of the simple. Furthermore, the historical case of Mary Rogers was, in truth, 'outré'. The lack of concern displayed by the New York constables in the crime for which, initially, no reward had been offered caused such a scandal that it led to a proposal from the city council for their reform on the preventive lines of the Metropolitan police (rather than Poe's French force). In the event, fears of political control over the force led New York City to reject the proposal. None the less, in 1844 the State Legislature instituted a uniformed preventive corporation, which was again rejected by the City, which set up its own, short-lived, force. See Clive Emsley, *Policing and its Context, 1750–1870* (London: Macmillan, 1983), p. 106.

23. This distinction further distances Poe from the real-life detective inasmuch as, according to Bernard Cobb, one of the reasons for the foundation of the Department was the failure of the New Police to ensure that, when they caught their criminals, they obtained the evidence requisite for their conviction. See Bernard Cobb, *The First Detectives and the early career of Richard Mayne, Commissioner of Police*, p. 26.

24. The rules of evidence had obviously developed over the centuries, but it was only in the eighteenth century that they came to be collated, studied, discussed and written down. The first specialized study of the subject was Lord Chief Baron Gilbert's *Law of Evidence*, written in the 1720s and published in 1754 (source of the 'best evidence' rule). During the nineteenth century, a shift to the United States as the centre for evidence scholarship was initiated by Simon Greenleaf's *A Treatise on the Law of Evidence*, based on the author's lectures at Harvard Law School, and published in 1842. See William Twining, *Theories of Evidence: Bentham and Wigmore* (London: Weidenfeld and Nicolson, 1985), pp. 1–7.

25. Op. cit., p. 70.
26. Op. cit., p. 72.
27. Sage, *Horror Fiction . . .* , p. 163.
28. Bentham, *Rationale of Judicial Evidence* (London, 1827), p. 276, quoted in Sage, p. 163.
29. Twining, p. 37.
30. See op. cit., p. 54.
31. Op. cit., p. 36.
32. Op. cit., p. 53.
33. Sage, *Horror Fiction . . .* , p. 165.
34. Cf. the conclusion to Hume's *Treatise . . .* : 'We have therefore no choice left, but betwixt a false reason and none at all . . . . The *intense* view of these manifold contradictions and imperfections in human reason has so wrought upon me, and heated my brain, that I am ready to reject all belief and reasoning, and can look upon no opinion even as more probable or likely than another. Where am I, or what? From what causes do I derive my existence, and to what condition shall I return? Whose favour shall I court, and whose

anger must I dread? What beings surround me? and on whom have I any influence, or who have any influence on me? I am confounded with all these questions, and begin to fancy myself in the most deplorable condition imaginable, environed with the deepest darkness, and utterly deprived of the use of every member and faculty' (p. 253).

35.   Twining, p. 55.
36.   Op. cit., p. 54–59.
37.   Op. cit., p. 20.
38.   Op. cit. pp. 62–3.
39.   I have chosen not to discuss this tale in detail because of the many excellent accounts of its complexities which exist (e.g., Jacques Derrida, 'Le Facteur de la Vérité', *Poétique* 21 (1975), Barbara Johnson , 'The Frame of Reference: Poe, Lacan, Derrida', in *Literature and Psychoanalysis: The Question of Reading: Otherwise*, ed. Shoshana Felman [Baltimore: Johns Hopkins University Press, 1982], pp. 457–505, and, obviously, that of Lacan referred to above). The question of the personal relation between Dupin and the Minister D——, as well as other matters, is interestingly discussed in Godden, 'Edgar Allan Poe and the Detection of Riot', and in Jean-Claude Milner, *Détections fictives* (Paris: Seuil, 1985), pp. 9–44.
40.   Bentham, p. 74, quoted in Twining, p. 57. The reason for this is that the 'doctrine of chance' is applicable only to finite series of possibilities, whereas events in the world as given in testimony – as in the text – have a potentially infinite range of permutations.
41.   See Mabbott, III, pp. 719–20.
42.   An account of these issues and a proposal for a non-referential, narratological approach to evidence in terms of the pragmatics of evidence-giving and courtroom process (the narrative of both the evidence and of the trial as a whole) may be found in Bernard S. Jackson, *Law, Fact and Narrative Coherence* (Roby, Merseyside: Deborah Charles, 1988), to which I am grateful for guiding me, alongside Twining's work, in this highly complex field.

CHAPTER 7   SENSATION

1.   I am most grateful to Anthea Trodd for drawing my attention to this passage in her *Domestic Crime in the Victorian Novel* (London: Macmillan, 1989), pp. 90–5; cf. Henry James, *The American*, 1877, 1907, Ch. 22.
2.   Anthony Trollope, 'On English Prose Fiction as a Rational Amusement', in *Four Lectures*, ed. Morris L. Parrish (London: Constable, 1938), p. 108, quoted in Sue Lonoff, *Wilkie Collins and His Victorian Readers. A Study in the Rhetoric of Authorship* (New York: AMS Press, 1982), p. 4.
3.   Alfred Austin, 'The Novels of Miss Broughton', *Temple Bar*, XLI (May 1874), 197, quoted in Terry, *Victorian Popular Fiction*, pp. 1–2.

4. *Punch*, 20 July, 1861, quoted in Richard D. Altick, *Evil Encounters: Two Victorian Sensations* (London: John Murray, 1987), p. 4.

5. Mrs. Oliphant, 'Sensation Novels', *Blackwood's*, XCI (May 1862).

6. Anthony Trollope, *Autobiography* (Edinburgh: Blackwoods, 1883), p. 226.

7. *The Edinburgh Review*, LXX (July 1864), 53, quoted in Winifred Hughes, *The Maniac in the Cellar: Sensation Novels of the 1860s* (Princeton, N.J.: Princeton University Press, 1980), p. 167.

8. See Altick, pp. 139–40. The first self-styled 'sensation drama' was Dion Boucicault's *The Colleen Bawn* (New York, March 1860, London, September 1860), which broke records for a continuous run in London.

9. See Philip O'Neil, *Wilkie Collins: Women, Property and Propriety* (London: Macmillan, 1988), p. 77.

10 Anonymous review of *Armadale*, *Westminster Review*, LXXXVI (October 1866), quoted in Norman Page, *Wilkie Collins: The Critical Heritage* (London: Routledge & Kegan Paul, 1974), p. 160.

11. D. A. Miller, '*Cage aux folles*: Sensation and Gender in Wilkie Collins' *The Woman in White*' [1986], in Catherine Gallagher and Thomas Laqueur (eds), *The Making of the Modern Body: Sexuality and Society in the Nineteenth Century* (Berkeley: University of California Press, 1987), pp. 117–18.

12. Richard Barickman, Susan MacDonald & Myra Stark, *Corrupt Relations: Dickens, Thackeray, Trollope, Collins, and the Victorian Sexual System*, (New York: Columbia University Press, 1982), pp. 33 et seq.

13. See Mary S. Hartman, *Victorian Murderesses* (New York: Schocken, 1977).

14. Quoted in Altick, pp. 136–7.

15. Quoted in op. cit., pp. 120 & 129.

16. The above quotes may all be found in op. cit., pp. 133–8.

17. Mrs. Oliphant, 'Sensation Novels', *Blackwood's* (1862), quoted in Page (ed.), *Wilkie Collins: The Critical Heritage*, p. 118.

18. Miller, '*Cage aux folles* . . . ' pp. 107–8.

19. Op. cit., p. 109.

20. Quoted in Hughes, *The Maniac in the Cellar*, p. 58.

21. Anonymous article, *Westminster Review* (October 1866), quoted in Altick, p. 148. The notion of a virus had already been used by Henry Mansel in his important article on sensation fiction in the *Quarterly Review* (April 1863).

22. W. F. Bynum, 'The nervous patient in eighteenth- and nineteenth-century Britain: the psychiatric origins of British neurology', in Bynum *et al.*, *The Anatomy of Madness*, I, p. 99.
    Anatomy of Madness, I, p. 99.

23. See Skultans, *English Madness*, p. 27.

24. See op. cit., p. 32.

25. Thomas Syndenham, *Epistolatory Dissertation* (1681), quoted in Ilza Veith, *Hysteria: The History of a Disease* (Chicago: Phoenix, 1965), p. 141.

26.   Edward G. Boring, *A History of Experimental Psychology* [1929] (New York: Century, 1957), pp. 127–8.

27.   James Braid, *Neuropnology or the Rationale of Nervous Sleep* in Arthur Edward Wait (ed.), *Braid on Hypnotism: The Beginnings of Modern Hypnosis* (New York: Julian Press, 1960), p. 113.

28.   G. E. Berrios, 'Obsessional disorders during the nineteenth century: terminological and classificatory issues', in Bynum *et al.*, *The Anatomy of Madness*, I, pp. 169–70.

29.   Lord Hale, *History of the Pleas of the Crown* (published 1736, but finished before 1676), in Nigel Walker, *Crime and Insanity in England*, I (Edinburgh: Edinburgh University Press, 1968), p. 38.

30.   Op. cit., p. 77.

31.   Op. cit., p. 93.

32.   Op. cit., p. 94.

33.   Op. cit., p. 99.

34.   See Ruth Harris, 'Murder under hypnosis in the case of Gabrielle Bompard: psychiatry in the courtroom in Belle Epoque Paris', in Bynum *et al.*, *The Anatomy of Madness*, II, pp. 197–231.

35.   Juliet Pollock, 'Novels and their Times', *Macmillan's Magazine*, XXVI (August 1872) 358, quoted in Terry, *Victorian Popular Fiction*, p. 60.

36.   Lee Holcombe, *Wives and Property: Reform of the Married Woman's Property Law in Nineteenth-Century England* (Oxford: Marion Robertson, 1983), p. 55.

37.   Collins was in fact quick to respond to the accusation in his preface to *No Name* (1862) when he informed the reader that 'The only Secret contained in this book is revealed midway in the first volume' – Wilkie Collins, *No Name* [1862] (New York: Dover, 1978 [1873]), p. 10.

38.   Mary E. Braddon, *Lady Audley's Secret* [1862] (London: Virago, 1985), p. 319.

39.   Wilkie Collins, *The Woman in White* [1860] (Harmondsworth: Penguin, n.d.), p. 101.

40.   Op. cit., p. 105.

41.   Anna Katherine Green, *The Leavenworth Case* [1878] (New York: Dover, 1981), p. 91.

42.   Op. cit., p. 81.

43.   Op. cit., p. 309.

44.   Trodd, *Domestic Crime in the Victorian Novel*, pp. 2–6.

45.   M. B. Saint-Edme, *Dictionnaire de la Pénalité* (Paris, 1828), pp. 430–1.

46.   Trodd, p. 32.

47.   See D. A. Miller, 'From *roman policier* to *roman-police*: Wilkie Collins's *The Moonstone*', *Novel*, XIII. 2 (Winter 1980), 153–70.

48.   *Spectator*, XLI (25 July 1868) 881–2; *The Nation*, VII (17 September 1868) 235; quoted in Page, *Wilkie Collins: The Critical Heritage*, pp. 172, 174.

49.   Op. cit., p. 155

50.   Op. cit., p. 162.

51.   Wilkie Collins, *The Moonstone* [1868] (Harmondsworth: Penguin, 1966), p. 155. Future references given in the text.

52. Miller, '*Cage aux folles* . . . ', p. 113.
53. Barickman *et al.*, *Corrupt Relations*, pp. 8–9.
54. Lee Holcombe, *Wives and Property*, p. 35.
55. See Claude Lévi-Strauss, *Les Structures Elémentaires de la Parenté* (Paris: Seuil, 1967) for the importance to the fundamental family 'atom' of the symbolic debt set up by the maternal uncle's renunciation of his sister in marriage which, in this case, passes to the subsequent generation.
56. Barickman *et al.*, pp. 49, 26.
57. See Hesselius' explanation of the Rev. Jennings' suicide in LeFanu's 'Green Tea'.
58. Sigmund Freud, 'Psycho-Analysis and the Ascertaining of the Truth in Courts of Law' [1906], *Collected Papers*, II (London: 1933), p. 13.
59. Freud, p. 18.
60. See Veith, *Hysteria* . . . , pp. 201–6.
61. Quoted in op. cit., p. 211.
62. Skultans, *English Madness*, p. 92.
63. Veith, p. 209.
64. Quoted in op. cit., p. 134.
65. Michel Foucault, *Madness and Civilization. A History of Insanity in the Age of Reason* [1961] (London: Tavistock, 1971), p. 138.
66. Barickman *et al.*, *Corrupt Relations*, p. 21.
67. Hughes, *The Maniac in the Cellar*, pp. 162–3.
68. O'Neil, *Wilkie Collins*, pp. 14–18.
69. Op. cit., p. 19.
70. L. S. Hearnshaw, *A Short History of British Psychology, 1840–1940* (London: Methuen, 1964), p. 17.
71. Op. cit., p. 17.
72. See J. H. Conn, introduction to Wait (ed.), *Braid on Hypnotism*, pp. 4–5.
73. Quoted in Hearnshaw, p. 23.
74. Wilkie Collins, *Armadale* [1866] (New York: Dover, 1977), p. 591.
75. See Jeffrey Weeks, *Sex, Politics and Society: The regulation of sexuality since 1800* (London: Longmans, 1981), p. 104.
76. See Hans Eysenck (ed.), *The Experimental Study of Freudian Theories* (London: Methuen, 1973).
77. Miller, 'From *roman policier* to roman-police . . . ', pp. 155–6.

CHAPTER 8   THE MASTER

1. Arthur Conan Doyle, *The Complete Sherlock Holmes* (Harmondsworth: Penguin, 1981), p. 299. Future references to this edition are given in the text.
2. A. K. Green, *The Leavenworth Case*, p. 184.
3. These limitations are most succinctly expressed by Gryce's complaint: 'have you any idea of the disadvantages under which a detective labors? . . . Strange as it may appear, I have never by any possibility of means succeeded with one class of persons at all. I cannot pass myself off as a gentleman.' Op. cit., p. 106.

4. Ousby, *Bloodhounds of Heaven*, p. 153.

5. Knight, *Form and Ideology in Crime Fiction*, p. 86.

6. H. F. Wood, *The Passenger from Scotland Yard* (London: Chatto & Windus, 1888), p. 70. Future references to this edition are given in the text.

7. Emsley, *Crime and Society in England, 1750–1900*, p. 191.

8. Stewart demonstrates clearly how much Doyle is indebted to Gaboriau, not only for the very notion of a detective hero and for a basic structure, but for textual details such as the attitude to the police, the role of theory, the following of the 'scent', the attention to detail and the 'deduction' of a profile from the footprint – see Stewart, . . . *And Always a Detective*, pp. 256 et seq.

9. Michael Shepherd, *Sherlock Holmes and the Case of Dr. Freud* (London: Tavistock, 1985), p. 20.

10. See Catherine Louisa Pirkis, *The Experiences of Loveday Brooke, Lady Detective* [1893] (New York: Dover, 1986). For details of this and other post-Holmesian lady detectives, such as the pastiche Mrs. Julia Herlock Shomes (1894), see Patricia Craig and Mary Cadogan, *The Lady Investigates: Women Detectives and Spies in Fiction* (Oxford: Oxford University Press, 1986).

11. Quoted in Shepherd, p. 12.

12. J. Bell, 'The Adventures of Sherlock Holmes. A Review', *Bookman*, 2. 73; quoted loc. cit.

13. Howard Haycraft, *Murder for Pleasure* (London: Peter Davies, 1942), p. 54.

14. We might also note that Holmes also reveals his debt to the 'romance of the detective' precisely in those tales, which are not few, in which there is hardly any 'detective work', the crime plot serving more as a pretext for an old-fashioned *fait divers*, such as the story of 'The Man with the Twisted Lip'. Likewise, the tales are sprinkled with a Paschal-like celebration of the modern and its ideology.

15. See Shepherd, p. 10.

16. See Ronald Pearsall, *Conan Doyle: A Biographical Solution* (London: Weidenfeld & Nicolson, 1977), for example pp. 186–8; an example of this 'spirit photography' may be found facing p. 121.

17. Mrs. Oliphant, 'Novels', *Blackwood's*, CII (Sept. 1867).

18. Clive Bloom, 'Capitalising on Poe's Detective: the Dollars and Sense of Nineteenth-Century Detective Fiction', in Clive Bloom *et al.*, *Nineteenth-Century Suspense: From Poe to Conan Doyle* (London: Macmillan, 1988), p. 14.

19. See Conan Doyle, *The New Revelation* (London: Hodder & Stoughton, 1918), pp. 38–9.

20. Bram Stoker, *Dracula* [1897] (Harmondsworth: Penguin, 1979), p. 447. Future references to this edition are given in the text.

21. Review, *Athenaeum*, 26 June, 1897, quoted in Peter Haining (ed.), *The Dracula Scrapbook* (London: New English Library, 1976), p. 48.

22. John Forrester, *The Seductions of Psychoanalysis* (Cambridge: Cambridge University Press, 1990), p. 2.

23. Stoker, *Dracula*, pp. 229–30.

24. Quoted in John Forrester, *Language and the Origins of Psychoanalysis* (London: Macmillan, 1980), p. 11.
25. Sigmund Freud, 'Psychical (or mental) Treatment' [1890] *Standard Edition of the Works of Sigmund Freud*, (London: Hogarth Press, 1953) VII, p. 283.
26. Forrester, op. cit., p. 67.
27. See op. cit., pp. 167, 206.
28. Sigmund Freud, *The Origins of Psychoanalysis. Letters to Wilhelm Fliess*, intro. Steven Marcus, (New York: Basic Books, 1977), p. 305.
29. See Shepherd, *Sherlock Holmes and the Case of Dr. Freud*, p. 13.
30. Malcolm Bowie, *Freud, Proust and Lacan: Theory as Fiction* (Cambridge: Cambridge University Press, 1987), p. 26.
31. Op. cit., p. 43.
32. Freud to Jung, June 1909, in William McGuire (ed.), *The Freud/Jung Letters* (Princeton, NJ: Princeton University Press, 1974), pp. 234–5.
33. Forrester, *The Seductions of Psychoanalysis*, p. 18.
34. McGuire (ed.), *The Freud/Jung Letters*, p. 228.
35. Op. cit., pp. 230–1.
36. Sigmund Freud, 'Fragments of an Analysis of a Case of Hysteria ('Dora') (1905 [1901]), in *Case Histories I: 'Dora' and 'Little Hans'* (Harmondsworth: Penguin, 1977), p. 162.
37. See John Forrester, *The Seductions of Psychoanalysis*, pp. 42.
38. See Freud, op. cit., p. 162n.
39. Forrester, op. cit., p. 53. By the same token, we should note, in relation to the primal narratives referred to above, that Freud described his perhaps most far-reaching attempt at an analysis of mythic origins, 'Moses and Monotheism', as a 'historical romance' and the 'nuclear complex in neuroses', later the Oedipal complex, as a 'family romance'.

Index

in Doyle, 104, 216–21; in
  Wood, 217–18
defining the genre, 3–10, 60,
  98, 104–6, 109–10, 137, 172,
  193–4, 209, 228, 241n
structure of: 3–6, 10, 98, 116; in
  Gaspay (Richmond), 110,
  112; in Russell (Waters),
  117–19; in Hayward (Mrs.
  Paschal), 124–5; in Poe, 138,
  160–1, 168–70; in Collins,
  174–5; in Doyle, 221–2
'detective',
  as literary epithet, 18, 105–6,
  109–10, 129–31, 135, 166–7,
  172, 193, 209
detectives: anon. in *X.Y.Z.*, 132–4;
  Audley (Braddon, *Lady
  Audley's Secret*), 183–8; Byde
  (Wood, *The Passenger from
  Scotland Yard*), 217–18; Cuff
  (Collins, *The Moonstone*), 209,
  214; Brooke (Pirkis, *The Experiences of Loveday Brooke*), 129,
  219–20, 224; 'Inspector F.', 109;
  Inspector Field, 107–8; Gryce
  (Green, *The Leavenworth Case*),
  187–8, 213, 261n; Mrs. G——
  (Forrester, *The Female Detec-
  tive*), 120, 128–9; Hartright
  (Collins, *The Woman in White*),
  187; Hesselius (LeFanu, 'Green
  Tea'), 255n; Jennings (Collins,
  The Moonstone), 200, 204,
  206–8; *see also* Hayward (Mrs.
  Paschal), Doyle (Holmes), Poe
  (Dupin), Gaspay (Richmond),
  Russell (Waters)
and intelligence: 117, in Dickens,
  106–8; in Russell (Waters),
  120–1; in Hayward (Mrs.
  Paschal), 123, 126–9; in
  Green (*X.Y.Z.*), 132, 134; in
  Poe, 138; in Pirkis (Brooke),
  219–20; in Doyle, 220–1
methods: in Dickens, 108–9,
  252n; in Gaspay (Richmond),
  112; in Russell (Waters),
  119–20; in Hayward (Mrs.

Paschal), 126–9; in Forrester
  (Mrs. G-), 128–9; in Green
  (*X.Y.Z.*), 132, 134; in Poe,
  138–9, 151, 165–9; in Collins,
  202, 207; in Doyle, 216–21; in
  Wood (Byde), 217–18
as narrative authorities: 3, 10,
  60, 72–3, 75, 91–2, 98, 101,
  174–5; in Poe, 139–140; in
  Green (Gryce), 187–8; in
  Collins, 193, 204, 207–9; in
  Doyle, 220–1
relation to police and law: 8,
  129; in Gaspay (Richmond),
  112–16; in Russell (Waters),
  118–19; in Hayward (Mrs.
  Paschal), 122–5; in Poe,
  137–40, 151, 161–2, 255n;
  in Braddon (Audley) and
  Green (Gryce), 184–8; in
  Collins, 194–5; in Doyle,
  215, 224–5
in sensation fiction, 130, 184–209
  passim, 215
Dickens, Charles, 61, 69, 105–9,
  252n
dime novel, the, 131, 254n
Donnelly, Michael, 83, 86, 249n
double, the, 151–9, 170–1
Doyle, Arthur Conan, 3, 4, 229
  Holmes, Sherlock: and crime,
    224; and Freud, 10, 237–9;
    and intelligence, 220–1;
    and mastery, 220–6, 237–8,
    240; methods, 216–21; and
    police and law, 215, 224–5;
    and predecessors, 10, 18,
    104–5, 117, 129, 135, 214–16,
    219, 221, 225, 240, 262n;
    and realism, 160, 225–8;
    and sexuality, 213–14; and
    science, 104, 216–20; and
    structure, 221–2
Dupin, the Chevalier Auguste C.,
  see Poe

Elliotson, John, 204–5
empiricism, 8–10, 47–8, 121–2,
  142–3, 152–4, 157–9,